KU-336-662

An Nguyen

The Penetration of Online News

Past, Present and Future

VDM Verlag Dr. Müller

BIRMINGHAM CITY
UNIVERSITY
DISCARDED

Impressum/Imprint (nur für Deutschland/ only for Germany)
Bibliografische Information der Deutschen Nationalbibliothek: Die Deutsche Nationalbibliothek
verzeichnet diese Publikation in der Deutschen Nationalbibliografie; detaillierte bibliografische
Daten sind im Internet über http://dnb.d-nb.de abrufbar.
Alle in diesem Buch genannten Marken und Produktnamen unterliegen warenzeichen-, marken-
oder patentrechtlichem Schutz bzw. sind Warenzeichen oder eingetragene Warenzeichen der
jeweiligen Inhaber. Die Wiedergabe von Marken, Produktnamen, Gebrauchsnamen,
Handelsnamen, Warenbezeichnungen u.s.w. in diesem Werk berechtigt auch ohne besondere
Kennzeichnung nicht zu der Annahme, dass solche Namen im Sinne der Warenzeichen- und
Markenschutzgesetzgebung als frei zu betrachten wären und daher von jedermann benutzt
werden dürften.

Coverbild: www.purestockx.com

Verlag: VDM Verlag Dr. Müller Aktiengesellschaft & Co. KG
Dudweiler Landstr. 125 a, 66123 Saarbrücken, Deutschland
Telefon +49 681 9100-698, Telefax +49 681 9100-988, Email: info@vdm-verlag.de
Zugl.: Brisbane, University of Queensland, PhD Dissertation, 2007

Herstellung in Deutschland:
Schaltungsdienst Lange o.H.G., Zehrensdorfer Str. 11, D-12277 Berlin
Books on Demand GmbH, Gutenbergring 53, D-22848 Norderstedt
Reha GmbH, Dudweiler Landstr. 99, D- 66123 Saarbrücken
ISBN: 978-3-639-08155-8

Imprint (only for USA, GB)
Bibliographic information published by the Deutsche Nationalbibliothek: The Deutsche
Nationalbibliothek lists this publication in the Deutsche Nationalbibliografie; detailed
bibliographic data are available in the Internet at http://dnb.d-nb.de.
Any brand names and product names mentioned in this book are subject to trademark, brand or
patent protection and are trademarks or registered trademarks of their respective holders. The use
of brand names, product names, common names, trade names, product descriptions etc. even
without
a particular marking in this works is in no way to be construed to mean that such names may be
regarded as unrestricted in respect of trademark and brand protection legislation and could thus
be used by anyone.

Cover image: www.purestockx.com

Publisher:
VDM Verlag Dr. Müller Aktiengesellschaft & Co. KG
Dudweiler Landstr. 125 a, 66123 Saarbrücken, Germany
Phone +49 681 9100-698, Fax +49 681 9100-988, Email: info@vdm-verlag.de

Copyright © 2008 VDM Verlag Dr. Müller Aktiengesellschaft & Co. KG and licensors
All rights reserved. Saarbrücken 2008

Produced in USA and UK by:
Lightning Source Inc., 1246 Heil Quaker Blvd., La Vergne, TN 37086, USA
Lightning Source UK Ltd., Chapter House, Pitfield, Kiln Farm, Milton Keynes, MK11 3LW, GB
BookSurge, 7290 B. Investment Drive, North Charleston, SC 29418, USA
ISBN: 978-3-639-08155-8

Dedicated to the four most important people of my life:

— my mum and dad, Loc and Tuan;
&
— my wife and daughter, Minh and Khue,

with all the best of love.

BIRMINGHAM CITY UNIVERSITY

Book no   34688579

Subject no.   070.435/ Ngu

LIBRARY

Content

List of Figures

List of Tables

Acknowledgements

This book would hardly take its shape without the contribution of numerous people and organisations. My thanks go first to my former team at the University of Queensland (UQ) in Australia: Dr Elizabeth Ferrier, Dr. Susan McKay, Prof. Tom O'Regan and Prof. Mark Western. I am especially indebted to Tom for his constructive criticisms of the earlier drafts and to Mark for his conscientious and invaluable instructions in the research design and data analysis process.

I acknowledge the funding for this research by the Australian Government under its IPRS scholarship scheme and by the University of Queensland under its UQIPRS scheme. I strongly appreciate the professional help of Angela Touhy and other administrative staff at the UQ School of English, Media Studies and Art History. I thank Meg Tighe and Warren Laffan at the UQ Social Research Centre for their enthusiastic assistance during sampling and data collection. I am particularly grateful to my "Vietnamese corps" at UQ – Doan Nhat An, Phan Thanh Binh, Le Canh Duong, Hoang Hong Thuy Duong, Nguyen Tam Lac Huong, Do Trung Kien, Nguyen To Nguyen, Do Thanh Nhon, Nguyen My Phuong, Phi Dang Son, Nguyen Hong Thanh, Dang Ngoc Toan, Dao Ngoc The Vinh and some others – for their responsible help in the bulk of manually numbering the questionnaire forms, putting them into envelopes and bringing them to the post office as well as in data entry. I miss those winter days and nights – full of jokes and laughs without losses of the accuracy needed for this tedious but demanding job. I also thank my colleague, Billy Crosgray, at the University of Stirling for his help in the layout of this book.

In a diversity of ways, this book is influenced by the many people who have been shaping my views on journalism. These include my "old journalism people" at the former UQ Department of Journalism, especially Prof. Kerry Green, Prof. John Henningham, Dr.

Stephen McIlwaine and Dr. Levi Obijiofor. I would like to express my heartfelt gratitude to Steve for being an always reliable source of caring advices and to John and his wife, Helen, for their kindly support during the years I was in Australia. I must remember my former professional mentors in Ho Chi Minh City, Vietnam – Mr Tran Quoc Toan of the *New World* magazine and Mr Quoc Vinh of the *Saigon Times* group, the two senior journalists who taught me the very first lessons in journalism in the 1990s.

Finally, I would like to dedicate this book to my big family, my greatest source of pride, motivation, inspiration and support. This book is to my mum and dad, Loc and Tuan, whose immense efforts during their most resourceful years allow my siblings – Tri, Hien-Kim, Hieu-Son, Dung – and me to have what we have today. In the extreme hardship of the post-war Vietnam, they would not even be sure of a day when I obtain a bachelor degree, let alone a day when I become a scholar with a PhD and anything like this book. This work is also to my enchanting wife, Ngoc Minh, who has been living away from me for most of the time since our honeymoon, with an enduring sympathy and an admirable sacrifice. Last but not least, this book is a welcoming gift for our happy and smart first daughter, Khue Minh Thi Nguyen, whose first birthday coincides with the planned publication date for this book.

An Duc Nguyen

Introduction
The appeal of online news: untapped issues

> A fantasy trip into the future may give a feeling for such a communication medium. Sitting at the breakfast table, you might cause the latest headlines to appear on a small display screen simply by touching a key. These headlines may have been written five minutes before. Pointing at a headline might get the story displayed.... Suppose you encounter a name of a person you would like to know more about: ask for a bibliographic sketch. Suppose you do not completely understand the economic reasoning behind an action of the International Monetary Fund: there might be available a short tutorial on some aspect of international economics.... Suppose you want to search the want ads or supermarket ads. Instead of shuffling pages, you may just ask to have ads displayed in a particular category... Suppose a high school student wishes to search the equivalent of the local public library for information needed to write a term paper. He can quickly search for the equivalent of the card catalogue and soon be browsing in relevant material – E. Parker, 1973 (quoted in Dozier & Rice, 1984, p. 104).

Three and a half decades after communication scholar Ed Parker made this journey into the future of mass communication, a "fantasy" has probably become a marked reality of contemporary societies throughout the world, thanks to the spectacular penetration into daily life of the Internet. Exactly twenty years after Parker's vision, the introduction of web browsers in 1993 quickly moved the then 24-year-old Internet out of the military and academic world into the household around the globe. According to Morgan Stanley Technology Research, it took radio 38 years to reach 50 million users in America. Television had to wait 13 years and cable television 10 years to hit this benchmark number. For the web-enabled Internet, the time was only five years (cited in Green, 2002). The surge has not stopped: according to the Computer Industry Almanac (via http://www.clickz.com/stats/), the global online population reached 1.08 billion in 2005 and is projected to jump to 1.8 billion by 2010. The new medium's impact is so overwhelming that Nicholas Negroponte "measured" it at "10.5 on the Richter scale of social change" (quoted in Dizard, 2000, p. 5). As early as 2000, Manuel Castells had already declared: "The Internet is the fabric of our life" (quoted in Lister et al, 2003, p. 188).

The way news is produced, packaged, distributed, communicated, retrieved and used might be experiencing one of the most important socio-cultural shifts brought by this new medium. More than what E. Parker imagined, news users now can not only point and click to read headlines written five minutes earlier or search and get whatever information they want. The medium provides a diverse range of other innovative utilities to news users: they can personalise their news experience in any desired way; retrieve as much news as they need from any corner of the world; explore issues of interest with as much depth as desired; get all existing communication formats in the same news package; show fierce responses to the media over a disturbing news item; pass their own news and views to potentially millions of people in cyberspace; and so on. All this could be done at any time and from anywhere at their convenience, within a matter of seconds, and for almost no cost. Since the early 1990s, the "fantasy trip" has become like this:

> Imagine an electronic newspaper delivered to your home as bits. Assume it is sent to a magical, paper-thin, flexible, water-proof, wireless, lightweight, bright display. The interface solution is likely to call upon mankind's years of experience with headlining and layout, typographic landmarks, images, and a host of other techniques to assist browsing.
>
> (...)
>
> The entire conception and construction of the newspaper is digital, from beginning to end, until the very last step, when ink is squeezed onto dead trees. This is the step when bits become atoms. Now imagine that the last step does not happen in a printing plant, but that the bits are delivered to you as bits. You may elect to print them at home for all the conveniences of hard copy (for which reusable paper is recommended, so we all don't need a large pile of blank newsprint). Or you may prefer to download them into your laptop, palmtop, or someday into your perfectly flexible, one-hundredth-of-an-inch-thin, full-colour, massively high-resolution, large-format, waterproof display (which happens to look exactly like a sheet of paper and smell like one, too, if that's what turns you on). While there are many ways to get you the bits, one is surely broadcast. The television broadcaster can send you newspaper bits (Negroponte, 1995, pp. 52-56).

With this image of the Internet as a powerful news medium have come many hopes and fears about a future dominated by it. Many scholars are enthusiastic about the prospect of a more informed public that is no longer an "underdog" in shaping the outcome of public affairs, while some others are concerned that we might be entering an era of further social exclusion due to a worsened information gap between different socio-economic groups, and an increasingly crazy world where information overload can potentially lead us to being too desensitised to be involved and critical. Some even go so far as predicting that the unlimited resource of news and information produced by citizens for citizens will result in a gradual death of professional journalism. In the news industry, traditional journalists and news executives have been taking to the medium with both excitement and fear – excitement about its new socio-technical capacities and fears of being driven out of existence because of these capacities. Since the intrusion of the web, the debate on the potential impact of online news has never ended. But the general sentiment has been that the technological "power" of online news is so appealing and compelling that it will effortlessly transform society and established norms, replacing older and supposedly less efficient news forms (Boczkowski, 2004).

The rationale for this for book: five research questions

This book on the diffusion and social impact of online news sets out with a departure from such a technology-determinist viewpoint, based on the historical observation that technologies are not like an embryo that grows in a predetermined and programmed manner regardless of its environment (Dimmick, 2003). For years in its hot days of the 1960s, for example, cable television was predicted as the agent for an ideal society to be created. Most prophets of the time saw cable the new medium as a sudden technological development with naturally "revolutionary capabilities" thanks to its copious bandwidth and its two-way interactivity. They thought of the vast possibilities of specialized cultural programming to enhance citizen knowledge. They envisioned a wired nation in which all citizens, social services and political leaders could be linked together and home-based work would eliminate physical travel. They even imagined dramatic social benefits to accrue from the new communication technology such as less crime and rioting (thanks to adequate information), more equal participation (thanks to specialized cable channels), a better-educated citizenry, and an enhanced democratic process. The outcome of this "miraculous" technology has been clear today – there is no specialised programming and

3

there is just a one-way, nationally distributed delivery of programs to mass audiences. The only interactive cable service was closed by 1985 due to high production costs and few users (Kyrish, 1994, pp. 5-13).

Technologies, thus, do not act alone and might not be the primary determinant of social change. The future directions of online news development and its social impact cannot be predicted if we do not take into account the many social, cultural, political and economical factors that shape this development. It is apparent that the Internet as a whole has deeply penetrated daily life but it is still unclear whether, and to what extent, the Internet as a news medium has substantially been integrated into daily life and altered established news routines. The spectacular failure of cable television suggests that in order to assess the potential development of online news, we need to explore the interaction between its technical superiority with its socio-cultural context, looking at the issue from both ends of the news chain: the media actors who create the online news artefact and the public who adopts and uses it.

From a producer-centric perspective, despite the now ubiquitous presence of news on the Internet, we might question the extent to which online news potentials have been brought into play. The process of materialising technological promises (the production process) is under the influence of many beyond-technology factors and, however "powerful" the technology might be, the social artefact generated in this process does not necessarily embody all its potentials. Television and radio, for example, have the technical potential to become interactive media but mostly follow the one-way, top-down model today. Or the lack of profit could lead cable television services to nowhere near its potential. By the same token, can media practitioners overcome their traditional values to make a complete break from their traditional practices and interests to develop a full online news product with immediacy, multimedia, interactivity, customisation, hypertextual links and so on? Or do they just develop it as no more than an extension, or even replication, of their newspapers, radio news bulletins, or TV current affairs shows? Given their often defensive innovation culture (Boczkowski, 2004), have they proactively done their best to bolster the innovative potential of the new news? These issues are obviously crucial as they determine the social shape of online news that users are offered.

4

Thus, to predict the future of online news, it is worthwhile to look at its past and present development in the newsroom to explore what technical and non-technical factors have been affecting its social shape. As this book will show, there has been a substantial body of research dealing with the social production of online news, especially content analyses of news sites, but most of these studies have explored online news as a completely new phenomenon or, at the most, as a continuity of videotex news services of the 1980s (see Boczkowski, 2004; Gunter, 2003; Li, 2006a for overviews). In this work, I will follow previous classic research (Defleur & Ball-Rokeach, 1989; Winston, 1998), hypothesising that the development of online news – like any other communication form – is a long evolutionary process that could span throughout centuries across cultures and societies, being affected by a range of socio-technical accelerators and brakes. If such an evolution exists, the factors influencing online news production found throughout this evolution can be expected to continue to determine its future development. The first key question of the book, therefore, is:

RQ1: How has online news evolved in the newsroom and what are the social factors affecting this evolution in general and the social shape of online news in particular?

From a user-centric perspective, online news adoption and use is more than just a "give one, take one" or push-pull process. The web is a mine of in-depth news/information, but do people really want it and if they do, do they have enough time to click from one page to another for the same news item? Even when the web's strengths are highly regarded, to what extent does this affect the adoption likelihood and use levels of online news? Some people might adopt it more because, for example, it is simply convenient to combine this with other utilities of the Internet than because it is immediate, searchable and so on. Even with some common sense, we can think of a diverse range of possible reasons for non-adoption of online news: satisfaction with the news feeds from other sources, having insufficient resources, or simply being tired of onscreen reading, just to name a few. By the same token, the common fear that the "powerful" Internet could replace traditional sources in daily life might turn out to be an overreaction. It is the media technology that needs to find ways to fit into the user's diverse socio-psychological context – i.e. it is not user who has to "sacrifice" all established elements of their daily life just to take up a new technology. Television, for instance, might be technologically superior to radio but people simply do not want to abandon the kingpin of news in the car – the built-in radio set – to watch television only. Thus, without understanding the user factors affecting the adoption and use of online news, we will have no reliable means to predict its future diffusion and social impact.

Unfortunately, the first dozen years of online news has seen limited academic attention to user-centric diffusion issues. Much empirical research so far has treated online news and/or non-news information adoption and use as one dimension of overall Internet use patterns rather than a form of use that is of interest in its own right (see, for example, Atkin, Jeffres, & Neuendorf, 1998; Ferguson & Perse, 2000; Lin, 2001; Liu et al, 2002; Mikaki et al, 2002; Papacharissi & Rubin, 2000; Rhee & Kim, 2004; Zhou & He, 2002a; and the series of Internet use surveys within the World Internet Project). Meanwhile, most studies with a substantial focus on online news use mainly follow pre-web studies of computer-mediated communication to explore the usability of information presentation on computer screens. These include issues such as how users respond to the portrait and landscape display of screen documents (Schierhorn et al, 1999; Wearden, 1998; Wearden et al, 1999; Wearden & Fidler, 2001); how the length of initial summaries and links to sidebars (i.e. the amount of summary information) influence users' reading decisions (Vargo et al, 2000); how the scroll-down online interface, hypertextual links and other features of the hypermedia format affect the time efficiency and cognitive processes of online news use (Lowrey & Choi, 2006; Oostendorf & Nimwegen, 1998); how the lack of editorial cues and the serendipity of news use in the online environment affect news knowledge acquisition (Tewksbury & Althaus, 2000; Tewksbury, Weaver & Maddex, 2000); how news judgement and knowledge acquisition in print reading differs from that in online reading (Althaus & Tewksbury, 2002; Mensing & Greer, 2006; Li, 2006b; Tewksbury & Althaus, 2000); and how source attribution (Sundar, 1998) and the presentation of audio/video materials (Sundar, 2000) affect users' perception of online news quality and credibility.

Of course, the cause and effect of online news consumption affect each other throughout consumers' experience and findings from the above studies have important implications for the future of online news. The issue is that these studies are essentially medium-driven in the sense that they deal with *what the medium has done to the user* rather than *what the user has done with the medium*. The many social and technological factors that have a potential impact on an individual's decision to adopt and allocate his/her resources to consume online news remain largely untapped today. There are quite a number of substantial studies that have been tracking online news trends such as those by the Project for Excellence in Journalism, the Pew Research Centre for the People and the Press and the Pew Internet & American Life Project but data from these organisations are largely descriptive in nature[1]. When I started this work in 2002, there were only a few preliminary attempts to both theoretically and empirically chart the adoption dynamic of online news (Aldisardottir, 2000; Bromley & Bowles, 1995; Chyi & Larosa, 1999; Conway, 2001; Mueller & Kamerer, 1995; Weir, 1995). Since then, more relevant studies have been published (Chan & Leung, 2005; Coats, 2002; Horrigan, 2006; Kaye & Johnson, 2002; Li, 2003; Lin & Salwen, 2006; Weiss et al, 2003; Wu and Bechtel, 2002) but it was not until 2005 that the first book dedicated to a comprehensive analysis of online news audiences (Salwen, Garrison & Driscoll, 2005) was published. Even this book, however, mostly examined general online news adoption rather than going into deeper use levels and related aspects.

What has been more substantially studied is the impact of the Internet on traditional news media. As this is a key concern among many stakeholders. we have seen research into the issue by commercial/industrial organisations – such as Gomez Advisors and InterSurvey (Lent, 2000), GartnerG2 (Saunders, 2002), the US Interactive Advertising Bureau (Lee & Leung, 2004) and Strategy Analytics (*The Register*, 2004) – as well as by policy-making institutions (European Commission, 2002; European Commission, 2003) and academics such as Nie and Ering (cited in O'Toole, 2000), Kayany and Yelsma (2000), James, Wotring and Forrest (1995), Lee and Leung (2004) and some others. However, most of this literature, again, is more or less medium-driven, being conducted from a medium-centric perspective and based on the belief that with its technical potential, the Internet is a functional alternative to and thus can displace/replace traditional news media (Dutta-

Bergman, 2004). As the above discussion suggests, because a new medium has to find its ways to fit into people's established routines, there are reasons to believe that old and new media can coexist to meet users' needs in their diverse social and psychological situations, a point that is at least supported from the history of the mass media. A stronger focus on this possible complementary relationship is therefore much needed. Only a few studies have taken this user-centric approach (Dimmick, Chen & Li; 2004; Dutta-Bergman, 2004; Lin & Salwen, 2006; Stempel, Hardrove & Bernt, 2000; Robinson et al, 2000).

In addition, it might be noted that most studies on online news uses are from the US. Only a few are from Europe (Aldisardottir, 2000; D'Haenens et al, 2004; Oostendorf & Nimwegen, 1998) or Asia (Chan & Leung, 2005; Lee & Leung, 2004). In Australia, a thorough examination reveals that the whole world of online news audiences has been almost ignored, except for the studies that this author published while conducting the research and writing for this book (Nguyen, 2008a; Nguyen 2008b; Nguyen, 2007; Nguyen & Western, 2007; Nguyen, 2006; Nguyen & Western, 2006; Nguyen et al, 2005; Nguyen, 2003; Redden, Caldwell & Nguyen, 2003)[2]. This work, therefore, is also intended to be a considerable attempt to address the need for more international research into online news adoption and use. Taking an international perspective, it raises four user-centric research questions:

RQ2: What are the general patterns of online news uses and gratifications?

RQ3: To what extent and in what way do the much-touted attributes of online news contribute to the way users adopt, use and integrate it into daily life?

RQ4: What are the social determinants of public adoption and use of online news?

RQ5: Is there a complementary relationship between online news and information and traditional sources?

The approach and structure of this book

In order to explore the above issues, I will integrate a range of theoretical perspectives from journalism, sociology, psychology, economics, consumer behaviour, and media and communication studies. The producer-centric issues (RQ1) will be approached by using historical analogies as a forecasting method (Klopfenstein, 1989), while the four user-centric questions (RQ2 to RQ5) will be explored with empirical data from two national surveys in Australia. The first is a survey among 790 Australians that I conducted in July and August 2004 to answer RQ2, RQ3 and RQ4. The second is the Australian Social Attitudes Survey – 2003, conducted with 4,270 respondents in the last four months of 2003, which will be utilised to answer RQ5. Each of the four questions will be divided into sub-questions in its relevant chapter. While the data were generated in Australia, they will be placed and/or analysed in the context of research findings from other countries to generate an international perspective. Also, the implications of all the user data will be discussed in the context of the most recent industrial development of online news around the world (up until May 2008). For a cogent flow, this book will be divided into the following chapters:

Chapter 1 is an in-depth historical journey into the pre-web days of online news to find general social and economic factors affecting its production process. Merging a number of models and theories of media formation, including the evolutionary perspective and the social-conflict paradigm proposed by Defleur and Ball-Rokeach (1989) and the concepts of "supervening social necessities" and the "law" of suppression of radical potential by Brian Winston (1998), the chapter has two points to make in relation to RQ1. First, despite the fact that the term "online news" has become the buzzword to refer to Internet news services since the introduction of the world-wide web in the early 1990s, consumer online news services have been evolving through a number of social forms for 160 years. Web news is in essence a continuation of many news services created out of the media's response to a range of new point-to-point telecommunication technologies – namely the telegraph, the telephone, facsimile and videotex. Second, and more importantly, this evolution process has been taking place in circumstances in which technological possibilities have often succumbed to the many socio-economic conflicts between the media and societies and between the media themselves. Despite technical superiority, many earlier online news forms vanished due to a range of social "brakes" such as moral norms and values, the laws, social needs, economic factors and the like.

The most marked feature of that evolution of online news is the fear-driven defensive innovation culture among traditional newspeople. Because of the many vested interests resulting from their establishment in the market, traditional media often feel threatened by disruptive technologies. When a new and potentially innovative medium emerges, the general reaction among them is the fear of their near-monopoly being disrupted, leading the new to be too often positioned as potential foes rather than friends. This perceived possibility of becoming irrelevant stimulates their adoption of new technologies but the subsequent excessive focus on defending their well-being has led the radical potential of the new to be often blindsided with the result being that many online news services (such as videotex of the 1980s) are not developed to their fullest extent. Chapter 2 will detail how this fear-driven innovation culture has been affecting the shape of web news in its first fifteen years. Until recent years, unique features of web news have rarely been observed or offered on a cheap and very limited manner on mainstream sites. Looking at industrial developments since the mid-2000s, however, the chapter argues that as the Internet has established itself as a major news medium and a viable advertising space, the same culture of fear might have started to ignite a second, more rigorous development stage of online news, one in which its diverse potentials will be more actively and aggressively embraced and exploited.

Such a development highlights the need for a more thorough understanding of the online news audience and its response to the "power" of online news, which the rest of the book will deal with. Chapter 3 is a general theoretical assessment of the potential diffusion of today's online news (i.e. Internet news), with regard to its much touted "power" from a user-centric approach. Placed in the innovation diffusion framework (Reagan, 2002; Rogers, 1986; Rogers, 2003; Rogers, 2004), online news – as a continuous innovation with little financial and technical requirement and many potential benefits – can be seen as being well-qualified in terms of the five well-known innovation attributes: relative advantages, compatibility, (low) complexity, trialability and observability. To argue for this, a six-dimension user-centric profile of online news will be constructed, based on a discussion of why people use the news and what they use it for. Some oft-mentioned "relative disadvantages" of online news will also be discussed. The chapter concludes that, although having been insufficiently exploited by the news media, the current artefact of online news still has a considerable potential to foster wider adoption thanks to the intrinsic nature of the Internet.

From this, Chapter 4 attempts to answer RQ2, exploring the general responses of the public to online news inside and outside Australia. It first reviews the vital rise of online news adoption/use across the developed segments of the world in the first years of the 21st century. This will encompass the world-wide spread of online news use as well as the unprecedented and powerful emergence of online public participation via a number of web-based platforms such as weblogs and online forums. The key point here is that since the early 2000s, the Internet has established itself as a mainstream news medium, with its growth still on the way. A review of the still limited international research shows that online news attributes – particularly its ease/convenience of use, its immediacy and its content richness – have made an important contribution to this impressive uptake of online news. The chapter then goes on to report the general findings of the 2004 survey to depict the patterns of online news uses and gratifications in Australia, covering the implementation and appreciation of online news. Findings on potential obstacles to online news adoption among Internet users will also be presented. Putting all the findings together in a further analysis, the chapter will draw on the concept of interpersonal influence in the innovation diffusion process to conclude that online news is likely to continue its impressive uptake in a more substantial way in the future. Detailed discussions of the 2004 survey's methodological matters will be presented in this chapter.

Going beyond mere descriptive statistics, Chapter 5 will explore the effect of online news attributes on the way adopters use and integrate it into their daily life. Aiming to answer RQ3, it first introduces two models related to the adoption and use of online news – the five-step innovation-decision process (knowledge, persuasion, decision, implementation, and confirmation) in diffusion theory (Rogers, 2003) and expectancy-value theory in uses and gratifications research (Palmgreen, 1984; Palmgreen & Rayburn, 1985). Each theory will be discussed with its strengths and weaknesses in relation to the nature of online news, on the basis of which an integrated model for the micro-process of online news adoption/use is proposed. Based on this model, the chapter three crucial sub-RQs on how online news attributes influence the way users become cognitively and affectively attached to it and the way they allocate their resources to using it. The 2004 data are then analysed, using logistic regression, to answer these questions.

Leaving the medium-related factors, Chapter 6 will be devoted to RQ4, investigating the influence of socio-structural factors on online news adoption and use. The baseline here is that the extent to which a user actually perceives the exclusive features of online news as compelling and to which these perceived advantages are needed, used and enjoyed by him/her depends very much on who he/she is, where he/she is from, what he/she wants in relation to news and so on. On this basis, the chapter will integrate innovation diffusion theory – or its emphasis on socio-economic status, personality and communication behaviours as determinants of innovativeness – with the structural approach to media audience formation, which places a heavy weight on an individual's social situation, his/her associated media-related needs and the media options accessible to him/her (McQuail, 1997; Weibull, 1985). This theoretical discussion ends up with three groups of social predictors: news orientation/behaviour, social locators and experience with the Internet. The 2004 survey data will then be analysed to explore their influences. At the end of the chapter, the attributes of online news are explored again with major socio-structural factors being controlled.

Chapter 7, which aims to answer RQ5, explores the relationship between online news and information and traditional sources. First, Maxwell McCombs's (1972) Principle of Relative Constancy, the most influential framework in studying media competition, will be revisited and criticised for its many methodological and theoretical flaws in the light of media use theories. Taking a complete separation from the common assumption of previous research, the chapter draws on different user-centric perspectives to argue that even if media spending is fixed over time, no new medium can act to completely replace an old one simply because no medium is functionally equivalent to another in an absolute sense. Displacement might happen but this will not lead any traditional news business to an end. Instead, old and new media compete and will finally coexist after each finds a firm niche in the media environment. They would complement each other because each has its own distinctive features in serving a particular human need that other media also serve in a different manner. I will use the Australian Social Attitudes Survey to explore this complementary relationship between old and new media within the specific domain of news and information.

Finally, Chapter 8 will summarise and present a further discussion of the main findings of the study, placing them in the context of the latest development in the online news world to forecast its future. First, I will construct and present a forecasting model of public adoption and use of online news in the years ahead. Second, based on the user data in this research, I will discuss some potential good practices that might help online journalism to foster a wider and more substantive adoption of online news in the years ahead. Throughout this, I will introduce and discuss a promising operation model for the 21st century newsroom proposed by Paul Bradshaw. The likely continuation of the defensive innovation culture of the news media will also be discussed in relation to these good practices. Third, based primarily on the final forecasting model, I will argue that online news is widening the digital divide and this divide will not narrow or disappear in the long run as many scholars have argued. Fourth, the normative implications of the recent rise of online participatory media for the future of journalism and the public sphere will be explored. Finally, the book presents a brief discussion of some other potential consequences of online news – including the possible transformation of traditional news forms, the changing notion of news, and professional problems that journalism might face in the years head – along with a call for future research.

Notes

1. There is certainly a great deal of relevant commercial research but findings from this research body are not usually publicly available and, if available, are presented more at the descriptive than theoretical-testing level.

2. I acknowledge that most of these papers – except Redden, Caldwell & Nguyen (2003) – have been revised, updated and restructured to be included in this book either as full chapters or parts of chapters. I thank the publishers of these publications for their permission to include them in this book.

Chapter 1

Technologies in the social sphere: lessons from the 160-year pre-history of online news

As a way to set the scene for this book, this chapter looks at the past of online news itself to further elaborate the key point made in the introduction: placing an excessive emphasis on technological power at the expense of its social conditions can be misleading. Merging a number of theoretical perspectives on media formation – including the evolutionary perspective and the social-conflict paradigm proposed by Melvin Defleur and Sandra Ball-Rokeach (1989) as well as the concepts of "social supervening social necessities" and "the law of the suppression of radical potential" by Brian Winston (1998) – this chapter has two major purposes:

First, it provides an alternative – and potentially contentious – viewpoint to the literature which has traced the history of online news back to the late 1960s, when ARPANET, the precursor of the Internet, was created (Cameron et al, 1995; Fidler, 1997; Pavlik, 1998; Shedden, 1998). In particular, despite the fact that the term "online news" has become the buzzword to refer to web news services since the early 1990s, consumer "online" news services, like any other news form, have been evolving through a number of social forms for more than 160 years, all of which follow the introduction of new point-to-point communication technologies of their time, including the telegraph, the telephone, the fax machine and videotex.

Second, this evolution process has been taking place in circumstances in which technological capacities and social conflicts among the media themselves and between the media and other segments of society act both as accelerators and brakes. While the mentality that technological superiority is so appealing and compelling that it effortlessly transforms society and established norms recurs in this history, not all online news forms

15

survived. While some brought about significant changes in human communications, some vanished due to a range of social and technological "brakes" such as the law, economic factors and the like. The producer-centric implications of this pre-history of online news for its future – especially the long-established fear-driven innovation culture of traditional newspeople and its impact – will be briefly discussed to serve as a theoretical basis for a detailed account of the emergence and development of web news in the next chapter.

The birth and development of mass media: a conceptual framework

The history of any medium is an evolutionary process. In one classic work, *Theories of Mass Communications*, DeFleur and Ball-Rokeach (1989) utilised "the evolutionary perspective" to successfully argue that the emergence of the mass press, the development of motion pictures and the establishment of broadcasting all followed an evolutionary path from one form to another. Briefly, the evolutionary perspective assumes that the organisation and development of a society take the shape of a biological mechanism, which involves "natural selection, survival of the fittest, and the inheritance of acquired characteristics" (DeFleur & Ball-Rokeach, 1989, p. 33). The basic idea is that social forms, as integrated and interconnected parts of a society, are invented and undergo gradual changes to meet human aspiration for effectiveness in goal-attaining. Applied to media history, this "social Darwinism" is reflected in the fact that new technologies have been tried, in different social forms, to meet the widespread need for swifter and broader-reach communications systems. This evolution of the media involves the gradual and inevitable *accumulation of small changes* (1989, p. 47). Not all of the social forms tried survive, but they all have some features inherited in today's media. The modern newspaper, for example, "is a combination of elements from many societies and many periods of time", which includes the Roman distribution of public newssheets before the Christian era and the use of wood-carving technologies for paper-printing in China and Korea long before their appearance in Europe (1989, p. 49).

The evolutionary perspective, however, does not provide an insight into how media are born and developed, and how the "survival of the fittest" occurs. Concerning this, DeFleur and Ball-Rokeach provided another notable explanation in which the entrance of

16

a social form of mass communication into human life is determined by social conflicts. Similar to the evolution theory, the social-conflict paradigm involves a process of change. However, the change comes out of a dialectic process in which, different components of society, being in constant mutual conflict due to different interests, compete with each other and resist the competitive efforts of each other. Changes take place either when one side prevails or when some compromises arrive. DeFleur and Ball-Rokeach's approach shares some features with Brian Winston's somewhat more specific model of media development. Like the former, who argued that any cultural complex, such as a mass medium, cannot be born and become a part of daily life without a set of necessary social conditions, Winston (1998) explained the historical development of media within a social sphere. Accordingly, a medium emerges and develops in a social sphere in three transformation stages. At the risk of oversimplification, this could be understood as follows:

In the first transformation, the *ideation* process, *scientific competence* is tested through *technological performance* (Winston, 1998, p. 4). In this stage, solutions are tested and devices built. It might take years before an idea becomes a tested device. The telephone, for example, was theoretically conceptualised over two decades before Bell. The second transformation decides whether the tested devices, termed *prototypes*, can enjoy a wide diffusion. It is not technological effectiveness that always decides. In Winston's view, abandoned devices "might work just as well as the device eventually 'invented' but will achieve no measure of diffusion because there is *no externally determined reason for its development*" (1998, p. 8; emphasis added). The decisive forces to move a prototype out of the lab into the society are termed *supervening social necessities* (1998, p. 6). These necessities might be created by either (1) other technological innovations (such as the railway stimulating the need for telegraphic devices); or (2) a concentration of social forces (such as the rise of corporations and modern offices accelerating the use of telephones and typewriters); or (3) commercial needs for new products.

That a prototype enjoys supervening social necessities, however, does not guarantee that it will become a part of human life, or an "invention" as Winston called it. A prototype has also to conform to existing values and fit into established social patterns. As Winston argued, if supervening social necessities act on the diffusion of an innovation as "the accelerator ... transforming the prototype into an 'invention' and pushing the invention out into the world", then there is also a "brake" which he called *the "law" of the suppression of radical potentials* (1998, p. 11). This is the third stage of transformation, in which the new device's potential damage to existing values is socially restrained. An invention, however needed it is, might not be accepted if it does not operate in a way consistent with established social norms. Indeed, the second and third stages are overlapped – i.e. they could happen at the same time.

In the discussion that follows, the major elements in DeFleur and Ball-Rokeach's and Winston's approaches will be integrated. To explain the evolution of consumer online news services, the starting point taken here is the view of the media institution as a business. As a business, the media are market-driven and are in "the visible hand" of money and markets (Abrahamson, 1998, p. 14), which creates social conflicts between themselves and sometimes between them and other components of the social sphere. As DeFleur and Ball-Rokeach (1989, p. 36) pointed out within the American context:

> The mass media in America are competitive enterprises devoted to making profit. They compete with each other and pursue their interests in a complex web of restraints placed on them by the courts, federal regulative agencies, the moral codes of the society, their organisational structures, and the advertisers who support them. In addition, the press and government have a long history as adversaries. There are other arenas of conflict as well. These include controversies concerning the rights of the press versus the rights of citizens to privacy, the rights of government to protect its secrets in times of national emergencies, the rights of citizens to a fair trial, the rights of consumers to be protected from false claims in advertising, and so on.

With constant profit motives and under permanent competitive pressures, the media attempt to create new and commercially better news products to meet "supervening social necessities" or what I would sometimes term "supervening market demands". At the heart of this process are two major interrelated components: the technologies that make media forms possible and the people who generate these forms. Usually, the media business is not involved in the ideation process that results in technological prototypes. It can take decades before some people in the social sphere, whom I will follow past research (e.g. Boczkowski, 2004) to label as "media actors"), to realise the potential of a technology in

18

developing new media "artefacts". Their involvement starts when an existing technology is seen as potentially profitable and/or destructive to their business. But it is not always established media investors/practitioners who initiate or run new media experiments. Quite often, entrepreneurs with no prior experience in the content provision business but with expertise in new technologies are the first to realise their potential for content production and distribution.

With this in mind, we could further conceptualise "supervening market demands" as something imaginary in the first place. These are what media actors *perceive* or *assume* to be, but are not necessarily, existent in the market. The first set of real "supervening market demands" for a media form/service is, therefore, not one within the whole society but in the smaller context of the media institution. These demands derive from the urge to make more money from the new and/or to protect money made from the old. As media entrepreneurs try the new, they would find out whether their imagined "supervening market demands" are correct. In many cases, the experimented services succeed as real demands exist or can be created. But in others, they are abandoned as a consequence of either no real market demands or the law of suppression of radical potentials. The second scenario happens when market demands do exist but cannot be met due to unforeseeable technical limits, moral modes, regulatory mechanisms, social values, and so forth. Some initially unacceptable technologies, however, could eventually survive after continuous improvements to address their social and/or technical drawbacks. Others become relics of the past but might still have some traits inherent in modern communication forms. This underlines the evolution of communication forms, with "survival of the fittest" in the market being the most important ruling principle.

The history of consumer online news services largely follows this path, having gone through many stages of development in different and increasingly complicated social forms of which web news is the latest and most advanced. And even within each form of online news services, an evolutionary path is normally found. But before that, what is a consumer online news service anyway?

What is "online news"?

Despite its prominent status as a buzzword since the web's intrusion, the term "online" is an example of the underdevelopment of vocabulary in discussions about the speedy development of the so-called new media in the past four decades. It has been widely used, at least since the early 1990s, to refer to communication on the world-wide web, which is so overwhelming an Internet application that it is often taken almost synonymously as the Internet. But "online" as a communication term appeared in the literature quite a long while before Tim Berners-Lee invented the web in 1990 and before its penetration into the news industry in the mid-1990s. For example, in the early 1980s, it was already used to describe the new phenomenon of electronic publishing (Laakaniemi, 1982). According to Fidler (1997), it was born in the early days of telephone systems.

So what does "online" exactly mean? This deceptively simple problem has received no single solution. The core element in most definitions of "online" communication today is the presence of an interactive computer network. Among the 26 web definitions of "online" that I collected by using the "define" function on Google at the time of writing (24 April, 2006), only one was presented with the absence of the computer network. One typical example is the definition by John Pavlik (1998, p. 141), who contended that "online" refers to "communication that occurs between users at two or more computers connected over a local or wide area network". But there are disputes over whether computer-assisted interactivity between users and the computer itself as the receiving terminal should be considered essential parts of online services. This can be seen in the mid-1990s Australian debate over what an online service is. When the Australian Broadcasting Authority (ABA) started its investigation into online content regulation, it defined an online service as

> a system of information accessed through the use of public telecommunications network which allows the transfer in both directions of text, graphics, sound and video between a user, other users and the system (ABA, 1996).

Many of the nation's individuals and organisations sent their critical feedback so that the authority ended up with three crucial amendments: (1) not all content is presented in multimedia forms; (2) there are alternative terminals other than the computer; and (3) online services can be one-way but the interactive nature should be considered "a fundamental attribute" of online services. The final definition thus reads:

> An "online service" is a service that makes content available by means of a telecommunications network which enables the transmission of information between users and between users and a place in the network (ABA, 1996).

In other cases, interactivity is not considered a central element. Roger Fidler, for instance, saw online communication in a much broader sense, as "services, interactions, or transactions that require continuous connection to an electronic communication network" (1997, p. 291). More recently, Lister et al (2003, p. 389) defined "online" simply as "to be logged on to a server".

One possible way to escape this "conceptual matrix" is to go through a gradual exclusion process by looking first at the dominant characteristics of the communication media from which those under the "online" umbrella are considered distinctive. We then can see that "online" is often depicted in contrast to the three major traditional mass media – print, radio and television. Of these, print media like newspapers, magazines, books and so on have a very distinctive physical image that could be easy to separate from online media. The task, then, is to distinguish online media from radio and television. What is tricky here is that all the three are based on electronic communication technologies and thus are difficult to discriminate. However, the question of what online media are could be further narrowed by subsuming radio and television under their usual umbrella of "broadcasting media". Thus online media can be understood as electronic media that do not follow the traditional broadcasting model. And when talking about "broadcasting", we are in essence talking about a content delivery/distribution method. A sensible definition of online communication, therefore, could be based on how it is different from traditional broadcasting in terms of distribution-related matters.

If this is agreeable, then the next task is to work out what broadcasting actually means. If broadcasting is understood as "to disseminate widely" as in dictionaries, then making content available and accessible on the Internet is in essence an act of broadcasting (ABA, 1996) and so is publishing a newspaper, which is certainly at odds with common wisdom. As a jargon in communication studies, however, broadcasting is not so simply

21

conceptualised; rather, it is a more specifically and narrowly understood as the act of sending a message *simultaneously* to *every end user* within the sender's broadcast domain. Whenever content is beamed into the air from a radio or television station, *every possible end-user* (viewer or listener) within the sending station's reach will inevitably receive it if the reception device is on – and the user has to consume it at that time, except when he/she has some time-shifting instrument such as the video-cassette recorder. Broadcasting, thus, operates on a simultaneous point-to-multipoint communication network, in which end-users are connected to the sender only and not to each other.

This is where we can see the difference between broadcasting and online media. In an online environment like the Internet, there are two major ways of delivering content. The first is to store content in a central computer and make it available for users from connected computers to retrieve when they want. The second is narrowcasting or "multicasting": pushing content to a specified group of users in the network such as sending email news alerts to subscribers. In both cases, the delivery methods are different from radio and television broadcasting because (1) once made publicly available, content does not *inevitably* reach *all possible receiving nodes* within the network (i.e. it does not automatically arrive at all computers actively connected to the Internet like radio and television content reaching every radio or television set within its broadcast domain if the set is turned on); and (2) content does not need to be consumed at the same time as it is delivered. These online services are consumed more or less on demand – the content needs to be actively sought and retrieved by network-ready users and the provider has much less control when and where it is used.

What makes both of these online delivery methods possible is the nature of the Internet as a point-to-point communication network. In this network, all users are physically (but not necessarily socially) connected to each other and the sender acts as only one node to which any other node can connect on a one-to-one basis when necessary. In this light, online services are different from electronic broadcasting primarily because of their reliance on point-to-point connection and thus point-to-point content delivery. This connection-based distinction between broadcasting and online services makes sense from an etymological perspective because the birth of the term "online" took place shortly after

22

telephone systems were introduced, when as many people had to share the same line, the use of such notices as "I'm on (the) line" was popular (Fidler, 1997). In essence, these notices denote a mode of being connected – here being connected to another node on the (point-to-point) telephone network. Not less importantly, such a distinction can serve to depict non-web services that are often termed as "online" today – such as email newsletters, wireless content services to mobile devices – because the underlining delivery methods of all of them are point-to-point. Indeed, the nexus between point-to-point and point-to-multipoint communication is a basis to distinguish online from broadcasting services in Australia's Broadcasting Services Act 1992 (ABA, 1996).

For these reasons, in this work, "consumer online news services" are defined as *a set of news services distributed directly to a consuming public via point-to-point communication networks*. These news services have for the most part been delivered "on the line" – i.e. over hardwire-connected telecommunication networks such as the telegraph and the telephone – but have also been made available in wireless environments in recent years. It must be noted that *distribution* here does not have the same meaning as *transmission*. A consumer service must be one that directly targets the consumer market (like today's web news). This means that telegraphic news provided by wire services to the provincial press in the 19th and early 20th century should not fall into the territory of consumer online news services. Neither does the facsimile transmission of newspaper proof pages from a typesetting area to a far-away plate-making area, which started in Japan in 1959 and spread over the western world in the 1970s (Russell, 1981). In both cases, these news transmissions are, although "online", just stages in the production process of the final news artefact that reaches the consumer market – the newspaper.

Put in another way, the history of online news traced in this study is a history of media actors' continual efforts in taking advantage of point-to-point telecommunication networks to directly deliver news to end users in the market. From a producer-centric perspective, understanding online communication on the basis of distribution means is also sensible, if not crucial, for several reasons:

First, distribution methods have always been at the heart of the news media's operation in their history. As noted, conquering time and space in communication has been a central element in the development of human societies of all times and places (DeFleur & Ball-Rokeach, 1989; Marvin, 1988). The media business, in its long-established search for commercially viable news products, is not beyond this aspiration (Snowden, 2003).

Second, the social shape of a media form depends very much on its underlining distribution method, although this is too often ignored in media research (Star & Bowker, 2002). Whether a media form allows one-way or two-way communication, or whether it is multimedia-presented or primarily on a single modality (the printed word, human voice or image), is determined by the capacity of the distribution technology. For instance, the shift from circuit-switching to packet-switching in the telecommunication network is the foundation for the Internet to enable advanced features such as multimedia content.

Third, separating "online" from "offline" distribution provides a crucial tool to explore many issues of power and control that determine the success of online news ventures in its history. The core fact here is that delivering an online news service usually requires the provider to use a third-party telecommunication service – e.g. the telegraph carrier, the telephone company or the Internet service provider. In contrast, for radio and television, the distribution is direct from the news provider to the consumer. This means that "online" and "offline" news providers will have very different levels of power in controlling the economic, political and technological nature of their services.

If we can agree on these points, then consumer online news services, like any other news form, have evolved in a number of forms for 160 years.

Consumer news services over the telegraph

The first form of online news services did not come from any mainstream organisation but from technology-savvy independent media entrepreneurs in the early days of the telegraph. The story began not long after Samuel Morse and his competent assistant Alfred Vail successfully demonstrated the power of the telegraph on May 1, 1844. As the first telegraph line on the 20-mile Washington-Baltimore route was established and made available for private use in 1845, there arose a group of "telegraph reporters" who, belonging to no particular editorial staff, were not "necessarily committed to (serving) the newspaper press" and "could transmit news to any customer interested in telegraph news" (Blondheim, 1994, p. 44). As one advertisement of these services reads, it served both the press and "commercial gentlemen and others desiring regular and special intelligence or private correspondence" from a distant point (quoted in Blondheim, 1994, p. 44). By satisfying "numerous paying customers by one report, at the price of one transmission", these on-demand multicasting services diverted much profit from Morse's telegraphic enterprises. To respond to the threat, one of Morse's three commercial telegraph apostles, Henry O'Reilly, set up his company's news service, which supplied "consolidated, uniform" reports along his western lines and the New York-Albany-Buffalo line to newspapers and private operators in areas that these lines passed. By 1873, in addition to serving 600 newspapers around America, the New York Associated Press had earned substantial money from special bulletins of "updated" commercial news, which were cooperatively distributed three to four times to major markets during business hours by the Western Union Company (Blondheim, 1994).

Consumer telegraphic news services also spread to other countries with a high level of telegraph development. In Canada, by 1871, the Gold and Stock Company had become a source of news about stock quotes, gold prices and other trade events for 800 bankers and brokers (Winseck, 1999). In England, the Electric Telegraph Company began to deliver telegraphic news to not only 120 provincial press members but also to other private subscribers in 1854 (Winseck, 1999). This news service covered parliamentary matters, commercial events, stock exchange prices and entertainment information such as gambling, racing and sports news. By the early 1860s, Reuters had the exclusive right over distributing "commercial and shipping news to private subscribers within 15 miles of London" (Kieve, 1973, p. 71). In 1872, the Exchange Telegraph Company (Extel) started to offer a wide range of specialised news, information and entertainment content to the financial and other communities. With its controversial monopoly over the flow of news and information from the London Stock Exchange and later-established connections to stock markets in the US and France, Extel was able to deliver exclusive stock-related data to brokers, traders and other financial workers. By the mid-1880s, Extel had over 600 subscribers (Winseck, 1999).

What were the drivers of the emergence of these services? Technologically, telegraph news services were by no means easy to use. They used codes that would be quite demanding to decipher and they would hardly look appealing in comparison with the newspaper of the time. Despite this, they thrived because there was a "supervening market demand" for news at the time, which is comprehensively depicted in Menahem Blondeim's *News over the Wire*. On part of the public, there was a long "hunger" for timely and non-local news – especially news about political and commercial events on both national and international scales (Blondheim, 1994, pp. 11-29). In the US as well as in European countries, this became more urgent than ever in the decades before the telegraph, which saw a dramatic expansion in trans-Atlantic trade facilitated by a revolution in transportation. This stimulated the media's need for timelier and broader-scale news. Competition for "being the first" between newspapers to attract readers became increasingly harsher, as seen in the following description of how pre-telegraph newspapers responded to the overwhelming market demand for news:

> Initially newspapers employed private expresses to hasten the transmissions of news from Washington – first the pony express, later the locomotive express. In the former case, swift, full-size horses were dispatched in relay. In the latter, locomotives were chartered for special runs. Horses were most effective for short distances, with fresh riders, and of course only when unencumbered by heavy loads, let alone a coach. The rail express required a heated locomotive ready to run (on) an open track, with synchronized connections on other rail lines at the ready.
>
> … Even more complex facilities were necessary for speeding news from overseas markets. Unlike congressional and political agendas, which arrived with regularity, trans-Atlantic transports carrying the latest European news were unscheduled; … the expected time of arrival could be established only within a matter of days. There were also enough unscheduled voyages, with each arrival possibly bringing crucial economic and political data, to warrant constant watch of harbour offings for the latest arrivals. The time-consuming process of docking and later of quarantine suggested to the enterprising news-gatherers that they could save time by pre-boarding vessels and stripping them of their news cargo prior to their entry into the harbour (Blonheim, 1994, pp. 27-28).

Even with the pony express, steamboats and locomotives, the urgency of news did not diminish. In such a context, the emergence of the above news services is understandable. By the time the telegraph was introduced with a cheap and almost immediate correspondence, it was probably a "long overdue" invention. The market was ready – and as a common sense, when the market was ready, there would appear suppliers. In other words, to use media sociologist Helen Hughes's phrases (Blondheim, 1994, p. 38), it was the "quickening urgency" of news that gave rise to the earliest online news services.

Approaches to telegraph ownership and regulation were also crucial. In France, consumer telegraphic news services did not appear as the government saw the new technology as a political, not commercial, instrument. In the US, after a short period of state ownership, the Baltimore-Washington line was released for general public use, which saw the immediate emergence of telegraphic reporters, many of whom had already been serving as correspondents for the press (Blondheim, 1994). In England, the facilitation took place the other way around. After the state-run Post Office took ownership of telegraph systems in the 1870s, it created "a more open and transparent regime" to liberally license private networks and content providers, which was grounded on a "first come, first serve" basis to avoid undue favouritism. As a result, the decade saw a vital surge in the number of consumer news services over the wire like Extel (Winseck, 1999, p. 149). Extel, after many unsuccessful legal efforts to eliminate competition by preventing new content provision licences from the Post Office, ended up acquiring many of these companies.

Another socio-political situation that facilitated this development was the common lack of legal, organisational or technical grounds to distinguish telecommunication and content services during the 1840-1910 period in Canada, Britain and the US (Winseck, 1999). With concerns about the possible rise of irresponsible journalism and the circulation of libellous content, for example, the Supreme Court of Canada ruled that "it would seem that telegraphic companies are similar... to publishers ... (because) they are all engaged in one and the same transaction, viz.: collecting, transmitting and publishing matter collected, the aid and participation of all being necessary to the publication" (quoted in Winseck, 1999, p. 147). All this partly explained why the major players in the early consumer telegraphic news market were not the press but technology-savvy telegraph reporters and telegraph companies, although the former was well-aware of the strong need for breaking news and had larger budgets for and more experience in "speeding the pace of news" than any other party (Blondheim, 1994, p. 28).

[Indeed, the new technology was unfolding as a tremendous threat to the future of the press. Prominent publisher James Bennett was so overwhelmed by the telegraph's immediacy that he declared the death of the newspaper: "The telegraph may not affect magazine literature but the mere newspapers must submit to destiny and go out of existence" (quoted in Blondheim, 1994, p. 37). Thus, the provision of updated news to private subscribers by telegraphic reporters and telegraph companies means that, for the first time in history, newspapers had to experience the unpleasant reality that they could no longer dominate the news field. But during the early days, with no control over telegraph lines, they had to use others' telegraphic news services because they would otherwise have to pay much more to send their own reporters to the field. This was a remote reason for the birth of wire services such as the Associated Press.]

From the radio concept of telephony to audiotext news services

As in the case of telegraphy, the telephone was made use of to distribute news more effectively not long after "Bell's electrical toy" was invented in 1876. It started from "the radio concept of telephony" – the idea of delivering news and other content over the telephone line. As Briggs (1977, p. 43) explained:

> ...following the brief period before its two-way capabilities were fully appreciated, (the telephone) continued to be publicised as a device to transmit music and news as much as or more than speech; long after its multiple private and organizational uses had been exploited, it continued to offer the prospect of shared entertainment, information and instruction.

The concept was initially realised in the social form of, again, unprofessional news reports via early telephone operators. Aronson (1977) stated that during these days, it was not professional journalists but telephone operators who were the first to transmit news throughout many urban communities in the US – "news about crises, like fires and floods, missing persons reports, man-wanted bulletins, crimes and so forth". These services resemble today's web news in the sense that they made content available in a (human-operated) central database for users to retrieve over the phone line.

Telephone news services of these days, like their telegraphic counterparts, emerged and developed out of the thirst for news among the public. In fact, Bell's original purpose in inventing the telephone was to make it possible for people to talk to each other from distances. However, while he had not perfected the device as intended, he was under constant pressure from his supporters to make money (Aronson, 1977). This is why Bell had to envision the telephone as a means to distribute news and other content such as music and drama. He was right. The telephone news services were "too successful": operators, due to a number of technical problems, could not handle the excessive numbers of calls to meet the demand for news (Carey, 1982). As Aronson explained:

> … in the larger cities and towns the large numbers of subscribers and the small numbers of operators made it virtually impossible to provide the personal service that continued to be rendered in rural regions. Company officials were aware of the changing nature of urban telephony as it grew but they found it impractical to continue the previous kind of service. Increasing complexity, the size of the traffic, the nature of the equipment, as well as operating arrangements for handling the load demanded more formality in managing the calls…. In cities, most calls involved little of the unusual, and the main consideration was prompt, accurate handling (1977, p. 33).

Despite this and despite Bell's abandonment of his radio concept after perfecting his invention for long-distance conversations, telephone news continued to develop into more organised forms. One specific type of news, election statistics, was especially important in boosting the formation of what Marvin (1988, p. 217) called "the most ambitiously organised American effort to use new electric technologies to deliver the news" of the late 1890s. In the 1892 presidential election, through a coordinated effort of telephone companies in New York and Chicago, over 380 carefully edited telephone bulletins were sent out from a central point in New York to large waiting crowds at clubs and hotels in a wide area covering New England, most of the Middle Atlantic states, Wilmington, Washington, and Baltimore on the south, and Chicago and Wisconsin to the northwest (Marvin, 1988). For the Bryan/McKinley election (1896), "thousands sat with their ear glued to the receiver the whole night long, hypnotised by the possibilities unfolded to them for the first time" (Briggs, 1977, p. 43). During this election, telephone news became more diverse, with three distinctive services mobilising hundreds of operators: news delivery to local hotels and clubs; news delivery to local exchanges (to which groups of around 20 subscriber lines connected via special telephones set up for election news announcement); and central call-up exchanges (by which individual subscribers could call to retrieve election information from operators). See Marvin (1988) for more about the continuity and refinement of these services in the 1912 election.

The services were appealing. For one thing, as Marvin (1988, p. 217) pointed out, "election returns had been distributed by the telegraph since its invention, but the telephone added speed, immediacy and convenience". For another, in the case of those following the news from their own homes, there was no need for intermediaries as "no codes were necessary" (Briggs, 1977, p. 43). Amid the excitement, newspapers became "enamoured" with the telephone's distinguished capacity "to communicate the thunder of events directly to an audience with an immediacy greater than that of the telegraph or newspaper alone" (Marvin, 1988, p. 221). Many soon formed partnerships with telephone service providers to meet this demand. Among the major suppliers of election returns for the mentioned telephone news bulletins was the press. Other publications such as *The North American* in Philadelphia delivered their news summaries to the telephone companies so that callers could retrieve them "at any hour of the day and night" from operators (Aronson, 1977, p. 32). Telephone news was so familiar that subscribers soon "came to feel that they had the right to receive such information when they called Central" (Aronson, 1977, p. 33). These call-in newscasting services spread to rural America after telephones were brought there in 1894, and lasted until the radio age.

It was, however, not in the US but in the Austrio-Hungarian empire that the ultimate development of the radio concept of telephony was first found. Nearly two decades after Bell's proposal, the concept was developed into the more perfect form of the "telephone-newspaper," introduced in Budapest in 1893 (Denison, 1901). After obtaining exclusive rights for telephone development in the country, Theodore Puskas – an inventor and ex-collaborator with Thomas Edison – divided this city of 500,000 residents into 30 circuits, each connected to 200-300 subscribers of his *Telephon Hirmondo* (Aronson, 1977). At the receiving end, for a minimal fee, subscribed family members could listen to news simultaneously through a wooden box and earphones (Gilbert, 1999). Gathering news in the same way as other newspapers (Denison, 1901), the programmed news service successfully operated for 23 years in a way that is surprisingly not different from today's television and radio programming:

> Each day a schedule or program was announced to the subscribers. The day began with a news bulletin and with summaries of the newspapers. In the midmorning, summaries of stock exchange prices were repeated at regular intervals while the Exchange was open. There were hourly news summaries for those who had missed earlier bulletins, and at noon there was a report on preceedings in Parliament. During the afternoon, "short entertaining stories" were read, "sporting intelligence" was transmitted, and there were "filler items" of various kinds. In the evening, there were theatrical offerings, visits to the opera, poetry readings, concerts and lectures – including repeats of Academy lectures by well-known literary figures. There were also "linguistic lessons in English, Italian and French which was hailed "as a great benefit to the young generation"... At (the central) office..., there were over 40 "reporters and literary men" in addition to the 'the persons who actually speak to or transmit the news to the subscribers, and who are chosen on account of their good voices and distinct articulation (Briggs, 1977, pp. 51-52).

It must be noted here that while *Telephon Hirmondo* can be seen as a proto-broadcasting system because of its real-time content delivery (Marvin, 1988), it might also fit into the definition of online news in this work because the content was delivered over a point-to-point communication network only to selected users, i.e. not all telephone network-ready users in Budapest. Its operation scope, however, was not limited and was increasingly broadened. By the latter half of 1900s, according to a witness, this "newspaper with only an abstract existence" was employing over 200 people (including non-editorial personnel such as office boys, linemen and janitors) "in the busy winter months" to serve "a veritable web" extending 1,100 miles of wire and "more than 15,000 of the best homes in the Hungarian capital" (Fitzgerald, 1907, p. 507). In addition to private homes, it was "invariably turned on in the doctor's waiting room, in barber shops, cafes, restaurants, and dentists' parlours – wherever people resort, in fact, sit waiting for any purpose whatever" (Fitzgerald, 1907, p. 507).

Telephone newspapers, however, never appeared in other European countries, which is puzzling for several reasons. First, Hungary had an awful telephone infrastructure. As Colton (1912) observed: "Hungary seems a strange place in which to seek for anything novel in the telephone line, for next to Italy, which has 62, 000 to serve a population of 33,500,000, Austria-Hungary has the worst telephone service and the least of it to be found in all Europe". Second, the practice of multicasting content over the telephone was well understood in other European countries. Indeed, Theodore Puskas might well have come to the idea for his Budapest service at the International Electrical Exhibition of 1881 in Paris, where "long queues gathered ... to listen to music transmitted by telephone from a mile away" (Briggs, 1977, p. 43; see also Marvin, 1988). In Britain, irregular phone delivery of theatre and concert performances had already been in place in Birmingham, Liverpool and Manchester in 1894, when a company named Electrophone started to regularly deliver entertainment content and religious services to telephone households and hospitals in London. Even this service met with this limited success, attracting a total of 600 subscribers after ten years of operation (Briggs, 1977).

However, the strange absence of telephone news services in non-Hungary Europe is, again, understandable in the light of what DeFleur and Ball-Rokeach defined as a social conflict with existing values or what Winston referred to as "the law of suppression of radical potential". British observers usually attributed this to higher costs, no legal entitlement for the same right of access and the social difference between Budapest – a city of pleasure, and London – a city of business, where "time is everything" and "a man could not sit the whole day with apparatus to his ear waiting for some particular news or exchange prices" (Briggs, 1977, pp. 53-59). Briggs saw more issues beyond these. One was a sense of cultural resistance from the contemporary institutions, which saw the undesirable prospect of those "laid-on services" that, as *The Electrician* wrote, might lead people "sitting in armchairs and pressing a button" to a life of "no wants, no money, no ambition, no youth, no desires, no individuality, no names and nothing wise" (quoted in Briggs, 1977, p. 56). Another reason was the vested interests of related businesses, especially the press. Unlike the Budapest service, Electrophone had to exclude news from its service, because this posed a threat to British newspapers, whose interests "were to remain strong enough during the 1920s and 1930s to prevent the BBC from developing a news service of its own" (Briggs, 1997, p. 56). In Budapest, the press initially boycotted Pukas's service but then quickly realised that this was not to replace them but could even stimulate public interests via brief news items that led to more newspaper sales. This was not realised in Britain until the 1940s[1].

Telephone news services did not die. They still find their "habitats" today, not only in developing countries but also in the developed world. The modern "telephone-newspaper" takes the social form of audiotext news, technically based on telephone voice information systems. By pushing buttons on their touch-tone phones, callers can easily and immediately access a central database and retrieve information of their interest such as breaking news, sports scores, stock quotes and soap-opera updates. Some newspapers such as the *Post-Gazette* in Pittsburgh even set up a toll-free phone number, on which public members can hear reporters reading news reports (Garneau, 1992) – a service strikingly similar to the 19th century telephone news. Starting from experiments in the late 1980s (Shedden, 1998), as late as 1993, about 420 American newspapers provided audiotext services – some for free (with inserted advertising) but most with a subscription fee (Piirto, 1993). *The Atlanta Journal and Constitution* received nine million calls in 1990, compared with 5.2 million in 1989 (Boczkowski, 2004).

The reason for this revival, once again, can be explained in terms of market demands and competition. To the consumer, the service is easy and convenient to use while the information database is rich enough to meet many news and information needs, especially the demand for classified advertising. To local businesses, being recorded on audiotext services with their products gives them a competitive edge. To publishers, the service involves low investment, ease of use and low risks while being able to either generate considerable money from subscribers and businesses. At the very least, these audiotext services create goodwill among readers, which boosts readerships and circulations (Piirto, 1993). As *The Atlanta Journal and Constitution*'s audiotext general manager put it: "It's a lot like colour. You don't make a profit using colour but it helps maintain readers" (quoted in Boczkowski, 2004, p. 32). Finally, the popularity of these audio news services was impressive enough to generate some excitement and fear in an increasingly diversified media landscape. As seen in a comment made by George Wilson in May 1989:

The flood of new electronic products and services that the regional Bell telephone companies are creating will be nothing less than tomorrow's system for distributing information to every American home... Depending on how they are used, these distribution systems will strengthen or shatter the traditional links between newspapers, their advertisers, and their readers. In short, the phone companies could reshape the media triangle (quoted in Dizard, 2000, p. 164).

The faxed newspaper

The facsimile machine has also been made use of as a technology for news delivery but it did not enjoy immediate applications as in the cases of the telegraph and the telephone. Invented by Alexander Bain in 1842, the fax machine was not tried for home-delivery newspapers until the 1930s. *The Milwaukee Journal* started the experiments in 1934 and *The New York Times* followed suit (Pavlik, 1998). Fax newspapers of these days met with a failure due to many reasons including poor transmission quality, the unpopularity of fax machines and limited transferable content (Pavlik, 1998, p. 58). In the 1940s, the technology began to work well and the fax machine was gaining increasing popularity, giving rise to new hopes for the fax newspaper. As commented by the then NBC director of research in *Journalism Quarterly*: "The bright promise of a newspaper printed in your home has occupied a firm place in the bag of tricks with which prophets of the electronic future have delighted their audiences for years. This service is to be made possible by facsimile broadcasting – the transmission of reproductions of printed matter and pictures by radio into the homes" (Beville, 1948, p. 7). However, fax newspapers of these days still could not make money because not many consumers wanted to spend money on them. As Albert Blade, a newspaper executive editor, recalled: "The technology worked. Experts writing in magazines said it was the coming thing.... But they could not get people pay for it" (quoted in Butler & Kent, 1983, p. 4).

Fax newspapers, however, were revived in the late 1980s and early 1990s with many newspaper giants as pioneers. Junk fax advertising was becoming popular; some services such as FaxFacts (supplying technical support, marketing information and installation instructions from industrial companies) and FaxTicker (providing access to information on a portfolio of fifteen stocks by using their personal identification number) were making money. The technology was gaining prominence in national election campaigns

34

when candidates tried to send their messages as quickly as possible. And newspapers quickly jumped on board (Dizard, 2000). In Japan, *The Daily Japan Digest* was published as a faxed newsletter to provide summaries of important news in the country to decision-makers and businesses in the US (Stokes, 1992). In the US, *The New York Times* in 1992 republished a faxed newspaper to primarily serve cruise ships, which was then expanded to a broader consumer market, including hotels that its print version could not reach (Pavlik 1998; Dizard, 2000). It also faxed to subscribers other kinds of raw information such as tax forms and presidential speeches (Teinowitz, 1993). Other American newspapers offered, either free of charge or with some fee, faxed reprints of articles or faxed advertising. Some other papers went beyond these simple services. *The Hartford Courant* "pre-cycled" its content by faxing out a 1,500-word summary of stories of its next day stories to paying subscribers (Dizard, 2000, p. 47). Others (e.g. *Fortune, Upside, Cruising World, MediaFAX*) provided fax-on-demand services, based on computer storage of documents for users, especially businesses, to retrieve via a touchtone phone and fax (Kauffman, 1994; Piirto, 1994).

Technically, the fax survived in the age of the Internet at least because it was easy and convenient to use and modern fax machines of the 1990s were chip-filled machines with more sophisticated capabilities. Also, at least until the 1990s, fax technologies enjoyed a universal technological standard that Internet technologies did not. Economically, the cost of the fax machine was trivial for consumers and, as fax consumerisation was becoming "the fastest-growing service in the new telemedia environment", the machine became a "newly competitive service" for newspapers (Dizard, 2000, p. 47). Also, as the above services show, there were niche markets for publishers both to reach old customers and attract new ones. In 1995, the US market for faxed news services were valued at nearly half a billion dollars and this was projected to grow by 40% annually till 2000 (Martin, 1995). By the late 1990s, however, the growth of faxed newspapers became slower, with niche market or on-demand fax information services being the main successful players (Dizard, 2000). Indeed, they "never took off", with "several (folding) for lack of profits ... and most of those that continued publishing became neither significant revenue centres nor objects of much enthusiasm among those interested in a digital future" (Boczkowski, 2004, p. 32). However, they did not "(die) unmourned" in the 1990s as Kovaric (2001) suggested: a recent visit to the corporate websites of giant publishers like *The New York Times* or *The Wall Street Journal* reveal that many still continue their fax news services today in addition to digital platforms. It would be interesting to see whether they would survive in an age when customised news/information is delivered to the email box.

Pre-web computer-mediated online news: from teletext to videotex

With the introduction of the computer into the news-production process, consumer online news services took some far more complex forms during the 1970s and 1980s. Apart from auditext and fax-on-demand services, all other computer-based online news services have been subsumed under the catchall, although controversial, term of videotex (without the *t* at the end).

"Videotex" in its very generic meaning involves delivering news and other content from a central database through the telephone line on to the TV or the computer screen of the news consumer and takes two major social forms – the text-only service and the text-and-graphics service (Patten, 1986). The former, called information banks or online databases (electronic collections of information), began with *The New York Times*'s database of story abstracts in 1969 (Shedden, 1998). They were then developed into full-text commercial infobanks during the 1970s by many news organisations, the first of which was *The Global and Mail* Canada. In 1997, there were 6,200 databases all over the world, up from 3369 ten years before that (Pavlik, 1998). However, as the web hastily penetrated daily life, the late 1990s began to see these services struggling to survive (Tenopir & Barry, 2000). Rather than dying, however, some databases that used to serve a wide public with popular content have evolved into specialised information services, with library users as their most substantial consumer base. Others – such as Northern Light – turned to the web and mixed the free and fee models for their business. Still some others – like Reed Elsevier's Lexis-Nexis – charge low fees in exchange for displaying limited advertisements.

The more popular and advanced text-and-graphics services are what "videotex" generally is understood to be today. There are two distinctive groups of services within this domain, one consisting of those content and communication services delivered on to the computer screen and the other on to the television screen. The computer-based videotex group is associated with proprietary services such as America Online, CompuServe, Prodigy, Delphi, Genie, Applelink, EWorld and the Source. Starting from CompuServe in the 1970s, these "online service providers" – as they are called – provided pay subscribers with a dial-up access, via a modem, to a range of content and communication opportunities, from updated news, weather, stock quotes, shopping information, encyclopaedia, games to email, teleconferences, bulletin boards, chat rooms and so on. These were based on their own packet-switching technologies and interfaces that have been evolving from being merely text-based to being GUI (Graphic User Interface)-based. They attracted millions of users around the world and some are still doing well today after adjusting their business strategy from being proprietary services with hourly charges to being more like Internet service providers operating with monthly flat-rate fees on the web. For practical reasons, however, this study will not delve into the development of these services. The focus here is videotex services delivered on to the television set, which are almost dead today.

The story of TV-based videotex (hereinafter shortened as videotex, unless when clarification is needed) began from the experiment and development of a news form called teletext at the BBC in 1972 (Logue, 1979). In an oversimplified description, teletext works as follows: a page of text is processed and edited at a terminal with a computer database before being digitally encoded and beamed over the air as audio signals. At the receiving end, the news consumer needs a decoder to accept the sent data and display the pages on his/her television screen. A news consumer can easily, through handling the buttons on the decoder, request any information that is available at the providing end. Teletext of the 1970s was hailed as a coming revolution in information delivery and consumption as well as in other realms of daily life. Although enjoying some successes, it quickly became a backward technology in the eyes of many media actors after the introduction of videotex.

In contrast to being beamed over the air, videotex data (both text and graphics) were sent through a telephone network to a user's modem, which was connected to a decoder controlled by the user with a keypad (Tydeman et al, 1982; Rogers, 1986). As a result of being distributed via the phone line, the volume of content in videotex services was much richer than teletext. Whenever the user needs some information, he/she needs to adjust the keypad so that the information displayed on the TV screen can be called up. Videotex thus has far more advanced features. While a teletext user could call up only a few hundred pages of text-only information from a computer database, videotex allowed the display of text and graphics on the screen, the user's self-control of the information flow, and a vast capacity for information storage and news updates. The social form of videotex is also characterised by the capacity for two-way communication – a feature that no previous news media had. With a videotex service, the user can send and receive messages to and from the central computer as well as can communicate with users at other terminals in the network. For more detail about the technologies and features of teletext and videotex, see works by Barr (1985), Mayne (1982), Money (1979), Montague (1981), Roizen (1980), Smith (1980) and Tydeman et al (1982).

Videotex news began in Britain with the Ceefax service in 1976 (Shedden, 1998), following some fairly successful teletext ventures. They quickly spread across Europe and to other developed countries such as the US and Japan. Except in France, however, most of these services were closed down by the late 1980s, leaving behind them billions of lost dollars. In the US alone, an estimated $2.5 billion "(vaporised) into thin air" (Lefcowitz, 2001). Why?

The story of videotex is a clear example of how the media as a business adapt to and take advantage of new technologies to protect their commercial viability. It happened in a period when videotex was seen as the coming revolution in the news industry thanks to the mentioned outstanding features. Many media scholars and practitioners of the 1970s and 1980s believed videotex would bring revolutionary changes to human communications in general and the news media in particular (Fidler, 1997; Mayne, 1982; Pool, 1983; Smith, 1980). It was advocated as a technology that would change the nature of economic practices, public awareness, education and training and other social norms.

In the language of the 1980s, the convergence of the two popular technologies of the telephone and television "could be a marriage of the century" and would become "the quintessential medium of the 21st century" (quoted in Kyrish, 1996, pp. 8-9; see this excellent review for more about the pervasive "revolutionary" language on videotex).

For the newspaper industry, videotex generated both excitement and fear. On the one hand, the exclusive features of videotex made it a desirable new horizon in which the first to enter could be the best to make money in the future. AT&T predicted that by 1990, eight million households in the US would have been installed with a videotex terminal and in another estimate, a $10-billion market was projected (Lefcowitz, 2001). Videotex, in other words, was a golden opportunity for newspapers in their long search for better and more commercially viable news products. On the other hand, this happened at a time when newspaper circulation had been declining for years, strengthening the obligation to adapt or die. Videotex was powerful enough to mean that, as Anthony Smith (1980, p. 244) put it, "the decade of the nineties (was) going to be one in which the traditional newspaper may face decline, extinction or at least complete internal self-appraisal". A survey in 1982 addressing the potential use of videotex found that one-third of the respondents said "if (they) could get the contents of a newspaper on a TV screen... (they) might stop buying a newspaper" (Butler and Kent, 1983, p. 7). The threat was perceived to be serious enough for the Newspaper Association of America to take legal actions to prevent AT&T and other regional phone companies from entering the content provision arena via videotex (on the basis that it would produce unfair competition in the nascent electronic publishing realm) (Boczkowski, 2004). The following description by Fidler (1997, p. 144) of the secrecy of his mission in the Knight-Ridder team to develop the first videotex news service in the US, *Viewtron*, further reveals how the panic was on:

> A four-person development team, of which I was a member, had been selected covertly from staff of newspapers and subsidiaries within the Knight-Ridder group. James K. Batten, the vice-president for news, ... asked each of us in private meetings to volunteer for a venture that he believed was of the utmost importance to the future of the company... He explained that Norman Morrison, Knight-Ridder's director of information systems, had alerted the company to the potential threat posed by videotex technology. After executive visits to England, he and most of the other officers had become convinced that the threat was real and believed that Knight-Ridder must act quickly... The secrecy surrounding our mission was so tight that only Batten, a few other senior Knight-Ridder

executives, and our designated team leader, John Woolley, knew all our identities before we assembled for the first time at the Portman Hotel in London.

(Viewtron started its commercial operation in October 1983 and closed down in March 1986 after a total loss of about $150 million.)

So what went wrong? Winston's ideas of supervening social necessities and the law of suppression provide an explanation here. As noted, there seemed to be a clear supervening market demand on part of the user, as surveys consistently found the public willingness to use videotex. These, unfortunately, were false necessities and the positive research quickly became considered "woefully overblown", as media critic John Zonderman put it (quoted in Lefcowitz, 2001). Mindy McAdams explained this in an informal but concise way:

> The story is that the companies that ran these tests did a lot of expensive market research, asking people who had never seen a computer, or anything else like videotex, what they would like in terms of information that would be delivered as electronic text. The people answered, and the horrible videotex systems were built to deliver what the people said they wanted… They tried it, they hated it and they refused to use it (1995).

In reality, as soon as the novelty of the innovation wore off, people stopped using the systems. This was due to a number of social and technological problems. First, the cost was too high and unrealistic, including cost for the necessary device, which went up to $600 (McAdams, 1995), and the subscription fee, which was initially set at about $30 per month at Viewtron (Fidler, 1997). Second, the service was too difficult to use and sometimes annoying to subscribers. Data transmission speeds were "painfully slow"; it was "a strange, seemingly endless labyrinth of information" with no obvious structure for the user to browse easily for their favourite content; and the page looked "dull and uninviting on TV screens" (Fidler, 1997, pp. 151-159; see also Lefcowitz, 2001).

Third, and probably most importantly, newspapers were not active enough in bringing videotex's potential into its full strength. For one thing, videotex services were no more than repurposed newspapers with very little original content, which is at odds with the need for specialised news and information among its early adopters (Boczkowski, 2004).

Also, important stories, especially exclusives, were not provided first because of the fears that they would fall into the hands of competing outlets. For another, newspapers' imagined "supervening market demands" for videotex was just wrong: while the information need among subscribers was not well met, the most frequently used service, electronic mail, was not fully served. As Fidler (1997, p. 148) recalled, Viewtron research showed a clear trend that interpersonal communication with other subscribers was the more exciting and more highly evaluated feature than content "but that was not what anyone was prepared to hear at this time ... (because) nearly everyone involved in the trial saw Viewtron as an advertising-supported electronic newspaper ... (and) its potential role as an interpersonal communication medium was considered secondary". By comparison, the France-based Minitel service – a rare survivor of videotex – succeeded partly because it quickly shifted from a focus on news and other content to one on interpersonal exchange, after realising that the latter was what would drive the adoption of videotex among users.

Interest in videotex news, however, came back in the early 1990s, when personal computers gained an increasing popularity and telecommunication providers were now allowed to enter the electronic publishing market. Partly under the recurring fear of being left behind, newspapers' videotex services briefly resurged in the years immediately before the web – this time not on their own systems but via online services like America Online (Fidler, 1997; Boczkowski, 2004). By the mid-1990s, the success of these experiments was limited, with a huge survey of 10,000 consumers finding a significant amount of dissatisfaction. As the Internet was opened to the general public and the web penetrated daily life, as briefly mentioned in the introduction, it was quickly chosen as the delivery platform of the future by newspapers and other traditional media. Thus, although failing, videotex laid the foundation for today's Internet-based news; its place in media history is "a crucial missing link on the road to the Information Superhighway" (Lefcowitz, 2001).

The mutual shaping of technologies and society: lessons learnt from the pre-web evolution of online news

This book raises a question concerning the evolutionary path of online news and the social factors that shape this evolution from a media-centric perspective. By connecting different news media forms that were previously seen as discrete developments, this chapter has shown that the recent emergence of web news is not a sudden "overnight" event but is the latest in a chain of continuous episodes in the evolution of consumer online news services over the past 160 years. In this history, all the point-to-point communication technologies in human life have been tried since their early days for news delivery. The social forms of online news have evolved from simplicity to complexity – from the use of a single new technology to the integration of the old and the new, from text-only to text-and-graphics deliveries, from one-way to two-way communication, from man-operated to the computer-operated central databases, from pull to push and so on. Some of them survive and find their niche markets today while others vanished due to a range of social and technological brakes. While the definition of online news as news over point-to-point communication network is open for historians and media researchers to debate, this is at least a prehistory of electronic publishing and part of the history of media convergence. (And if this definition of online news is not acceptable, then the above discussion is at least a timely attempt to call for more scholarly attention to the issue. Is "online" a too generic term to be helpful in any sense?)

Whether one agrees or disagrees with the above definition of online news, however, the media development chain tracked in this chapter reinforces the crucial point that predicting the future of a medium solely on the premise of its technological power is a naïve approach. However "powerful" a communication technology is, the decisive force to determine its diffusion is the many characteristics of the social sphere that are present at the time of its introduction. In other words, technologies' impact depends more on the convergence of socio-economic forces than on their innovative potentials (Marvin, 1988). The clearest example is the telephone newspaper. As much as it sounded an awkward technology by today standards, it was a substantial improvement for mass communication at its time. But it enjoyed a substantial reach only in Hungary and did not exist in other parts of Europe and immediately failed in the US. Other examples include consumer telegraphic news services, which were popular in the UK and North America but not in France in the latter half of the 1800s; or the coming "revolutionary" videotex, which was successful in France but failed in other Western countries in the 1980s.

To chart the socio-economic kinesis underlining this process, it is important to go beyond the nature of the technology to think of three inter-related sources of social influences: the historical context in which the technology is introduced, the people who create the media form based on this technology, and the people who use it. To be consistent with the producer-centric perspective in this chapter, this diffusion dynamic could be explored on the basis that under constant profit motives and/or permanent pressures to ensure commercial viability, the media as a business have always been playing a central part in determining the success of new communication forms. This involvement, however, does not ensure that the media will make the best out of newer communication technologies to improve products and services because it depends on a wide range of other factors:

First, the extent to which a new technology is made use of depends much on the issue of who controls it, which in turn is determined by the historical socio-political context of the technology, including the ideology applied to the technology and its resulting ownership regulation (public versus private; exclusive versus inclusive rights). These factors affect both investors' willingness to pour resources into new media and the number of potential players in shaping the social form of the technology. For example, the flourishing of consumer telegraphic news in the UK in the 1870s was based on a "laissez-faire" and egalitarian ideology and approach in conferring access rights to lines by its owner, the Post Office. Or, *Telephone Hirmondo* enjoyed a wide diffusion in a city of limited telephone penetration partly because it was legally given the exclusive right to control the city's telephone system, thus having a sufficient consumer base to deliver its own news and other content services. This issue of control could create a serious conflict between communication infrastructure and content providers that might act as an impediment to the diffusion of new media, as can be seen in the legal lobbying efforts by the American newspaper industry to exclude telephone companies from videotex development in the 1980s.

Second, and obviously, users play a critical role in shaping new media forms via affecting media actors. To succeed, media actors would usually have to adjust and compromise what they think with what users really need. As a response to users' demand, for instance, American telephone companies of the late 1890s substantially diversified their online services of election returns from 1892 to 1896. This point is clearer in the case of Minitel, which was more open to quickly realise the importance of communication utilities in videotex and then, unlike its American counterparts, to aggressively incorporate them in the service. That is, the social form of Minitel was determined substantially, although indirectly, by its users' needs and tastes. In other words, society is the greatest lab for new technologies to transform from "prototypes" to "inventions". Thus, although technologies do play an important role in the diffusion of new media, they are involved in *a dynamically continuous process* that is marked by the *mutual influences* between their technical capacities and the interests and values of their actors and their users.

This leads us to the many issues associated with the third – and the most direct -- social force in determining the social form of new media technologies: those who finance and produce them. Above, I reviewed that the media often attempt to generate products and services that are perceived to have better quality and/or "supervening market demands". However, this process is vulnerable to many inherent socio-cultural problems that media actors themselves face. A key issue is that the media generate new news products on the basis of what they are interested in and how they perceive the new technology, which is largely informed by their existing practices, cultural norms and values. In other words, media practitioners are associated with systemic restraints that have a strong effect on the social shape of the technology – such as work routines, commercial motives, professional values, and so on. Sometimes, these restraints led them to being unable to "imagine" their consuming public and its supervening demands, which in turn results in the failure to develop the right product out of a technology.

A popular restraint in the pre-history of online news is the fear of new technologies. With an established position in the market, traditional news organisations are by and large the most resourceful to invest and foster the development of a new medium. Ironically, it is also due to this established position that traditional practitioners are usually not genuinely eager to harness the power of new media. When a new and innovative medium emerges, the general reaction among traditional media is the fear that the new will disrupt their near-monopoly and could make them become irrelevant in the long run. As they let this fear drive their experiments with the new technology, traditional media actors are often not seriously interested in exploring its new socio-technical possibilities, especially those that do not appear as a direct threat to their traditional business. Also, as the new is done with the ultimate aim to protect the old in the future, resources are often poured into new media ventures with a caution that the new should not become a direct competitor to the old. This is worsened by the fact that a fear-driven move to embrace new media usually leaves traditional practitioners with inadequate time to be technically, professionally and commercially prepared for new technologies.

All this was clear in the American experience of TV-based videotex, where technologies did not translate into market demands not simply because the market did not exist. For one thing, it was because of a wrong assumption that videotex users will have the same need for news and information as those of the traditional newspaper. What users seemed to want seemed to be the two-way communication more than content utilities of videotex systems. Viewtron and other American videotex services could have followed the same route as Minitel over the long run – the problem was that these experiments were put to an end, rather than explored for possible alternative avenues, as soon as it became clear that this "revolutionary" technology was not going to kill their core business, news provision. Indeed, videotex in the end was a failure with "mixed blessings" for American newspapers. When announcing the end of Viewtron, for example, James Batten declared: "Videotex is not likely to be a threat to newspapers in the foreseeable future" (quoted in Boczkowski, 2004, p. 28). The same sign of relief was found in the statement by James Holley, president of Times Mirror's Gateway videotex service, on its closure: "We reached the point where we learned enough to know that (videotex) was not a threat to our newspapers or our cable companies or our magazines which is what drove us into this project in the first place" (quoted in Ettema, 1989, p. 108).

In this light, it is still too early to support the common claim that the Internet will become the dominant news medium of the future. If history is a repetition process and the past can be seen as a prologue, the above suggests that despite the potential "revolutionary" technical nature of the Internet, it might become just another medium to deliver news if it its commercial aspects are not clear. The next chapter will shed more light on this by applying some of the above historical and sociological lessons to the penetration of web technologies into the traditional newsroom in the past 15 years.

Notes

1. Since most Internet services are delivered via the web platform, I tend to use the terms "Internet" and "web" interchangeably throughout this work, except when clarification is needed. For example, "web-based" news and "Internet news" are often used to refer to the same thing, although strictly speaking, the web is only one part of the Internet.

2. A similar "telephone newspaper" called The Telephone Herald appeared in Newark, New Jersey, the US for a brief period between 1911 and 1912. It was a brief success cum failure due to many of the common problems discussed in this chapter, including lack of control over the telephone infrastructure which the Budapest service enjoyed. For practical reasons, however, this interesting phenomenon was not discussed in details. Readers with interest can refer to Marvin (1988) for a brief but incisive discussion of this American telephone news service.

Chapter 2

A repeated history: the media's fear-driven innovation culture and the development of news on the web

Using the historical lessons from the pre-web history of online news, this chapter presents a critical review of the emergence and development of news on the web since the 1990s, mapping its development into two stages that are driven by the same factor: the fear-driven defensive innovation culture among traditional media. Being threatened by the penetration of the Internet, traditional media hastily established their online presence in the 1990s but then, under the many uncertainties resulting from this rush online and the strong urge to defend rather than expand markets, have been reluctant to and/or unable to pour good resources into developing an online news artefact with its full potential. Online news has been force-fitted into the same old professional and business model that is at odds with its remarkable potential. Industrial developments in the past three years, however, suggest that as the Internet has established itself as a major news medium, traditional media – now even more threatened and urged to take actions to make up their already lost time – are on the verge of a new, more vigorous and rigorous development stage of online news.

Fear versus excitement: the news media's online migration in the 1990s

Up until the mid-1990s, the nascent world-wide web remained a true "Wild West" to the majority of news organisations. Apart from a few giants with substantial resources for experimenting with web technologies, most practitioners were not even sure what it was. When technology reporter John Markoff for *The New York Times* mentioned Mosaic – the first popular web browser – at the Nieman Foundation's first new media conference in 1994, he was interrupted by the moderator with a request to explain what the tool was (Boczkowski, 2004). The new medium was taken to as no more than a fad that did not deserve media executives' attention (Outing, 1999). The boom soon, however, began and took place at an unprecedented rate. In the US alone, hundreds of millions of dollars from traditional media organisations were poured into cyberspace projects to exploit a promising market which, according to Dataquest, grew from a scant $21 million in 1996 to $203.7 million by the end of 1998 (Brown, 1999). As an *Editor & Publisher* article described in 1996:

> The trickle has grown into a stream, the stream has swollen into a river, and nobody knows when the flood of newspapers into computerized information services will peak... Overwhelmingly, the highway these information services are travelling is the world wide web" (quoted in Boczkowski, 2004, p. 21).

A similar explosion was found in other well-wired countries. In Australia, Quinn (2000) reported that within only a few years, the online world quickly turned from "an oddity" to something "sexy and modern" in the eyes of newspapers' executives and journalists. In Europe, according to the director of Interactive Publishing Europe, "the first year (1994) was curiosity-driven (...). The year after that a certain amount of fear settled in (...) and 1996 saw the first really expert crowd at Interactive Publishing, with everybody having set up an online publishing site and talking page views" (Specker, 1999).

As a result, from virtually zero in 1993, there were 3,112 online newspapers, 3900 online magazines, 2108 radio sites and 1823 TV sites in 1998 – according to *Editor & Publisher* (cited in Sparks, 1999). By the dawn of the new century, the World Association of Newspapers (2001) reported that 5400 newspapers worldwide had a web edition and this number was on the way up. By 2002, *Editor & Publisher* reported a total of 13,536 sites set up by traditional news organizations worldwide (cited in Nguyen et al, 2005). For the first time in the history of journalism, all traditional news media were pushed into a head-to-head competition on the same platform. By the mid-2000s, "virtually all mainstream newspapers and broadcasters" in North America had an Internet site, with "an increasing number of community newspapers and local broadcasters joining the trend" (Eid & Buchanan, 2005). According to the World Association of Newspapers (2006), the worldwide number of newspapers with websites increased by 20% in 2005.

The imperatives for this "sex change operation", as Brown (1999) called it, are rather complicated but, at the risk of oversimplification, could be discussed in two interrelated categories – enormous opportunities provided and potential threats posed by the Internet as a news medium. An examination of the 1990s academic and industrial discourses in trade and scholarly publications reveal that three main opportunities were opened to traditional news media on the Internet. First, the spatial independence of the web (i.e. its global accessibility) was taken to as a rare opportunity to reach an almost infinite audience, which is what many traditional news organisations have been longing for. Second, in an environment where low entry barriers provide a chance for virtually anybody with a desktop to become a publisher, that could be done without high distribution costs. The third, and probably most important, reason was that the Internet was seen as an exciting avenue to develop better and therefore more commercially viable news products to serve the market. The Internet was widely perceived as an ideal platform for people to keep themselves informed of their daily interest in a more effective, efficient and enjoyable way thanks to a number of technological advantages that were briefly mentioned in the introduction to this book and will be discussed in detail in Chapter 3.

But perhaps the motive to make money from this new medium was not as stressing as the fear of becoming irrelevant in the Internet age. The 1990s was a decade in which the Internet was heralded as a coming communication revolution. Bill Gates declared in his 1995 best-selling book, *The Road Ahead*, that human beings were watching something historic happen, something that would "affect the world seismically, rocking us the same way the discovery of the scientific method, the invention of printing, and the arrival of the industrial age did" (quoted in Kyrish, 1996, p. 18). Negroponte "measured" the medium's impact at "10.5 on the Richter scale of social change" (quoted in Dizard, 2000, p. 5). Amidst all these claims, the Internet became a "fabulous monster", a term coined by journalist Bryan Appleyard (1999), in the mind of media executives and journalists of the 1990s. As in the videotex days, it was believed that the multipurpose nature of the Internet meant that people would find it increasingly indispensable in their daily life, and along with this, they would be likely to use and, and sooner or later, rely on ubiquitous online news services and their many "exclusive" features. Consequently, it was feared, time and money spent on traditional news services would reduce, and at some point, might even cease. Extinction, or at least a reduced importance, of old news media would appear.

The threat seemed to become all the more closer in the dotcom boom of the late 1990s, in which thousands of online service providers took advantage of the medium's easy and cheap publishing capacity to expand their e-business operations, drawing people to their sites with extensive databases of free news and information. That has not included the emergence of rich content services provided by Internet giants such as Lycos, Yahoo! and MSN, who used to have no place in the news industry. As Anderson (1995, p. 5) argued: "As a new medium with almost no distribution costs, the Internet has the potential to reshape the media world, letting new competitors in and forcing established giants to evolve or die".

All this happened at a time when traditional media had been in troubles for decades (Ahlers, 2006; Boczkowski, 2004; Dizard, 2000; Meyer, 2004; Pavlik, 1998). For the network television industry, for instance, the Internet started to "invade" the market at a time when it was already facing stiff competition from other new broadcasting media. In the US, the combined prime-time ratings of the big three television networks, which had once reached 90%, dropped to below 50% in the 1990s. In Australia, research by Roy Morgan (2005) shows that in stark contrast to the steep growth of the Internet during the 1994-2004 decade, the percentage of the population aged 14 or over watching commercial TV "in the past seven days" reduced from nearly 80% to around 67%. Meanwhile, new technologies continuously emerged, as Dizard (2000, p. 81) reviewed:

> Over-the-air television is under siege these days, as its audiences (and its revenues) are being depleted by cable television, home videocassette recorders, and the Internet. The pressure will accelerate as newer technologies such as direct satellite broadcasting and fibre-optic delivery of information and entertainment services compete for consumer attention.

All this created a wave of pessimists about the future of television among its practitioners and critics. In 1998, ABC president Robert Iger confessed: "We used to think that the possibility existed that the erosion was going to stop. We were silly. It is never going to stop" (quoted in Dizard, 2000, p. 1). Earlier, a media critic argued:

> No one believes the networks will ever relive their glory days, when they were the nation's 'electronic hearth,' around which more than 90% of the TV audience gathered on a given night. With dozens of existing viewing alternatives, and the prospect of perhaps hundreds of new TV channels through technological advances, even the most bullish analysts concede the networks will continue to lose audience share (Farhi, 1992, p. H-1).

Meanwhile, authoritative technology critic George Gilder (1994, p. 5) opened his book, *Life After Television*, with a blunt declaration of television's apocalypse:

> Proclaiming "multimedia convergence," "interactivity," "intelligent networks," "electronic yellow pages," "500 channels of pay-per-view," and vistas of "high definition TV" and "information superhighways" seers in television and telephone today give stirring speeches about the future of their industries. Contemplating their revenues of tens of billions of dollars, their laboratories full of new technology, their millions of mostly satisfied shareholders and customers, their multiplying masses of trade publications, and their cover-story blasts in national magazines, television and telephone executives all too often seem unaware that their basic technologies are dead.

But perhaps nowhere was the Internet-generated atmosphere of excitement and fear more evident than in the newspaper industry. Newspapers, in their competition with radio, television and newer media, have a long tradition in investing in new technology ventures just to overcome the geographical limits of their products and to reduce the production and distribution costs, which make up somewhere between 30% to 60% of their total operating expenses (Fidler, 1999; Patten, 1986; Pavlik, 2000; Picard, 1998). To newspaper practitioners, therefore, the world-wide web was an excellent platform to overcome these traditional limitations. Online publishing not only does not involve the expensive and vulnerable costs of newsprint and distribution but also requires less initial costs and much less complicated technologies (Pavlik, 1998; Sparks, 1999). Using the cost-cutting factor as a common sense, American publisher Levor Oldham declared: "Clearly, the future of newspapers is on the web" (quoted in Pavlik, 2000, p. 234). However, the major reason for newspapers to migrate online was that the Internet was becoming more a nerve-wracking medium than an exciting opportunity, in the mind of many – if not most – newspaper practitioners of the 1990s. There were several reasons for this:

First, the Internet means that newspapers are no longer the most capable adopters of new media technologies. Traditionally, since they have the cash to pour in multibillion-dollar "technological roulette" (Patten, 1986), newspapers are in a better position than any other media to stampede into high-tech ventures. In the 1920s, for example, along with universities, churches and some businesses, newspapers were one of the most powerful beginners in the feverish rush into radio (Allen, 1999; Patten, 1986). The same phenomenon was seen during the early days of television. In Canada, for example, Allen stated that "just like with radio, many of the first to climb on (the television) board were newspapers" (1999). In Australia, the first decades of television saw commercial broadcast licences being dominated by print conglomerates and it was not until the mid-1980s that strengthened cross-ownership laws led to what Tom O'Regan (1993) called a period of "entrepreneurial television". With the Internet emerging, however, entry barriers into the market were substantially reduced and an active role in adopting new communications technologies seemed to be no longer an exclusive preserve of newspapers.

Second, and more importantly, newspapers were perceived as the most endangered species because the traditional strengths of their core service, news and information, became all too vulnerable in the face of the Internet's technical capacities. The most threatened among these strengths was the provision of in-depth analysis and background information, which was what newspapers had been proud of and firmly survived on in the contest with radio and television. As Paul Zwillenberg, the online operation runner of Associated Newspapers in Britain, put it: "The trouble with newspapers is that they are a mile wide and an inch deep. Websites that work best are an inch wide and a mile deep" (quoted in *The Economist*, 1999). Coupled with this are features such as immediacy, multimedia and customisation which print media simply do not possess.

Meanwhile, classified advertising was facing a critical challenge from online publishing (Prosser, 1998). Classifieds have always been not only a key content asset of newspapers (people looked to the newspaper not only for news and information but also classifieds related to their daily life) but also a crucial part of their financial base. According to a report in *The Economist* (1999), classifieds made up around one-third of newspapers' total revenues during the 1990s. Online, however, classifieds work much better: searching is faster and easier than tracking down the printed page; and the global popularity of search engines allows a larger reach of classifieds than the geographical boundaries of newspapers (*The Economist*, 1999). In addition, low entry requirements could translate into more chances for advertisers to build their own sites and do their own advertising business (Rosalink & Melinda, 2001). At the same time, free classifieds were increasingly popular on sites owned by portal companies such as Yahoo! or Lycos, which provided access to intensive databases of searchable updated classifieds only to sell their banner advertising (Brown, 1999). On the whole, American newspapers' operating profit, which remained at 14% in 2000, was likely to be slashed to 3% if half of their classified advertising was lost in five years to net-savvy newcomers (Rosalink & Melinda, 2001).

Third, all this happened when newspapers had been witnessing a decline of readership for decades. According to the Readership Institute of the Newspaper Association of America (2001), American readership had been shrinking for more than 35 years. The World Association of Newspapers reported that US daily circulation dropped by 1.8% from 1996 to 2000. Meanwhile, industrial research found that all traditional news uses declined while Internet news consumption sharply rose (Hoag, 1998). In *The Vanishing Newspaper*, Philip Meyer (2004) used a statistical analysis of the downward circulation trend in three decades to declare that the last American newspaper to appear will be in April 2040. This situation was not unique to America. According to the WAN report, during the 1996-2000 period, when online news use became increasingly popular, circulation drop was found in, among others, Hong Kong (9.2%), New Zealand (6%), Australia (2.1%) and the EU (2.5%). In serious cases like Britain and France, the trend had been down for at least 30 years (*The Economist*, 1999).

Amidst all this, prophets of gloom and doom were dominant in the newspaper industry. In the US, at a conference of 1,100 journalists in 1998, online content pioneer Michael Bloomberg notified: "If you mix the ink and chop the tree, you'll be probably put out of the business" (quoted in Brown, 1999). Meanwhile, America Online CEO Steve Case declared that newspapers were "somewhere between beleaguered and dying" (quoted in Black, 2000). As *The Economist* (1999) reported: "In their worst nightmares, they fear that newspapers may be to the communications business what the horse and cart were to transport". In this context, it is not surprising that in 1996, representatives of American journalists gathered at a meeting organised by the Association for Education in Journalism and Mass Communication to conclude that newspapers were not the place for students to seek a career – the right place was the new media (Schultz & Voakes, 1999). Schultz and Voakes (1999) found that most of the newspaper journalists (55%) in their national sample said their print products would become a "less important part of American life" in 10 years. This percentage increased from only one-third in a similar study conducted eight years before that. Among the causes of this increase in pessimism, the researchers found the fear of new media.

The same fear was recorded in other continents. In Europe, for instance, as early as September 1997, a report on the impact of new technologies on the printed press was presented to the European Parliament, warning that newspapers were "in danger and in need of support (from public policies)" (van Dusseldorp, 1998t). Online news, the report said, was expanding amidst the trend that daily newspapers had continuously been losing readers for a decade and that most people between 18 and 24 were reading no daily paper at all. In Australia, former Fairfax CEO Fred Hilmer recently confessed that it was partly due to the Internet's threat that he had to consider selling the company's flagship broadsheets, *The Sydney Morning Herald* and *The Age*, in the 1990s – a sale that never happened but "would have been a rational decision" in his hindsight (quoted in Manning, 2007). In such as context, the best way for newspapers and other traditional media to guarantee a sustainable future was to catch the wave, as an American newspaper executive put it on returning from a conference on new media in 1995:

> With virtually everything about this new game uncertain… there may be only one immutable rule: If you want to be sure you can play later, you must play now. No communications company can afford to sit out and hope to catch up (quoted in Boczkowski, 2004, p. 38).

The not-so-impressive production of online news in its first decade

In short, while the hasty online migration among traditional commercial news media in the 1990s was driven in part by the desire to expand market, it was the urge to defend market that was the dominant imperative. Thus, just as the fear of videotex generated expensive experiments in the 1980s, the fear of the Internet as a potential destructive power to older news products has been a positive contributor to the emergence of online news in the 1990s. However, as in the videotex days, a combination of three fear-generated factors – the obsession by the new technology's destructive power, the application of old processes and values to the new and the reluctance to commit resources to experiments (see Chapter 1) – has resulted in online news services that can be likened to "new bottles with old wine", i.e. new products/services with nothing really new at all.

First, by "being faithless to be faithful" to the old, they were seldom able to build their news sites with a bold determination to make them distinctive from and/or superior to their old businesses. Under the many uncertainties about the viability of online news that quickly appeared after the snow-ball online migration in the mid-1990s, this has led traditional practitioners to be reluctant to pour resources into developing the remarkable potential of online news. Instead of adding original content to their online news services, for instance, they adopt the "safer" practice of reformatting already owned content – "shovelware" content – as a way to minimise the cost and to ensure that these services will not become disruptors of the traditional products that are still profitable and close to their heart (Boczkowski, 2004; Gunter, 2003; Hall, 2001). A major result is that the web's vast capacity for continuous updates and multimedia content/presentation has been largely ignored. Hypertextual links to content on other news sites were not popular either (Peng et al, 1999), probably because this poses a big, although indirect, threat to traditional products. Therefore, in studying forms of report among American newspaper sites, Barnhurst (2002, p. 477) commented that rather than reinventing themselves on the web, "print publishers use their Internet presence as a low-cost place holder that guards their US market position and erects a barrier to the entry of geographical competitors and ideological alternatives in the US news arena".

The same happened in Australian newsrooms, whose slow online move was labelled by a critic as a "crazy", "mean, stingy bad management" with a "downright stupidity" (quoted in Tapsall, 2001, p. 243). It was not until the 2004 Athens Olympic, for example, that the country's first news sites – theage.com.au and smh.com.au – started to experiment with a serious multimedia coverage. My diary of online news consumption in Australia during 2002-2006 suggests that while breaking news has been popular on major sites, most is cheap superficial information copied from wire services, especially the AAP. In fact, Australian online newsrooms have been accustomed to what is dubbed as the "file by three, home for tea" tradition (Este & Sainsbury, 2006). As Alan Howe – executive editor at the Herald and Weekly Times group – admitted:

> Editors live and die by their circulations. That's their success. It's measurable and it's measured, and it's a crucial part of the newspaper business model. But it has made a lot of editors very defensive about the Internet. I was guilty of it myself because editors focus on their papers rather than a part of the business which they may not fully understand, is not a profit centre and is not part of their measured audience (quoted in Day, 2006, p. 14).

Second, the lack of interest in exploring the real potential of online news and the resulting failure to commit adequate resources intensified their negative effect in the context that the fear-driven rush online left traditional newspeople with little time to work out innovative strategies to effectively use the resources they have committed to online news (Gunter, 2003). Facing uncertainties and lacking supporting resources from the top, the safer route for journalists is to "marry" the online and traditional worlds, bringing into the former much of their traditional thinking line that might be at odds with the former's uniqueness. As a result, Stovall (2004, p. 23) observed that "the news media's early approach to the web was checkered with visionary action, misguided concepts and curt dismissal". Worse, the traditional and online businesses are too often like, in Gordon Borrell's words, "Siamese twins" in their mind (Smolkin, 2006), leading to what Boczkowski (2004, p. 102) called "mimetic originality" – the turning of "the creation of newness ... into the creative production of sameness". In Australia, among the causes of the aforementioned "downright stupidity" are "the heavy investment in and reliance of newsrooms on made-to-measure news systems that predate the late 1990s rapid growth of

Internet services; ... and a lack of knowledge about ways to maximise the Internet as a communication, information, and publication medium" (Tapsall, 2001, p. 242).

The preservation of the "we publish, you read" mindset might have been the biggest mistake traditional newspeople have made online. By placing a primary interest in the traditional news and information function, they have largely failed to recognise the most fundamental change brought by the Internet, the two-way relationship between users and between users and journalists. The unprecedented growth of public interaction and participation on the Internet (see chapter 4) has not caught the serious attention of our traditionally bound and defensively minded newspeople until recent years. In a survey of American online editors on their 2000 election coverage, for instance, Singer (2003) found that 45 of 49 respondents cited providing information and bolstering the print or online versions' reputation as their primary goal while only four cited taking advantage of the interactive nature of the Internet to strengthen public participation. Their most popular first-cited source of pride during the campaign was updated news/election results (chosen by 16 of 44 respondents), followed by depth and detail (15 respondents). Chat/discussion forums were ranked far behind, being first cited by eight of the editors. Similarly, in the Netherlands, although online journalists show a stronger focus on interactive relationships with users than other journalists, the former still place far less weights on participation functions – particularly providing a forum for public discussions, building and sustaining communities, giving the public the chance to voice its opinions – than on traditional news-provision roles such as disseminating information as quickly as possible, producing news for the widest possible audience, providing analysis of complex problems or signalling events or trends (Deuze & Dimoudi, 2002). Similar attitudes to online participation can also be found in the UK (Thurman, 2008) and Australia (Nguyen, 2006).

As a result of this, participation opportunities and user-generated content remain rather scarce, at least until recently, on online news sites. Only a third of the American newspaper sites surveyed in Peng et al (1999) offered forums or live chats with staff journalists. Lin and Jeffres (2000) content-analysed the websites of 231 radio stations, 119 TV stations and 73 newspapers in 25 US metropolitan areas to discover that even the most commonly found interactive feature – email and feedback – was still offered by less than half (45%) of the sites. Letters to editors and bulletins or message boards were almost non-existent while chat rooms were offered by 9% of the sites. In another analysis of 300 local TV stations' websites in the US during November-December 1998, Chan-Olmsted and Park (2000) found limited communication structures and rare interactivity-based opportunities. In Australia, observers also note the severe poverty of participation opportunities on mainstream news sites (Bruns, 2005; Nguyen, 2006; Ward & Cahill, 2007). A small-scale study by Ewart (2003) found limited online connection between Queensland regional newspapers and their readers. Similar research findings can be found in other studies (Barnhurst, 2002; Dibean & Garrison, 2001; Gunter, 2003; Massey & Levy, 1999). In the UK, up until April 2005, facilities such as "have your say" options, blogs that enable comments and message boards were still provided by a small minority of the country's major news sites, according to an analysis by Neil Thurman (2008).

While most of the above data were collected during the 1990s and early 2000s, critics (Finberg, 2006; Salwen, 2005; Stovall, 2004) observe that the situation has remained largely unchanged until recent years, as evident in a comment by the general manager of the *Tampa Tribune*'s tbo.com when responding to the increasing power of broadband:

> Rather than getting starry-eyed about fat-pipe applications, I'd rather see us focus on doing a better job of the basics. The amount of local breaking news on many newspaper sites is abysmal. Their weather maps lack depth and dynamism. Their sports are boring. And their functionality – from search to calendar to recruitment databases – is barely passable. We should be ashamed of how poor our sites compare to Yahoo! and Monster in basic areas (quoted in Finberg, 2006).

All this presents a critical issue to think about the future of online news. As most online news ventures today are still not a source of profit and are quite often a source of financial loss, what will be the future of Internet news? Many scholars are sceptical about any soon-to-come vigorous capitalisation on online news ventures. For instance, despite some evidence of a gradual move away from the shovelware era, Salwen (2005, pp. 48-49) contended that with "advertisers ... (being) leery about whether online ads are being read" and online news subscription experiments having largely failed, "it is unlikely that online news outlets will expend resources to obtain original online news when less expensive news is available".

A potentially dangerous problem is that as they, to use Appleyard's metaphor, are focused on the "monstrous" rather than the "fabulous" aspects of online news (i.e. are more interested in how the Internet could destroy their businesses than how to become innovative leaders in this new area), those behind online news experiments are quite prepared to withdraw from them if their old core businesses turn out to be under no threat from the medium. This was clear after the boom and bust of dotcoms in the early 2000s, when the threat seemed to be waning and the prospect for making money from the web became even more uncertain. Thus, the early 2000s started to witness massive online staff reductions. In Australia, for example, News Corp decided to cut one-third of its online staff in January 2001, prompting the ABC to depict it as "a blow to Australia's bid to become a knowledge nation" (Ewart & Gregor, 2001, p. 43). Almost concurrently, News slashed its US-based News Digital Media workforce by 2000 (Balnaves et al, 2003). This was not something peculiar only to News: staff cuts, usually by hundreds, were happening across the American news industries, like "bloated holiday revellers on crash diets" (Wenner, 2001).

Fortunately, unlike videotex, the Internet is a diverse medium to which entry barriers are low enough to allow many actors outside the traditional media sphere to be aboard. In the online publishing world, traditional practitioners can no longer play the one-man game to freely decide when to end an experiment and "kill" the medium. Once they have started, they have only one way to go – the way forward. A closer look at industrial moves in the past few years shows that the same fear-driven innovation culture that has been a brake on online news development might well be driving a new and exciting stage of this development.

A second fear-driven development stage of online news under way?

Despite the industry's failure to create the best possible online news services, the Internet as a news medium has fast penetrated daily life, with its growth having shown no sign of stopping (to be detailed in the next chapter). As a result, the online world has started to convince advertisers in the past five or six years. Forrester research found that 84% of

American marketers planned to increase their online advertising spending by 25% in 2005 and estimated that this market would reach US$26 billon – or 8% of all advertising revenues – by 2010 (Davis, 2005). In Australia, online advertising grew by 64% between 2003 and 2004, according to the Audit Bureau of Verification Services (2005). Globally, Zenith Optimedia estimates that online advertising, with an annual growth of 75%, will go up from $18.7 billion in 2005 to $42.7 billion in 2009 (WAN, 2007a).

This growth seems to take place at the expense of the traditional media's advertising: Zenith and other research firms project that the global market share of online advertising will increase from 3% in 2002 to 14% in 2011, while that of newspaper advertising will shrink from 33% to 25% during the same period (WAN, 2008). Certainly, part of online advertising dollars will come to the online arms of traditional outlets, but they now lag far behind "digital natives" like Yahoo!, Google and even Craiglist. By the mid-2000s, only 30 cents of every classified dollar shifted from print media to the Internet in the US came back to their news sites (*The Australian*, 2005). In 2007, Ernst & Young research found that while Google could generate £2.40 per unique UK user per month from its website, the country's top national newspaper sites could only make £0.10-£0.13 (Utalkmarketing, 2008). As another indicator, PriceWaterhouseCoopers research for the Interactive Advertising Bureau (2007) shows that in 2006, search engines accounted for 40% and nearly 60% of total online advertising revenues in the US and the UK respectively. Concurrent with that is the continued decline in the reach of traditional media, especially newspapers in the world's most wired countries. WAN (2006) reported that during 2001-2005, circulation fell by 4.02% in the US, 4.58% in New Zealand, 0.97% in Japan, 4.25% in Belgium, 11.4% in Denmark, 9.63% in Germany, 11.62% in Greece, 7.38% in France, 10.58% in the Netherlands, 9.85% in the UK, 2.23% in Sweden, 1.73 in Spain, 5.25% in Italy.

With all this in mind, it is not surprising that recent figures from the NAA (2008) show that while the total online revenue of American newspapers grew almost 19% (from $2.66 to $3.17 billion) from 2006 to 2007, this failed to offset a much larger drop from $46.61 billion to $42.21 billion (i.e. a 9.4% drop) in print revenues during the same period. The bitterness of this situation is strongly felt, as seen in a recent comment by an American media critic on the state of the American newspaper industry:

> Newspaper owners these days routinely issue gloom-and-doom financial forecasts, usually accompanied by announcements of layoffs and other cost-cutting measures. Draconian steps are necessary, they declare sadly, because newspaper revenues keep falling. In these scenarios the Internet is usually portrayed as the villain, siphoning off print readers and ad money, but not adding online revenue fast enough to make up the difference (Richards, 2007).

Combined together, these market and technology trends have constituted a key driver of a new stage of online news development, one in which much of the fear of the 1990s is making a comeback in an even more pressing manner, generating the obligation to be more serious in exploiting the potential of online news among traditional media.

Evidence of such a comeback is not difficult to find. Tim McGuire (2005) depicted that "everybody from former journalists to editors to gurus to bloggers to the first grader down the street has been spouting opinions about dying newspapers, media death spirals, and the hopelessness of reaching young readers". Meanwhile, Terry Eastland, publisher of the *Weekly Standard*, claimed: "So, it's time to write, if not an obituary, then an account of their [traditional mainstream news media's] rise and decline and delicate prospects amid the 'new media' of cable television, talk radio, and the blogosphere" (quoted in Ahlers, 2006, p. 30). In early 2007, the owner of the *New York Times*, Arthur Sulzberger, said he was not sure whether his world-renowned newspaper would still be printed in five years' time (Newsam, 2007). And as late as January 2008, futurists at the World Economic Forum's annual meeting in Davos claimed that the printed newspaper will become a thing of the past by 2014. Also deeply impressed by the new wave of technologies is Michael Malone, who made this vivid and scathing comment:

> This is the last great divide, and my sense is that few newspapers will be able to make the crossing. If they kill their print editions now, they won't have the revenues to make a smooth transition to cyberspace; but if they keep wearing their paper albatrosses, they'll have less of a chance of succeeding in the new world. Thus, if all of the old-fashioned newspapers are going to die, nearly all of the forward-looking ones will, too.
>
> Before it is all over, the number of 'newspapers' left in America will probably less than 10 – and they might not be individual papers, but rather new entities created out of the current large chains. They will become the primary sources of

national and international news, delivered into multimedia form… As for the local papers, they will be shut down, their presses depreciated and scrapped, their offices leased out and the newsroom reporters scattered to the four winds of blogdom and specialty sites, where they will provide local news, commentary, movie times and maybe even those long lost Little League box scores (quoted in McGuire, 2005).

Certainly, newspapers and other traditional media do not accept such a bleak future without a fight. To respond to recent immense changes in the media ecosystem, they have started to act more vigorously and rigorously in the online world since the mid-2000s. A clear trend is convergence or multiple-platform publishing. In a study aiming at finding a way out for newspapers, the American Press Institute (API, 2006) advised newspapers to go beyond print products to adopt what it called the "portfolio strategy" – creating a suite of print and non-print products and services to intersect the population on a variety of planes. In accordance with this, the US news industry has seen massive joint ventures or mergers between traditional news organisations and online-only businesses. The year 2005 was probably the milestone for this trend. In this year, big news organisations spent massive amounts of money on buying online ventures: *New York Times* paid US$410 for About.com and hired 500 "guides" to write on special-interest topics; *Washington Post* purchased Slate.com, the renowned innovative webzine; Dow Jones acquired MarketWatch.com for US$520 million; and three newspaper chains bought a US$64 million stake in Topix.net (Walker, 2005). Perhaps more serious was the decision by Rupert Murdoch – the man who cut massive online staff after the dotcom boom and bust – to set online expansion as his global News Corporation's top priority from 2005, with A$1.3 billion ready to be poured into Internet businesses (Schultze, 2005a). In that year, he called up two summits of his top personnel around the globe to speak the "online language" and spent A$770 million to purchase the popular social networking site MySpace, plus A$60 to buy sports content site Scout (Schultze, 2005a).

In Australia, this move had an immediate effect on Murdoch's News Interactive, which in the latter half of 2005 started to experience what its former managing director, Nic Jones, called an "investment mode" (Schultze, 2005b, p. 17). Since then, News Limited has been thought of as a "media company" rather than a mere newspaper company, as Jones commented:

We are a content manufacturer. We're not a newspaper company, not a TV company; we are a media company... I see what we are doing online as just as important to the future of newspapers as anything happening in the newspaper" (quoted in MacLean, 2005, p. 20).

In late 2006, News's major competitor in Australia, Fairfax Holdings, was renamed as Fairfax Media to reflect a similar strategic move, whose key is "to build a culture that encourages innovation, considered risk-taking, creativity and agility – attributes not always associated with safe old newspaper publishers" (Kirk, 2006).

This convergence trend continues today. In the first three quarters of 2007, for instance, there more than 637 mergers and acquisition transactions in the US, which totalled more than $95 billion in value and far surpassed the total of $61 billion of the previous year (Project for Excellence in Journalism, 2008). Among these transactions were MSNBC's purchase of the community news aggregator Newsvine and ABC News's alliance with Facebook. As of January 2008, Monster.com, a job recruitment site, had struck partnership deals with more than 160 newspapers, including the difficult-to-persuade *New York Times*.

Amidst these developments, WAN (2007b) reported that more new, innovative newspaper products were launched worldwide in 2005 and 2006 than over the previous 30 years. More original content – including multimedia content and breaking news – and more opportunities for public engagement have been the most obvious moves. In Britain, filing stories online before print has been a marked trend since *The Guardian* and *The Times* initiated it in 2006. As of March 2008, *The Birmingham Post* of the Trinity Mirror group was the most recent British "web-first" news player (Luft, 2007). The new news site, reconstructed after consultation with local blogging communities, promises to carry out throughout the day breaking news, commentaries and analyses by both staff writers and a group of hired bloggers. Similar trends are recorded in Australia. In early 2006, Alan Howe started to add original content and build communities for the online versions within the Herald and Weekly Times group while news.com.au initiated an impressive weblog project, with regular contributions from both readers and senior editorial staff. Meanwhile, each of Fairfax Media's major news sites established an intensive and extensive Blog Central section devoted to user-generated content. Shortly after the web-first moves in Britain, Australian editors conceded that "the dam had broken" and the "file by three, home for tea" period was over (Este & Sainsbury, 2006). *The Sydney Morning Herald*'s editor, for instance, considered unique breaking stories online no longer a matter of "whether" but "when and how". His counterpart at *The Australian Financial Review* announced that his print version would be focused on analysis and its online version on breaking news – not mere breaking stories copied from wire services, but those with a few paragraphs added by his reporters (Este & Sainsbury, 2006).

Thus, if 1995 and 1996 were the takeoff years of web news, then 2005 and 2006 could be the beginning of its second development stage. The question is whether this is a mere fear-driven response or, as one might argue, is an "aggressive opportunity-seeking" effort. Again, there is evidence that as in the 1990s, the unfolding development stage is more or less driven by the motive to expand market via the Internet. In Australia, for example, Fairfax recently launched an online-only publication, brisbanetimes.com.au, which, for the first time in decades, acts as a direct competitor to News Limited's *Courier-Mail*, the only metropolitan daily in Queensland. On a global scale, the powerful World Association of Newspapers has been issuing a great deal of market research and analysis to encourage its members to creatively and aggressively embrace online news technologies as a new stream of revenues. However, the trade literature on the overall mood of traditional practitioners suggests that the "adapt or die" imperative is a, if not *the*, key driver of the new development.

For instance, the massive media mergers in 2005 were reportedly due to "the fear ... of missing the Internet ad boat" (Walker, 2005). Jay Smith, president of Cox Newspapers, recently commented that newspapers are in the most "open and receptive time ... in the last 40 years" because "nothing can motivate you like tough times" (Smolkin, 2006). When recommending the portfolio strategy, the API (2006, p. 16) stressed that it is "not merely an option" for newspapers but is "THE option – a necessity for survival". As the *American Journalism Review* editor commented:

> For years, newspapers have treated innovation like a trip to the dentist — a torture to be endured, not encouraged... Please. Tell the dentist to add a veneer and leave the rotting core alone...
>
> Now that's all changing, of necessity (Smolkin, 2006).

A similar language can be found in other countries. In the UK, when Michael Hill – the head of multimedia at Trinity Mirror – told a conference in January 2008 that newspapers had to accept the hard-to-swallow fact that breaking news had to come online first, he was protested with a question: "Why kill the goose that laid the golden egg?" His response was a joke that might tell it all: "The goose has got bird flu" (Bradshaw, 2008). In Australia, when talking about Fairfax Media's new strategies in the digital age, its new CEO, Dr. David Kirk (2006), quoted a remark by Miles Davis: "If you're not nervous, you're not paying attention". Similarly, when explaining his recent online move, Alan Howe said: "The Internet is now a critical part of our future. Either you embrace it or it will swamp you" (quoted in Day, 2006, p. 14). But perhaps nowhere this fear-driven mood is cast more dramatic than in Murdoch's confession to the American Society of Newspaper Editors in the year he decided to make up for his time lost online:

> Ladies and gentlemen, I come before you today with the best of my intentions. My subject is one near and dear to all of us: the role of newspapers in this digital age.
>
> Scarcely a day goes by without some claim that new technologies are fast writing newsprint's obituary. Yet, as an industry, most of us have been remarkably, unaccountably complacent. Certainly, I didn't do as much as I should have after all the excitement of the late 1990s. I suspect many of you in this room did the same, quietly hoping that this thing called the digital revolution would just limp away.
>
> Well, it hasn't... it won't ... and it's a reality we had better get used to – and fast (Murdoch, 2005).

Concluding notes

By applying the lessons from the pre-web evolution of online news, this chapter has further answered the first research question of this book on the evolutionary of online news in the newsroom. In particular, the chapter has shown that the pervasive fear of becoming irrelevant in the Internet age among traditional media practitioners has been acting both as an accelerator and a brake of web news development. On the one hand, it stimulated the massive online migration in the 1990s. On the other, the many uncertainties resulting from this fear-driven migration, in combination with the restraints of traditional journalism, have led the online news artefact to being far from its technical potential, with much of its unique capacity such as multimedia and interactive participation opportunities remaining a luxury in the online news world until recent years. Looking at industrial developments in the past three years, however, the chapter shows that the same culture of fear – and the associated urge to act to ensure future relevance and viability – has started to ignite a second stage of online news development, one in which the remarkable potential of the Internet will be more aggressively embraced by traditional news providers.

There are still reservations over this second stage of online news, to which I will return in Chapter 8. For now, the two-stage evolution of web-based news in this chapter highlights the need to understand the potentials of online news from a user-centric perspective. The unfolding second stage can only witness the arrival of an innovative online news artefact if its practitioners take to heart the crucial lesson from the first stage – i.e., for online news to serve the public and (the market) well, it ought to be done and developed with firmer knowledge and deeper understanding of what users want from and do with its socio-technical potentials. To avoid repeating the mistakes of the first stage, practitioners might have to overcome their technology-driven fear to rethink and reassess the "power" of online news in an informed manner. How has online news been penetrating into daily life? To what extent do the much-touted features of online news play a role in attracting users? Which of these features are the most important "killer applications"? What are the other factors that might shape the adoption and use of online news by the public? What does all this mean to online journalism practices? Rather than assuming the "power" of online news as a matter of course, journalists and media executives might have to seriously address these questions and work out what they need to do to make the most from this power. Most of the rest of this book will explore these user-centric issues.

Chapter 3

The potential diffusion of news on the Internet: a user-centric assessment

This chapter draws on innovation diffusion theory and media audience theories to present a general assessment of the potential diffusion of online news from a user-centric perspective. It first introduces diffusion theory with a focus on innovation attributes as a primary determinant of adoption rates. From this, the chapter goes on to place online news adoption in the context of Internet use to argue that as a continuous innovation, online news – with its many relative advantages, low complexity, high degree of compatibility, trialability and observability – has an enormous potential to foster wide diffusion in wired society. Throughout this process, a user-centric profile of online news – with six dimensions (use convenience, multimedia content and format, content richness, immediacy, on-demand news, and participation opportunities) – will be constructed to describe the relative advantages of online news in comparison with traditional media. The chapter concludes that despite the fact that much of the touted power of online news has not been fully exploited by the media, many inherent advantageous features of online news are available on the web today to foster wide adoption and substantial use among the public.

Innovation diffusion: an introduction

There are different ways of understanding how an innovation penetrates daily life. In economics, for example, diffusion is seen as a process by which innovations spread within and across economies (Baptista, 1999). This study follows a strong tradition in consumer behaviours and sociology, understanding innovation diffusion as a special communication process (Reagan, 2002; Rogers, 1986; Rogers, 2003; Rogers, 2004).

Particularly, according to Everett Rogers, diffusion is a process "in which an *innovation* is *communicated* through certain *channels* over *time* among members of a *social system*" (Rogers, 2003, p. 11-12). It is in essence a social process in which different individuals in the social system communicate messages about an innovation – defined as "an idea, object or practice perceived as new by an individual" – via mass media or interpersonal channels until they gain certain levels of certainty about the new idea and decide to put it into full use or not. Over time, the diffusion process follows an S-shaped curve, which rises slowly at first, then accelerates until half of the potential adoption population have adopted it, and finally slows down until there are no or few more adopters (Figure 3.1).

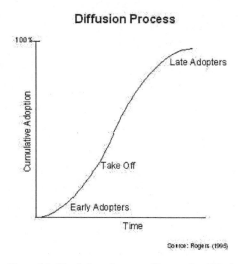

Figure 3.1: The S-shaped curves of innovation diffusion

Different innovations take different S-curves of diffusion – some are steep (indicating fast diffusion) and some fairly flat (slow diffusion). For example, it took the washing machine 40 years to increase its user base from one quarter of American households to three quarters; but the same leap took place less than 10 years in the case of the video cassette recorders and the colour television (Hall, 2002). More formally, the steepness of the diffusion curve represents the rate of adoption, "the relative speed with which an innovation is adopted by members of a social system" (often measured in the number of individuals adopting the innovation in a specified period). This adoption rate – seen as "the most important single indicator of effectiveness" of the innovation, i.e. the degree to which the implementation of the innovation attains its stated goals (Rogers & Scott, 1997) – is determined by a number of factors (Rogers 2003, p. 219-266), which can be relatively addressed in two major groups:

The first group consists of factors related to the communication channels of the innovation. The innovation-decision process is in essence an information-seeking and information-processing activity aimed to reduce uncertainty about the innovation. Throughout this process, people tend to make their decision not only on the basis of their initial contact and experience with it (via limited trials) but also on the subjective evaluation made by the mass media and those having adopted it in their near-peer networks (Rogers, 2003). Therefore, mass media channels usually play a crucial role in the initial stage of diffusion, forming the awareness and knowledge about an innovation. Because of this, the degree of large-scale promotion efforts by change agents contributes substantially to the success of an innovation during its initial diffusion phase.

As the diffusion process continues, a social learning process takes place: the innovation presents in an increasing number of different social settings, thereby attracting an increasing number of potential adopters, who learn about the innovation via their social environment (Rosenberg, 1972). When the number of adopters has reached the take-off point in the S-shaped curve (called the "critical mass" and represented by the shaded area in Figure 3.1), the communication, and therefore diffusion, of the innovation becomes self-sustaining in a sort of "epidemic" learning process. During this later period, interpersonal networks – more precisely, social feedback mechanisms, or "externalities", as economists call them (Hall, 2003) – play a more crucial role than the mass media, both in creating knowledge as well as influencing attitudes to the innovation. Because of this, the nature of the social system in which the innovation is introduced – especially its degree of network interconnectedness – can either slow or speed the diffusion process.

The second, and more important, group of determinants of the adoption rate contains factors concerning the nature of the innovation itself. One considerable factor is the type of decisions involved in its adoption process – i.e. whether it is up to the individual to choose it (individual-optional decision) or whether he/she has to share the decision-making power with some other people (collective decision) or whether he/she has to adopt it because some authorities have decided so (authority decision). Generally, the more people are involved in the decision, the slower the adoption – and thus the collective diffusion – process is. But more importantly, the innovation's adoption rate depends on how people evaluate its intrinsic attributes. There are different typologies of these attributes. In economics, they are classified into four groups: cost-related factors, benefits-related factors, structural factors (industrial supply and social environment), and uncertainty- or information-related factors (Hall, 2003). In the specific field of information systems, Davis (1989) identifies the two single most important factors determining the adoption of software package as (1) perceived helpfulness (the extent to which the package is perceived to improve one's work efficiency) and (2) perceived ease of use (the extent to which the use of the system is perceived to be free from effort).

In a more specific and inclusive typology, Rogers (2003) divided innovation attributes into five categories that are empirically interrelated but conceptually distinct – relative advantages, compatibility, complexity, trialability and observability, discussed in conjunction with other authors as follows:

Relative advantage is the extent to which an innovation is perceived as better than its precursor(s), including economic profitability, low initial cost, decreased discomfort, social prestige, time and effort savings, and the immediacy of rewards. In general, the more relative advantage an innovation is perceived to have, the faster it is likely to be adopted (Rogers, 2003). Cost is "almost always the primary factor" but this must go with the quality of the innovation; consumers will not be willing to pay even low fees if the quality of the new technology service is inferior but they will be happy to spend a large amount of money if the perceived benefits of the innovation are sufficiently compelling (Reagan, 2002, p. 79). Thus, factors concerning the innovation's cost-related risks, returns to the investment, and product efficiency – as reviewed in Neuendorf et al (2002) – can fall into the umbrella term of relative advantages. From Hall's (2003) standpoint, however, both costs- and benefits-related factors combine to create relative advantages.

Compatibility is the degree to which an innovation conforms to existing values, past experiences and needs of the receivers. This includes compatibility with (a) deeply embedded socio-cultural values and beliefs of the social system; (b) previously introduced ideas (people assess a new idea, reduce uncertainty and give it some meaning based on previous practices/ideas); and (c) existing (felt/or perceived) needs (Rogers, 2003). Past research has found compatibility to have a positive relationship with adoption rates although it is less important than, and sometimes not empirically distinct from, relative advantages (Rogers, 2003). The adoption of an incompatible innovation would involve adopting or adapting to a new value system, which is normally a lengthy process (Rogers & Scott, 1997). Compatibility can fall under the structural factors in Hall's typology. This is a reason, as seen in the pre-history of online news in Chapter 2, that the nature of the social system in which the innovation is introduced – particularly its established norms – is a matter of substantial importance.

Complexity refers to how difficult/easy an innovation is perceived to understand and use (Rogers, 2003). This issue of complexity is particularly crucial in the case of high-tech innovations, which typically involve four predominant types of fears: fear of technical complexity, fear of rapid obsolescence, fear of social rejection and fear of physical harm (Schiffman et al, 2001). Complexity could involve substantial costs as costs generated from the decision to adopt a new product include not only the price of acquisition but also complementary investments as well as learning/training costs (Hall, 2003). As seen in the case of computer network adoption (Caselli & Coleman, 2001; Greenan & Guellec, 1998), these costs tend to hinder the observability of the relative advantages (benefits) of the innovation – especially in organisational contexts – because such investment takes longer to be decided on. In addition to *attribute complexity*, there is a *trade-off complexity* – defined as the degree and number of conflicting benefits generated by the innovation (Neal, Quester & Hawkins, 1998). For instance, a microwave might be perceived to improve speed of cooking but to decrease cooking quality by many potential adopters.

Trialability is the degree to which an innovation can be experimented with on a limited basis (Rogers, 2003). An innovation is highly trialable if it involves low-cost or low-risk trial. The greater the opportunity to try an innovation, the easier it is for consumers to evaluate and ultimately adopt it (Nelson, Peterhansl & Sampat, 2002; Schiffman et al, 2001). This attribute is generally more important to earlier adopters than later adopters.

Observability refers to how visible the results of an innovation are to other people (Rogers, 2003). Schiffman et al (2001, p. 523) introduced *communicability* as an alternative term for *observability*, defining it as "the ease with which a product's benefits or attributes can be observed, imagined, or described to potential consumers". Neal et al (1998) defined a related element called the manifest fulfilment of a felt need (the more obvious the need an innovation satisfies, the faster its diffusion). For example, the potential need fulfilment and adoption results of a mobile phone are highly observable or communicable – its ringing can be heard and its look can be seen in many places (in restaurants, in offices, or on the train etc) but headache remedies are much less visible and less likely to be widely discussed in social networks (Neal et al, 1998). Both trialability and observability determine the fourth element of Hall's (2003) classification – those problems associated with uncertainty and information.

This list of innovation attributes has been extensively applied in studies of new media adoption. In *Mediamorphosis*, Roger Fidler added a sixth attribute, called *familiarity*, which he believed to be "equally critical to the comfortable and easy fit of new media within the general consumer market" (1997, p. 15). The key concept of this attribute is the innovation's link to earlier or existing forms. Photography, for example, was readily adopted because there had been similar ways of seeing and representing vision – such as the photographic portraits by itinerant artists in the days after the discovery of the effect of light on silver salt. The printing press was also not a complete break with the past but, for a long time, was based on the traditional hand-written letter forms and formats. In my view, however, this is indeed already encompassed in the notion of *compatibility* and therefore should not be counted as an additional element. (It also appears that Fidler did not fully comprehend the five listed attributes – for some mysterious reasons, he discussed an attribute termed *reliability* in place of *trialability* as one of Rogers's famous innovation attributes. This is a pity for a thoughtful book like *Mediamorphosis*.)

Together, the above five attributes explain from 49% to 87% of the variance in adoption rates in past research (Rogers, 2003). Ideally, "the innovations most likely to succeed – especially in the short term – include those with the least need for capital intensive investment, least dependency on existing spectrum or bandwidth, least subject to social norms or regulations, least complex, lowest cost to the adopter, the most advantageous, and most specifically applicable to needs" (Reagan, 2002, p. 82). However, an innovation does not need to satisfy all the defined attributes to be able to widely diffuse in a social system. An extremely complex and disruptive (i.e. highly incompatible with existing practice) technology like a computer can be well adopted because it is perceived to possess many relative advantages that address a wide range of work- and study-related needs. In most cases, the first two attributes – relative advantages and compatibility – play the decisive role (Rogers, 2003).

Online news as a continuous innovation

Placed in the framework of innovation diffusion theory, web news (hereinafter used interchangeably with Internet news) has a substantial potential to foster fast diffusion in both terms of communication facilitators and attributes. As for communication determinants, online news enjoys a range of favourable conditions. First, the web platform is a place where both traditional and non-traditional mass media operate. Self-promotion of online content and activities in traditional outlets is a common feature. Traditional news stories and programs are quite often followed by an invitation to do something online as a follow-up activity, such as looking for further content provision or interaction with media personalities. For example, at 9.30 every Monday night, right after the broadcasting of its weekly investigative program, *Four Corners*, the Australian Broadcasting Corporation invites its viewers to attend an online forum with involved experts and characters. Since 2005, it has offered a broadband version of the program, featuring "extras" such as raw materials, further interviews with experts etc.

Mass media sources, therefore, are like a "natural" push for the diffusion of online news. In the context of the harsh competition driving much of the traditional media's decision to migrate online as mentioned in Chapter 2, it can be even argued that no new news form

73

– and innovation – might have received the level of being mentioned and promoted in the mass media as has online news. Second, in terms of peer-network sources, one can communicate about online news with other people not only through daily "offline" interactions but also, as it will become clearer later, via the online delivery platform itself, whose interactive nature allows everybody to redistribute and discuss news of their interest. This high level of social presence or interpersonal utilities embedded in the consumption experience of online news is rarely found in other innovations, including previous mass media.

In terms of innovation attributes, as heralded here and there, online news might be seen as an almost perfect innovation. Before a systematic examination, however, the concept of innovation continuity – developed by both diffusion sociologists and consumer-behaviour scholars (Neal et al, 1998; Rogers, 2003; Schiffman et al, 2001) – must be considered. Accordingly, there are three major categories of innovations. The first consists of *continuous innovations*, those that require little disruptive influence on established patterns, i.e. only minor behavioural change. Examples include the Toyota Camry or the latest version of Microsoft PowerPoint. The second is *dynamically continuous innovations* – those new products/practices/ideas whose adoption is associated with a major change in some established behaviours that are relatively unimportant to the individual, or a moderate change in some important ones. Examples of this type include 8mm camcorders, cellular phones and compact disk players. The third type, *discontinuous innovations*, is the most disruptive, requiring an altering of some existing important behaviours or an adoption of new behaviour patterns. The facsimile machine, aeroplanes and VCRs are good examples of this innovation class. Obviously, the more continuous the innovation, the more likely it is to be adopted faster.

In new media studies, the distinction between continuous and discontinuous innovations is not always easy to make. This is because many new media technologies and services operate on existing media platforms, which Rogers (2003) called "trigger innovations" – those that lead a consumer to purchasing/adopting others. For example, a computer is a trigger technology that leads to the adoption of a range of other technologies such as CD-ROM or DVD. New media technologies, therefore, are usually more likely to be more or less continuous. The range of telephone-based innovations is an example – the telephone is a discontinuous innovation; the subsequent answering machines or call-waiting and voicemail technologies can be seen as dynamically continuous; and finally hold buttons or redial buttons or touch-tone services are continuous (Schiffman et al, 2001). This classification, however, is implicitly based on the assumption of "progressive adoption" – having the telephone before having voicemail or answering machines and so on. But what if the touch-tone service is considered within a population of those who have not adopted the telephone? Clearly, the service must be seen as a discontinuous innovation in this context. In other words, the same media technology or media service that is based on a single technology could be seen as either a continuous or discontinuous innovation, depending on which population we take into account.

This issue is crucial in a study of online news adoption, which is based on the Internet's infrastructure and thus the computer. For those who do not use the computer or those using the computer without using the Internet, online news is obviously a discontinuous innovation which requires not only the acquisition of a computer-based technology and many new skills and techniques but also a substantial change in a range of work/study, entertainment and communication behaviours. But for an Internet user, online news is more like a dynamically continuous innovation: while it does cause some substantial change to the way Internet users access and receive news, there is hardly any disruptive behavioural change – just a "smooth" transition from Internet connection/use to online news reading. The question is: Within which population (or "social system") should a study of online news adoption be placed? This depends on the nature of research purposes. Those who have an interest in how online news widens the information gap in society, for instance, might explore its adoption and usage within the general population. In this study, for the purpose of predicting the near future of online news, I will place online news adoption primarily in the context of Internet use. This is pragmatically sensible in the context that, as in any other developed country, the Internet has reached a sufficient proportion of the Australian population for online news to expand in the years ahead.

Within this in mind, the innovation attributes of online news seems to be almost perfect:

First, although online news is very different from existing forms of print or broadcast news formats, it can be seen as possessing a relatively high level of compatibility: retrieving and reading news on a web browser is not alien from potential adopters' past experiences because handling information on the screen is one primary use of the existing computer. In addition, all news content found in traditional media is available on the Internet to serve different needs. Second, because the technical expertise needed for different online activities is basically the same (opening a web browser, entering URLs, clicking on links, using search tools etc.), an Internet user does not need to learn any new skill to receive news online. In other words, it is very likely to be perceived with low complexity. Concerning high compatibility and low complexity, it might also be noted that most news web pages today have adapted the magazine page's format, "allowing the new and technocratic space of the Internet to appear in a far more familiar user-friendly guise" (Lister et al, 2003, p. 182).

Third, given that the number of news sites has reached tens of thousands and most are offered without charge, it is highly trialable to the Internet user. Fourth, the interactive nature of the web, where people can share and discuss news and information with their peers easily through a variety of platforms, enables many opportunities for online users to be "accidentally informed" and to observe the potential benefits of online news. Fifth, and most importantly, as mentioned in the previous chapters, online news possesses many features that are likely to be perceived as relative advantages over older forms of news that deserves a detailed discussion in a separate section.

The relative advantages of online news: a user-centric profile

For the most part, what the Internet can offer news audiences has been discussed in relation to how journalism should be done on the medium. Most of these discussions are centred on the construct of "interactivity". But this concept is something of a "definitional morass" (Massey & Levy, 1999). For some researchers, interactivity means technologically empowering consumers with content choice through, for example, embedding links to stories or topically relevant material or augmenting a story with multimedia elements. For others, interactivity equals creating interconnectedness between users and between users and journalists. Schultz (1999) argued that browsing the web, clicking a mouse or selecting from different hyperlinks is not in itself interactivity, which requires a chain of interrelated messages and the equality for anybody to receive/send messages. To Morris and Ogan (1996), interactivity takes on a broader meaning: genuine conversations through a continuum of media offers, from one-to-one email to one-to-many interaction and synchronous chatting, to a complex of all sender-receiver interactions. Still other research (e.g. Deuze, 2001; Ward, 2002) accepts the construct of interactivity as a mixture of both content and interpersonal interaction. An attempt to unify the concept – via a fivefold typology of complexity of choice, responsiveness to users, ease of adding information, facilitation of interpersonal communication and immediacy – can be found in Massey and Levy (1999). But the problem does not seem to have been resolved.

Without entering the debate, it is proposed here that we need not be too medium-driven to portrait online news just around its interactive nature. Whatever media actors can do with technologies, it is the users who will decide their success. Although the above accounts of online journalism practices have to some extent incorporated the image of the audience, being obsessed with interactivity leads them to little or insufficient acknowledgement of many other important factors that might affect the way news is adopted and used. For one thing, these perspectives encompass online news attributes in terms of what happens during the consumption process but ignore what results in and from that consumption. We might ask, for example, how online news is usually accessed, how this differs from other news media, and what this difference means to the chance for online news to be adopted and used. For another, each component of the mentioned typologies is assumed to be good for users but it remains unclear how each contributes to their news experience. In what way is the facilitation of interpersonal communication appealing for users? Why do users need journalists' responsiveness? Even for features that have been taken as important for granted (e.g. immediacy), it is still necessary to explore how they improve the news experience, online and offline.

For a study focusing on online news audience, therefore, there is a need to abandon the long-held hypodermic-needle notion of the audience as a set of mere passive receivers who unconditionally absorb the symbolic output of the all-powerful media. Since the 1950s, a rich body of uses and gratifications (U&G) research has shown that media use is for the most part a *purposeful* or goal-directed process in which a variety of personal utilities are the most important determinant (Dozier & Rice, 1984; Katz, Blumler & Gurevitch, 1974; McQuail, 1997; Palmgreen et al, 1980; Ruggiero, 2000; Schramm, 1949; Severin & Tankard, 2001). As active seekers of gratifications from media use, people pick up a medium consciously to meet certain needs derived from their own circumstances. More specifically, each individual "brings to each media event a host of unique life experiences (albeit within a wider social context) that collectively influence the uses of media and the gratifications derived from it, and that also determine the meaning of media content and the way in which texts are read" (Giles, 2003, p. 187). Because of this, the media have to compete for people's resources not only with other sources of need gratifications (e.g. social gatherings) but also with each other (Blumler & Katz, 1974). Each medium, content type or program must have its own distinctive features to act as a distinctive source of what Dimmick calls "gratification opportunities" (Dimmick & Rothenbuhler, 1984; Dimmick, 2003; Dimmick et al, 2004). It is in this light that I have drawn on different theoretical perspectives in the vast literature on media uses to propose a sixfold portrait of online news advantages, detailed below:

Ease/convenience of use

The process of media choice is substantially determined not only by a medium's gratification opportunities but also by how it fits in people's daily life to provide them. Therefore, the specific temporal and spatial context of use plays a crucial role in the medium's success. Whether a medium is chosen at a particular time of the day depends partly on its accessibility at that time, which in turn depends on both the individual's circumstances and the medium's use location and its timing/scheduling strategies (McQuail, 1997). For example, many people cannot read newspapers or watch television but do listen to radio when driving or doing some gardening work. This is important for both those with strong needs for news but a limited time budget and those who see news more as a pastime activity, or an "interlude of the day" (Stephenson, 1967). In short, a news medium that has many gratification opportunities but is accessible on a limited basis might not be considered appealing when compared with one with less gratification opportunities but more approachability.

Online news is well-qualified in terms of accessibility/approachability. For Internet users, the web might be a truly "any time, anywhere" news medium. One advantage is its 24-hour availability. A user does not need to wait, for example, till 6 pm to watch a national evening news bulletin. Instead, he/she can log on and consume the news at any time during the day – at his/her convenience. This time independence becomes all the more important in the workplace, where traditional news sources are generally not available. If something of great interest happens when one is at work, the Internet is often the only available news source to him/her. Research has shown that the prime-time audience of online news is that at work (Fitzgerald, 2002; Nguyen, 2003; Nua.com News, 2002). With the advance of wireless Internet and the explosion of handheld technologies such as PDAs, pod-cast devices or mobile phones, news of the future might be consumed from anywhere – on a plane, in a taxi, at a coffee shop or in the bathroom. At the time of writing, giant publishers in the US, France, Belgium and Finland are on the way with large-scale trials of newspapers delivered on to digital screens that can be rolled up and stuffed into a back pocket.

Probably more important is the joint effect of the nature of the web as a multipurpose medium and the ubiquity of online news. On the web, people conduct many essential daily activities and news can be easily distributed and redistributed via a wide range of platforms – including not only news sites or email newsletters but also news/information exchange networks, even websites whose primary service is not news-related, and so on. This makes for two advantages. First, there is a high chance of users being "accidentally informed" while doing something else – via a friend's email or an online forum, for instance. Second, and more importantly, news can be deliberately combined with many other online purposes. During chatting, for example, one might read news on a web browser while waiting for responses from the other end. Some others might register general news email alerts from one or a few favoured news services so that each time they open their mailbox (the most frequent online activity so far), the news is there waiting for them. This is especially handy for heavy users of portal sites like Yahoo! or MSN and a wide variety of ISPs, which often integrate news into a variety of content and communication services.

Also, there are an increasing number of web-based services and technologies that make online news consumption handy and time-saving. When one visits a major news site, for example, there is a high chance that he/she is offered to make it his/her home page. Other news consumption facilitating services (e.g. RSS, search engines) will become clear in the following discussion. Last, but not least, all this convenience would become much less meaningful if news on the web costs money. Fortunately, at least until now, most online news services are offered with no charge (except for some archived and/or specialised news content).

Immediacy

People use news to serve many cognitive and orientational purposes, i.e. to be provided with the needed orientation of self to society via utilities for surveillance and information, curiosity, decisions (e.g. issue and vote guidance) as well as for personal identity (self reference and reality exploration) (Katz et al 1973; Lasswell, 1948; Levy & Windahl, 1984; Levy & Windahl, 1985; McQuail, Blumler & Brown, 1972; Wenner, 1985; Wright, 1960). They also need the news media for social purposes, using news content as "ammunition" to support arguments in discussions or as an important means to strengthen social connection and status (by, for example, passing something interesting to friends and/or work colleagues). Thus, being able to obtain information about recent happenings at the possible earliest time can be seen as a crucial imperative for news use, whether this stems from mere curiosity or a desire to survey and explore the environment for important decisions (e.g. following the latest developments in the stock market to make decisions about where and how to invest), or to be the first to obtain and pass the latest updates on an issue of interest to like-minded peer networks. All this is why immediacy has been a major driver of the emergence and development of the penny press, the earliest online news services via the telegraph and the telephone (Chapter 1) and the broadcasting media in the 20th century. The simple fact is that people do not buy a last-week daily to obtain information about recent happenings. The more recent a piece of information, the more likely it is considered news.

In this light, the web can be seen as a superior medium. Although newspapers can have a few editions a day or radio and television can have certain flexible periodicity, they can do little in updating news due to limited resources (e.g. less viable commercial success or limits on timed programming). The technical ease of uploading news content on the web, in contrast, equals a considerable capacity for continuous updates – hour by hour or even minute by minute. Thus whenever a user wants, not only news content is immediately available but also the most updated news items are ready for consumption – usually via a breaking news section or right from the first contact with the front page, where breaking stories are often presented near the top of the screen. For those who are continuously on electronic mail throughout the day, this feature might become more compelling as email alerts of breaking news are sent regularly by many major news services during the day – sometimes as soon as it becomes available. To go back to E. Parker's 1973 prophecy mentioned in the beginning of this book, we now can read a story written only five – or even fewer – minutes earlier. Also, stories could be passed over to friends and peers in a number of easy ways (email lists, online forums, discussion groups, weblogs, personal or collaborative websites), thus increasing the social utilities of online updates.

Content richness

Content richness, especially depth of coverage, is another crucial aspect that increases the orientational and social gratifications of news. Certain people are only cursorily interested in news events and tend to watch television for superficial coverage of the main issues of the day. But many others, especially educated news users with higher socio-economic status, would place a stronger emphasis on story details and related information and perspectives. These people use news heavily for orientational gratifications – they need in-depth and background information to follow events more effectively and efficiently, to understand the world and its relationship to their inner self more thoroughly, to gain more knowledge for their work-related matters, to reduce uncertainties. Like immediacy, content richness is a crucial contributor to the perceived social gratifications of news – it could help to improve users' social identities via passing good information to peer networks or via presenting informed arguments in debates.

By giving the user more choices and more control of their news intake, the web is excellent in this aspect. An obvious asset of the web in relation to content richness is the hypertextual link. Receiving news on many news sites means no more worry about lacking background information and knowledge as new stories are often internally linked to previous coverage of related events or phenomena. An increasing number of sites also provide external links to sources, original documents, related news subjects and the like. Tremayne (2004) found that the mean number of links per story on ten US national news sites increased continuously from 2.99 in 1997 to 4.12 in 1998, 5.7 in 1999, 9.29 in 2000 and 9.36 in 2001. Furthermore, the seemingly unlimited space on the web allows news organisations to present events with greater details – via tools such as special reports or temporary sections or by adding content that does not fit in the print news hole or the broadcasting time slot.

Another crucial strength is that logging on to the web means the ability to receive news from all corners of the world. No longer does the user need to be restrained by the limited news feeds from the outlets available in their physical communities. One news item of great interest can be easily further explored through a few clicks to other news sites wherever they are based. A British user interested in the tsunami disaster in South Asia, for example, need not be constrained to British newspapers if he/she is unhappy with the way the disaster is reported in these publications. Similarly, a New York resident interested in an event in a local community in Sydney would only need a simple Google search to find and access the site of that community's local paper, its official website, or an information exchange network by its residents. "Content richness", in this sense, does not simply imply more news content but also incorporates a wider range of perspectives, including those from non-stream providers that will be discussed shortly.

News on demand

The availability of a vast mount of news and related information online does not necessarily lead to more use if people find it difficult to filter what is needed from what is not. Scheufele and Nisbet (2002, p. 57) argued that "human beings are cognitive misers or at least satisfiers; that is, they seek out as little information as possible to make any given decision". Indeed, with too many sources, the web could become a labyrinth of news and information that might cause a serious headache for focused news consumers. Even if an individual is a real news junkie, he/she still will not have enough time and other resources (e.g. physical health) to follow everything of interest. In other words, as much as people want more news and information available to serve their orientational and social purposes, they also want it to be easy to track and seek. That is, they need mechanisms to filter out the news that suits them and that directly provides them with what they genuinely need.

Fortunately, the web does remarkably well in several aspects to meet this demand. First, like the newspaper, the web allows random access to stories of interest. Instead of having to follow unwanted items of a radio or television news bulletin one by one, including sometimes annoying commercials, users now can receive what they want straightforward by browsing a user-friendly and magazine-like interface and clicking on sections or stories of interest. Second, search engines provided on news sites considerably facilitate public access to issues of interest. The appeal of searchable news might become more remarkable on popular portal sites that accumulate news from sources from every corner of the world. Google, for example, since 2002 has been offering a successful, although controversial, searchable news service that now scrawls, clusters and re-purposes content from 4,500 news sites around the world every fifteen minutes. Perhaps the most practical description of its benefits to users is that of Google News itself:

> Traditionally, news readers first pick a publication and then look for headlines that interest them. We do things a little differently, with the goal of offering our readers more personalized options and a wider variety of perspectives from which to choose. On Google News we offer links to several articles on every story, so you can first decide what subject interests you and then select which publishers' accounts of each story you'd like to read. Click on the headline that interests you and you'll go directly to the site which published that story.

Our articles are selected and ranked by computers that evaluate, among other things, how often and on what sites a story appears online. As a result, stories are sorted without regard to political viewpoint or ideology and you can choose from a wide variety of perspectives on any given story.

As of March 2008, Google News has had localised versions in over 40 regions/countries, being delivered in Arabic, Chinese, Dutch, English, French, German, Greek, Hebrew, Hindi, Italian, Japanese, Korean, Norwegian, Portuguese, Russian, Spanish and Swedish. Each regional version favours news about its geographical areas so that users can quickly and easily find the most relevant news/information to them. The US version of Google News recently took a step further, adding an experimental feature which helps users to enter a US postcode or town name and see a panel displaying news about that area.

Google News is yet only one among many similar news-aggregating services – such as Topix, RocketInfo News, Yahoo! News, GeoSearch News, and many others. Topix.com, for instance, is now tracking and pulling updated content from more than 50,000 news sources and categorising each story into one or more of 360,000 topic pages, where users can easily find news tailored to their interest. Starting in 2004, Topix was among the world's top 20 news sites in November 2007, according to ComScore research. Meanwhile, as of March 2008, RocketNews was accumulating news from 60,000 news sources, including newspapers, trade journals, scientific publications and weblogs. In the same month, MetaCarta's GeoSearch News – which lets users roll over pinpoints on an embedded Microsoft Virtual Earth map to specify a place of interest and then receive news stories relevant to that place – was launched with an initial pool of 1,400 sources. These services not only provide news on demand but also present the latest information at a desirable depth level.

Third, there are a number of other web-based technologies and services that make it easy for a user to receive and consume only the news tailored to his/her interest. This can be done simply by setting a trusted news page as their default homepage or saving URL links in the "Favourite" folder. At a more advanced level is the so-called "push technology", which requires users to register their tastes and preferences so that, without further prompting, any news relevant to this profile will be displayed on his/her computer screen as it becomes available). What a user needs is just a few simple registration steps that involve specifying his/her news tastes. The delivery platform can be either a customised email newsletter or a personalised news and information page on portal sites such as My Yahoo! and My MSN, which is linked to their email pages (or vice versa). In the words of online pioneer J.D. Lasica, with these net casting, or personal broadcast, applications, we "no longer have to surf for news and information; news finds us" (1997).

In recent years, there has been a shift from "push technology" to two newer and not less powerful technologies called RSS (Really Simple Syndication) and Atom. In its simplest meaning, RSS is a family of XML formats used to syndicate the latest headlines from multiple news sources and display them at one convenient location for use (called an RSS reader). In essence, an RSS reader is a "pull technology" that does the surfing for the user so that one does not need to visit each site individually to see what is new there. A user chooses the "web feeds" (i.e. the URLs of the news sites with the desired content) and the RSS reader will pull all the latest headlines (and associated summaries or full texts) from these sources. Atom is an alternative XML language to RSS, doing the same thing for users but tending to support more interoperability between different readers than RSS. Today, it is becoming increasingly rare to find a mainstream news site without an news-feed offer. In either RSS or Atom platforms, the latest news/information from a particular chosen feed (usually a news section of interest from a news site) will be ready for consumption when a user opens the reader. Like services such as Google News, RSS considerably facilitates news consumption through allowing users not only to "hierarchise" their news flow but also to combine customisation, depth and immediacy in a convenient and time-saving way. Many news sites – e.g. *USA Today* or Google News – have also started to deliver news feeds to mobile phones.

Participation opportunities

For many users, being able to be actively involved in the debate over public affairs is an important dimension in the social gratifications of news. Some might desire to protect socio-cultural values or perceive a civic responsibility out of their concerns about others and, therefore, will actively participate in relevant socio-political activities if resources are available (Steinberger, 1984). Many others, according to Bucy and Gregson (2001), look for specific, personally rewarding outcomes from corrective communications with power holders, including the desire to "talk back" to politicians, celebrities and even the powerful media system. The rewards might be symbolic (social status, proximity to material power, increased efficacy, becoming informed, monitoring material power and psychological rewards) or material (policy changes, governmental expenditures, peer recognition, professional status and media attention). There are still others who use effective participation as a way to foster social bonds in their interpersonal networks or those who simply write to express themselves and to feel they belong to a community.

And this is where the Internet shows its most marked contrast to traditional news media. In traditional models of communication, the information flow runs in one way from a centralised office to a mass public, who has to accept the passive position of an underdog. On the web, however, interactivity allows every news user to easily conduct two-way (one-to-one, one-to-many or many-to-one) communication. More particularly, the news user now can make their voices heard through publishing grassroots content, showing attitudes to news events, reacting to media treatment of public affairs and the like. According to Schultz (1999), on a mainstream news sites, this can be done through four major groups of interactive options for users: (1) email for asynchronous journalists-readers communication, reactive questions-and-answers sessions, quicker "letters to editors"; (2) live chats for reactive communication and interactive threads (guided by moderating hosts and defined topics); (3) online polls/surveys; (4) online forums organised as bulletin boards aiming to widen reader-reader communication. To this list, we need to add weblogs – a form of online journals with updated musings, presented in a chronologically reverse order, which has recently risen to the centre stage of participatory publishing (Bowman & Willis, 2003; Nguyen, 2006; see Chapter 4).

What is more important is that online participatory platforms need not be the mainstream media's exclusive preserve – i.e. the communication from the audience side does not live largely at the mercy of news professionals as in traditional models, where the means are restricted within letters to editors or calls-in to talkback radio and some television shows. Online, participation can easily take well beyond mainstream sites because publishing is now literally as easy as typing. In the case of weblogs, for example, all that an individual needs to do is simply to register for a free space on a hosting site, type what he/she thinks/hears/sees and hits the "publish" button – to reach potentially millions of people. In addition, as the result of low distribution costs, members of the public may gather and form their own publishing sites, where they have their say and listen to others in an unprofessionally mediated way. As Lasica (1996, p. 33) commented: "The zeitgeist of the Net – its unifying principle – is centred in interaction and interconnectedness, not 'I-will-publish, you-will-accept.' The Net is not a megaphone. The Net is a conversation".

The historical context of the online participation opportunities is important. Journalism has long been closing its door and turning a blind eye to the public's needs and concerns over its standards as well as over public affairs (Brand & Pearson, 2001; Grossberg, Wartella & Whitney, 1998; Henningham, 1992; Henningham, 1998; Kovach & Rosenstiel, 2001; Stannard, 1989). This attitude – combined with the increasing trend of ownership concentration, the cooperate strategy to "get more out of less" (focusing on affluent segments of the public rather than the general public) and the recent change in journalism tone from objective reporting to subjective and judgmental coverage – has rendered journalists' hard-earned independence and detachment from outside pressures to the risk of bleeding into isolation from communities (Kovach & Rosenstiel, 2001). Ironically, as Henningham (1992) pointed out, journalists themselves have long become a threat to press freedom – and thus substantially contribute to what Habermas (1996, p. 29) called the "refeudalisation of the public sphere" – a process in which "organisations strive for political compromises with the state and with one another, as much as possible to the exclusion of the public". All this turns the very justification for the existence of journalism – its mission to act as the independent watchdog of public affairs, to "let all with something to say to be free to express itself" so that "the true and sound will survive; the false and unsound will be vanquished" in a free, open and self-righting marketplace of ideas (Siebert, 1956, p. 45) – into a modern fallacy.

Consequently, public distrust and disrespect is found everywhere. In the US, the Pew Research Centre for the People and the Press (2005) found that the majority of Americans believed that when deciding what stories to report, news organisations care more about attracting the biggest audience (75%) than about keeping the public informed (19%) and more about "entertaining people in order to attract the biggest audience" (69%) than about "informing people in order to serve the public interest". In Australia, a 2005 survey revealed that 71% of Australians believed that "media organisations are more interested in making money than in informing society" and 67% thought that "the media is not objective enough" (Roy Morgan, 2005). Earlier, the 2003 Australian Survey of Social Attitudes found that around 80% of Australians were critical of media ownership concentration in their country and nearly 70% believed that the mass media must have less or much less power (Gibson et al, 2004). The situation is so critical that Nicholas Lemann had to moan that "the danger of these ongoing assaults (on journalism) is a general public that don't believe in us (journalists), don't want us any more" (quoted in Loewenstein, 2005). It is in the context of this image crisis of the news media that participation opportunities could take on its role as a potential driver of online news uptake (Bowman & Willis, 2003; Cornfield et al, 2004; Gillmor, 2003; Grossberg et al, 1998; McIlwaine & Nguyen, 2005; Nguyen, 2006; Rainie, 2005; Redden, Caldwell & Nguyen, 2003).

Multimedia content and format

Finally, the Internet is "a medium of media" – a place where other media happen (Levinson, 2003, p. 36). Online journalism is, in theory, "a journalism that uses the best devices of the novel – and the movie! and the radio! and the CD-ROM! and network communications – to tell stories" (Quittner, 1995). In its true meaning, multimedia is not simply a sum of media but is the integration of many communication formats into story-telling. Unlike traditional media that are usually dominated by one consumption mode or another, this capacity for the integrated formats on the web allows the online news consumer to be able to "do it all" – reading, watching, listening – at the same time. In an ideal sense, one can read stories that are audio-visually aided by not only excellent graphics, interactive maps and vivid Shockwave illustrations of events (e.g. the scene of the second plane crashing into the World Trade Centre on September 11, 2001) but also live or raw news video and audio clips. Examples include President Bush's inaugural speech or raw battlefield video reporting offered by Reuters in the second Iraq War.

The multimedia nature of online news provides the user with a good range of gratification opportunities. As a presentation format, multimedia mobilises all human senses into a distinctive news use process, thus improving what Wenner (1985) called *"para-social gratifications"* – a group of process-based, rather than content-based, utilities that users obtain from immersing in a perceived ongoing dialogue with media personalities. With it, users can immerse in the news event, "para-socially" interacting with a variety of media personalities, from television newscasters and political columnists to public figures in the news. In this way, it both enhances the efficiency and effectiveness of news involvement and boosts its playfulness, a quality which some scholars (Bogart, 1965; Bogart, 1989; Stephenson, 1967) see as the most important purpose of news. As content, multimedia can improve cognitive aspects during and after the news consumption process. The ability to combine the printed text with other media formats means users have more choices to add depth and/or breadth to the reported issue. Also, providing "multi-dose" and additional learning cues could improve the storage potential of obtained information and the ability to retrieve it from memory. (For some, however, this might not be the case because multimedia might be cognitively complex enough to overload the processing system, leading to superior recognition memory but inferior recall memory; see Gunter, 2003).

A total experience

With all the above advantages, the Internet appears to be able to become a news medium for a plethora of news user types. Even for those casual "news grazers", it still can offer much: free, easy and convenient access, a good chance to be accidentally exposed to news items, a high level of playfulness, the ability to scan/skim headlines and introductory text chunks, or simply the ability to leisurely or inattentively watch and listen to the news. But obviously, the value of online news is "ideal" for the serious user, and when all online news attributes are taken together, it generates a uniquely gratifying experience for news junkies. Ward (2002, p. 23) likened exploring a well-resourced web site to "playing a game of three-dimensional chess, (in which) you can sit in the middle of the site and go forward (immediacy), sideways (links to sites, related stories and interactivity) or down into the archive". Meanwhile, Lule (1998, p. B7) contended that the Internet brings Marshall McLuhan's infamous and controversial "The medium is the message" to reality, saying:

> Online news is different from all of those (traditional) media and oddly embraces them all. It offers the depth of a newspaper (or, with hypertext links and electronic archives, even more depth). It showcases the attitude and focus of a smart-mouthed magazine. It emulates the immediacy and interactivity of talk radio (with the added interaction of chat rooms, forums and email). It approximates the visual impact of television. This seemingly chaotic medium is exploding with messages.

Similarly, a journalist at the *Age Online* described online news consumption as a "total experience":

> I guess all of those kinds of multimedia things (devices) are making the net more of an experience (for the user) rather than just opening up a newspaper. You can go surfing and get audio and video, and read it... You can also interact in forums and things like that, so it is more a total experience" (quoted in Ewart & Gregor, 2001, p. 49).

This kind of "total experience" is becoming increasingly popular, especially on news-aggregating services. These services, as noted, not only provide depth, immediacy, multimedia, searchability and other on-demand services (e.g. RSS and Atom) but have recently moved towards interactivity and participation. Since 2007, for example, Topix users have not only been provided with the latest news from thousands of sources and opportunities to customise their news but also been enabled to add original content, edit or comment on stories which they know well.

The "relative disadvantages" of online news

Online news, however, is not perfect. Along with its relative advantages, online news has some potential drawbacks that might hinder its diffusion:

First, there are potential health problems caused by heavy computer use. For example, a three-year Japanese study of 25,000 workers found that staring at computer screens for more than five hours a day is likely to be the cause of physical pain and mental problems (Tobler, 2002). If more evidence of these health problems is found, many people might have to reduce much of their time in cyberspace, focusing on services that would not be available without the Internet – such as emailing and searching for work- or study-related information – and ignoring services like online news, whose functional alternatives can be easily found in the offline world.

Second, consuming news on the web is not always a comfortable experience. One source of discomfort is the reading and navigating process itself. According to Craig (2005, p. 89), small texts on the backlit computer screen "essentially (combine) the main sources of eye strain of both TV and newspapers". A survey found that 79% of Internet users scan rather than read, partly because online reading is tiresome and too demanding for the eye and is about 25% slower than print reading (Nielsen, 1997). Other research has shown that navigating through complex news sites might be frustrating to novice Internet users (Craig, 2005). As media critic Jon Katz speculated in the early days of the web:

> Reading a newspaper online is difficult, cumbersome and time consuming. There is none of the feel of scanning a story, turning pages for more, skipping easily back to the beginning. The impact of seeing a picture, headline, caption, and some text in one sweep is completely lost. With news glimpsed only in fragments and short scrolls, the sense of what the paper thinks is important disappears. You can't look at a paper's front page to absorb some sense, however limited, of the shape your town, city, or world is in. You can't skip through a review for the paragraph that tells you whether to see the movie or not or skim through movie listings for show times. Much of what still works about a paper – convenience, visual freedom, a sense of priorities, a personal experience – is gone. Online, papers throw away what makes them special (quoted in Mueller & Kamerer, 1995, p. 4).

Another source of discomfort is Internet speed. Waiting for a web page to be downloaded on to the screen might be frustrating to users. An extreme example is September 11, the biggest day of web news in its short history. As millions of people logged on for details, news sites were seriously jammed and the web "took a blow": people had to turn back to television and other traditional news media for news of the shocking event (Outing, 2001). This is still a big problem for the future of online news, especially in countries where access to broadband Internet is limited. Finally, advertising can become a common source of unpleasant experience. While the web allows random access to stories, popular online advertising practices such as the insertion of a flash ad into the body of a story can be annoying. Unlike advertising on television or newspapers, online advertising tend to be more distracting because of their use of colour, animation, pop-ups and so on. Further, as the physical distance between stories and advertisements is "more intermingled", online news reading becomes more unpredictably interrupted by ads (Yang & Oliver, 2004). In their survey, Yang and Oliver (2004) found that light Internet users were particularly vulnerable to this, perceiving hard news as less newsworthy after being exposed to interrupting silly ads.

The third, and most important, problem of online news is that its many advantages in promoting a well-informed citizenry are ironically associated with drawbacks that could produce an ill-informed citizenry. For one thing, reliance on customised news services might lead some online news users might to missing many important events that they should know about. Meanwhile, faster reporting means less time for reactions from the parties involved, shortening the life of many public issues (Bardoel, 1996). Another questionable advantage of online news is the hyperlink. Readers might want links for in-depth understanding of stories that they are interested in. But they only want links to trusted sources. If an online news organisation makes external links, will it stand behind the content of the sites and documents they link their users to? Does it have enough resources to filter everything? Quality control of the "free pass into unknown territory," as an American journalism professor calls the hypertextual link (Markus, 2000), is still open to scrutiny.

Perhaps more serious are problems associated with the ease of publishing and updates on the web. This might become a nightmare as there is no effective filter of the good and the bad, the true and the false. Beside good information, the web is full of hoaxes that can fool even professional journalists, let alone ordinary users. Also, there has been much anecdotal evidence that continuous updates mean less time for fact checking, resulting in a high chance of inaccurate breaking news (see Allan, 2005 for a prolific source of evidence related to this). One example, as reported by Frank (2000), happened in the US stock exchange on 24 August, 1999. In just a few hours, the stock of a company fell 50% as many panic-stricken investors sold their shares. The company, Emulex, was reported on the sites of established wire services as being under investigation by the Stock Exchange Council and that its chief executive had fled. Shortly into the collapse, the news was found to be a hoax – of course not because the reporters wanted to play a cheating game. The culprit was a shareholder in California, who, frustrated with one of his failing ventures, distributed a false press release about the investigation on the web (and eventually won $250,000). The breaking-news release was immediately snapped by the wire service reporters, who did not bother verifying and editing it before presenting it to the public.

The problem worsens as news sites have no good way to fix their errors in a manner that is apparent to users. The paradox lies in the technical simplicity of updates: "In five or 10 minutes an editor can correct a miscalculation that appears in three stories and republish them without a trace.... Insert the paragraph, update the death toll, rewrite the headline, add a quote. *'Updating' and 'correcting' can become indistinguishable in the churn*" (Palser, 2001; emphasis added). Meanwhile, in this global interactive environment, false news travels too fast. Those who went to CNN.com during the week of September 11 attacks, for example, could see a correction box for an earlier story in which two Arabian brothers were identified by some official sources as among the dead hijackers. In fact, these were not brothers and one of them died one year before the news item while the other was living in Florida. By the time CNN.com posted the correction box, the news had already been reported around the world. The problem might be worsened with the increasing popularity of news aggregators. As of 2008, for instance, the Google News crawler was still visiting the URL of an article only once – if more details, including corrections and updates, were added to the original article, they would not be reflected on the article's Google News page.

All of these potential drawbacks of online news could result in a credibility problem and thus might hinder adoption of online news among certain members of the social system, especially immature Internet users. It must be noted, however, that these drawbacks are likely to be outweighed by the above favourable attributes of online news. It might well be that because the "dark side" of online news is not substantially encountered over time, it is largely unnoticed in overall online news appreciation, or is not serious enough to lead a user to an abandonment of online news as the whole. To use the economic concept of "trade-off complexity" mentioned earlier, these disadvantages might be seen as a "price" that people accept to pay to enjoy the advantages of online news. This can be likened to the fact that people might buy a car without a set of safety instruments that they would desire, because this car has many other features of their favour – its look, its speed control system, and so on. Further, some of the aforementioned problems could be circumvented along with Internet experience – i.e. those with more Internet knowledge and skills can avoid them to the best possible extent. For instance, an online news veteran might develop a strategy to successfully ignoring ads inserted in stories or might find reading onscreen not too difficult (Yang & Oliver, 2004).

Concluding notes

This chapter has shown that from the user's perspective, online news has a great potential to foster a wide diffusion in the increasingly crowded online world. As a continuous innovation that can offer users a wide range of news-related gratification opportunities, it could be seen more or less as a superior news form to most traditional news media. Although online news has some potential defects, these could be outweighed by its many potential benefits. With this in mind, it is sensible to at least theoretically project that the Internet is by and large a compelling platform for human beings to meet their diverse needs for news (and indeed non-news information).

It should be reminded, however, that the relative advantages of online news have not been developed to their fullest extent. As discussed in Chapter 2, due to the fear-driven innovation culture among traditional news media, what the public has been offered on most news sites is still distant from what it can be offered. However, there have been some notable attempts among web-only news providers. According to Salwen (2005), even independent webzines with more limited resources than big commercial players – such as Salon and Slate – have established a distinctive online presence with dramatic social impact through their aggressive strategy to offer original editorial content, including exclusive news. Online news ventures of excellent quality have also been found among Internet giants such as Yahoo! or Google and public broadcasting services such as the ABC in Australia or the BBC in the UK. While having their own constraints, these outlets, either with no vested interest in the traditional world or with a purer public service function, have been pursuing active policies of differentiation in the online world, providing services that well exploit much of the Internet's potential to cater for different niche and mass audiences.

Perhaps more importantly, it must be noted that many online news advantages are due to the Internet's inherent nature rather than the effort made by producers. Its convenience of use and its ability to provide as much information as desired, for example, are intrinsic because the medium is a global network whose use is temporally and spatially independent. Or to some extent, immediacy is a matter of global accessibility – a recent news story of great interest might be unavailable on a local news site at a particular time but might be easily retrieved from sources based in other places, including the country or city where the relevant event takes place. This same global nature, as noted, is also a contribution to the depth of online news.

Thus, despite being short of its full potentials, the medium as it stands still has much to offer users with a unique news experience. The question is whether, and to what extent, online news advantages have been appreciated and how this appreciation has contributed and will contribute to its adoption and use. In the next chapters, I will explore these issues with empirical data from previous research and from a national survey of Australian uses of online news.

Chapter 4

The public's responses: general patterns of online news uses and gratifications

This chapter presents a general picture of the current status of online news uses and gratifications. First, extracting information from a wide range of academic, commercial and policy-guiding research data from around 20 countries, it reviews the uptake of online news among the global public in the 2000s, with some attention to the link between this uptake and the relative advantages of online news. Then, the chapter adds to the still limited literature on online news uses and gratifications by presenting a detailed report on the extent to which a wide range of online news services and/or attributes have been used and appreciated, using data collected from a national survey in Australia. In general, the empirical data from this survey and other relevant research in the literature show that (1) online news has been playing a relatively important role in Internet uses, with the medium having reached the status of a mainstream news medium in many developed segments of the world since the early 2000s; and (2) some its relative advantages – especially ease/convenience of use, immediacy and rich content – have substantially been used and appreciated while its potential problems do not seem to be a big issue for online news users. Based on a discussion of the influence of interpersonal networks in innovation diffusion, the chapter concludes that with its compelling nature and its interactive diffusion environment, online news will probably continue its impressive uptake in the years ahead.

The global uptake of online news consumption

In the context of the massive online news migration among traditional media and the emergence of many web-only news ventures (Chapter 2), the online news audience has been growing fast in both size and substance, with news being among the most popular online activities. Since the early 2000s, online news has reached a mainstream status in many developed segments of the world.

Nowhere is the unprecedented penetration of online news into daily life more evident than in the US. In September 2001, the US Census Bureau (2002) surveyed 57,000 households with more than 137,000 individuals to find that news (including weather and sports) was the third most dominant of 15 listed activities, being used by 62% of Internet users (approximately one-third of the population), just after e-mail (84%) and searching for products or services (67%). A year later, a Jupiter Research study of 4,341 Americans found news to be the sixth most popular activity on the web, being consumed by 53% of the online audience (Greenspan, 2002). This is confirmed by the University of California at Los Angeles – and now the University of Southern California – "Surveying the Digital Future" series, which shows that "reading news" has consistently been in the third position of the most popular online activities – after email and general web surfing – since 2000. In 2007, for instance, online news was used by 60% of Internet users – compared with 96% using email and 71% doing general web surfing (University of Southern California Centre for Digital Future, 2008).

The establishment of the Internet as a mainstream news medium in American life since the beginning of this decade is incisively asserted in the Pew Research Centre for the People and the Press's influential biannual surveys on media use. The 2002 survey within the series, for example, shows that despite a general decline in American use of news between 2000 and 2002, online news consumption was still up: 35% of the population (33% in 2000) logged on the web for news at least once a week in 2002 (Pew Research Centre, 2002a). At the time of the survey, 15.5% of the American population received online news every day and a further 10% examined online news three to five times a week — compared with 41% of the population reading a newspaper "yesterday" and only 13% being readers of weekly news magazines. The picture is clear: by 2002, the Internet as a news medium had substantially bypassed mainstream weekly magazines in the race for readers. The increase in the American online news population has shown no sign of stopping: 31% of the adult population got online news at least three days a week in 2006

– up from 13% in 1998, 23% in 2000, 25% in 2002 and 29% in 2004 (Pew Research Centre, 2006).

A similar reality is found in other countries. In Canada, according to a General Social Survey, 55% of 13 million Internet users in 2000 searched news online, making this the third most popular activity in the Canadian web sphere, just after e-mail (84%) and searching for goods/services (75%) (Dryburgh, 2001). As of 2005, "viewing news and sports" came fifth in a 22-item list, being reported as a reason for Internet use by 62% of users (Statistics Canada, 2006). In Europe, where news organisations were slower in embracing the Internet (Specker, 1999), a less vigorous but still strong development has been recorded. A special Eurobarometer report on Europeans' cultural participation stated that in 2000, nearly one-third of Europeans read articles on national newspaper web sites "in the past three months", making it the seventh most dominant of the 27 listed Internet services (European Commission, 2000). In late 2001, an eMarketer survey in 12 core European countries found news the second top online activity (after e-mail), with more than 70% of Internet users saying they logged on to keep abreast of important developments related to business and world affairs (Online Publishing News, 2001). More recent studies in specific countries reinforce these trends. In the UK, for instance, the Oxford Internet Survey found that looking for news was the tenth most popular of 32 listed online activities in 2005 (Dutton, Gennaro & Hargrave, 2005). Again, online news growth has shown no sign of stopping in this country, with the most recent Oxford survey finding that the proportion of British Internet users looking for news online considerably increased from 61% in 2005 to 69% in 2007 (Dutton & Helsper 2007).

In Australia, online news has enjoyed a similar rapid penetration since the launch of the country's first mainstream news site, *The Sydney Morning Herald*'s smh.com.au in April 1995. A policy-guiding study for the Australian Broadcasting Authority (ABA) in August 2000 found news the fifth most frequently used online categories on a 16-item list, being accessed by nearly half of the online population at home (with about 16% doing this "all the time" or "quite often") (ABA, 2001). As of November 2004, according to ACNielsen Consult, "news and reference" was the fifth most popular Internet activities among Australians (used by over 40% of the online population), after email, banking/financial

98

services, personal interests/hobbies, and entertainment (MacLean, 2005). The popularity of online news in Australia could be further elaborated by traffic to news sites. In an average month in 2005, all sites under Fairfax Digital attracted five million Australian users (i.e. 25% of the population) and eight million unique browsers (Fairfax, 2005). Meanwhile, Australia's top online news site, Ninemsn, attracted 894,000 unique visitors aged 14 or over in any four-week period between March 2005 and April 2006 (Roy Morgan, 2006a). It is noted, however, the Internet is still far behind traditional media in terms of its importance for Australians (Roy Morgan, 2006b).

Developed segments in Asia have been much on the same move since the early 2000s. In Japan, a 2002 study shows that news was ranked third among 33 types of web sites being accessed "in the past month". While all of the other four of the top five web site types (search sites, transportation/travel course/maps, weather forecasts and PC-related sites) more or less plunged from 2000 to 2001, access to online news surged from 37.8% in 2000 to 40.6% in 2001 (Mikaki et al, 2002). Socio-economically advantaged areas in China are no different. In Hong Kong, Zhou and He (2002a) found that users spent the fourth largest amount of online time on reading news in 2000 (90 minutes per week). In Taiwan, an island-wide survey of 2,015 people in December 2000 placed news reception on the third position on the list of the most time-devoted online activities: 17.42 minutes per day – just after searching recreational information (26.52 minutes/day) and searching professional or learning information (21.34 minutes/day) (Liu et al, 2002). In Macao, according to a survey conducted in early 2001 by Cheong (2002), news was on the top of a list of web-based information types, being sought by 62% of Internet users. In mainland China, a late 2000 survey among 2,664 respondents in Beijing and Guangzhou found that the second largest amount of online time spent by Internet users was on news – just after work- or study-related information (Zhou & He, 2002b). See Nguyen (2003) for further details.

In short, wherever and in whatever way they are collected or measured, the mere statistics above show that in most developed segments of the world, online news has reached a mainstream status and this growth has been an important contributor to overall Internet uptake. Along with this development is the recent vigorous rise of public participation via online participatory technologies, a phenomenon unique to the Internet that deserves a separate discussion section.

The unprecedented rise of online news prosumers

With the Internet fast penetrating daily life and a range of web-based easy-publishing technologies becoming increasingly popular, a two-way decentralised news and information environment has also established itself. This is most notably reflected in the vibrant rise of participatory publishing (hereafter PP), a social movement in which individual citizens or groups of citizens do their own "journalism", playing "an active role in the process of collecting, reporting, analysing and disseminating news and information" in order to "provide independent, reliable, accurate, wide-ranging and relevant information that a democracy requires" (Bowman & Willis, 2003, p. 9).

The explosion of weblogs is an overwhelming example of this development. As noted in the previous chapter, weblogs or blogs are a form of online journals where continuously updated musings about any topic, including public affairs, are date-stamped and presented in a chronologically reverse order. Before 1999, there were only a handful of blogs (Blood, 2000). Three years later, no one could be sure of the exact number but there was "a new blogger joining the crowd every 40 seconds" (Levy, 2002). By April 2007, the number of blogs Technorati was tracking went sharply up to 70 million, with over 120,000 new ones being created every day (i.e. about 1.4 blog every second) (Sifry, 2007). In terms of content volumes, the Technorati report states that there were about 1.4 million posts being created every day (i.e. over 58,000 posts per hour). Of the 100 most popular news and information sites, 22 were blogs, a substantial increase from 12 six months before that.

With that comes an increasing audience size and political influence of the blogosphere, especially in the US. In the second war on Iraq, blog sites became a source of news for 4% of online Americans (Rainie, Fox & Fallows, 2003). At the onset of the federal election in 2004, two surveys by the Pew Internet & American Life Project found that 7% of the 120 million American adult Internet users owned a blog or a web-based diary; and more than a quarter of them (27%, representing 32 million) read blogs – an increase of 58% from January of that year, with 12% having posted comments and other material on blogs (Rainie, 2005). By the end of 2006, 39% of American Internet users read someone else's blog – and while political blogs accounted for less than 10% of all blogs, one in five of those who received political news online had read political blogs (Horrigan, 2007). Since the National Convention of the Democrats in the summer of 2004, some bloggers have now been given press credits to access the US's most important political events and places, including the White House. As early as 2002, one of the world's most respected journalism schools, the University of California at Berkeley Graduate School of Journalism, started a course called "Creating an IP (Intellectual Property) Weblog".

The American blogosphere has been credited as the driving force behind some of the nation's recent biggest political scoops, one of which is the oft-mentioned saga of a former majority leader, Republican Senator Trent Lott. At the 100th birthday of the famous Senator Strom Thurmond, Lott made a comment that the US would have been much better off had the country chosen Thurmond as its President in the 1948 election. The note, which was racist by its nature as Thurmond's 1948 campaign was centred on an opposition to equal rights for blacks and whites, received only a brief coverage on ABCNews.com. But the rising weblog communities did not let it wither. Ignited by leftist Internet opinion leaders like Josh Marshall on Talking Points Memo, and quickly joined by influential conservatives like Glenn Reynolds, a law professor at the University of Tennessee (Thompson, 2003), the outraged debate went on with a focus on Lott's hateful past, calling on Republicans to oust Lott because of the dangerous implications of his comment. It was until then that the big media took notice and the event went mainstream and finally gave Lott no option but to resign. In February 2008, Josh Marshal won one of America's top journalism prizes, the Polk Award for Legal Reporting, for his blog's "tenacious investigative reporting" into the firing of U.S. attorneys by the Bush administration, which "sparked interest by the traditional news media and led to the resignation of Attorney General Alberto Gonzales" (quoted in Cohen, 2008). By that time, Talking Points Memo had a newsroom with seven journalists and was recording a 400,000 page views a day and 750,000 unique visitors a month.

Another spectacular story is the fall from grace of veteran CBS journalist Dan Rather (Eberthart, 2005; Kiss, 2005; Thornburgh & Boccardi, 2005). The story began on September 8, 2004, when Rather presented on CBS four documents allegedly written by a commander who oversaw President Bush during his service at Texas Air National Guard in the 1970s, which showed, among other things, that Mr Bush used influences to obtain a preferential treatment in an effort to evade the draft and join the Texas force. Within minutes of the broadcast, however, CBS's assertion that it "had consulted with a handwriting analyst and document expert who believes the material is authentic" (Thornburgh & Boccardi, 2005) did not stop serious doubts from being raised on a number of independent online forums and weblogs. A series of conservative bloggers conducted their own investigation, seeking advice from experts of 1970s typewriters and examining the material's fonts and formatting to conclude that it must be forgeries produced by a modern PC. Their reasons: it had Times New Roman font style, was proportionally spaced, and had a superscript "th". After a dozen days of stubborn reassertion of the authenticity of the documents, CBS finally confessed that "CBS News cannot prove the documents are authentic" and that it "was a mistake we deeply regret". An independent review panel was commissioned by CBS to investigate the whole process and arrived at the same conclusion as the blogosphere. Dan Rather stepped down from his well-respected news-anchoring career.

PP is not only about weblogs but a range of other platforms that have been increasingly known under the (controversial) catch-all term of Web 2.0 applications – such as email lists, bulletin boards, online forums, social-networking sites (e.g. Facebook, Twitter, Flickr), podcasts, collaborative publishing sites and so forth. Delivered and produced in different media formats (sometimes as simple as a 140-character message sent to a website via instant messaging or SMS and other applications), these PP platforms have registered their own victories in recent years. For example, when Slashdot.com, a collaborative "news-for-nerds" website of technological advances, turned seven-year-old in 2003, it had already recorded 10 million unique readers each month (with about half a million contributing articles). Another oft-mentioned case is Wikipedia – a collectively developed online encyclopaedia where every user can create entries of any scientific concept from "nanotechnology" to "culture", suggest definitions for them, edit and/or elaborate others' definitions. Starting in 2001, the free encyclopaedia had, by November 2005, been contributed to by some 350,000 people, with around 800,000 entries in English and more than one million in 25 other languages. It was one of the world's 15 most visited websites by the end of 2006. In the past several years, news stories on mainstream sites such as news.com.au have increasingly incorporated links to Wikipedia coverage of involved news subjects. In early 2005, Wikipedia took the next step: burning its content into CDs and DVDs for distribution in under-developed areas like Africa, where access to high-speed Internet is a luxury.

Not less spectacular is the success of NowPublic, another collaborative-reporting website that, after two years into its existence (by April 2007), attracted more than 82,000 citizen reporters in 140 countries, with half of its stories being original and half rewritten from online resources. Some other anecdotes would provide more telling examples of the rise and potential power of non-weblog PP outlets:

o   According to *The New York Times*, the doom of the Columbia space shuttle was first hinted on an online discussion group 11 minutes before the AP issued its first news alert concerning the event (cited in Bowman & Willis, 2003).

o   In the morning of July 7, 2004, when American TV viewers received on NBC the first news story about John Kerry's official announcement of John Edwards as his running mate in the 2004 American presidential campaign, they would not know that they were actually laggards. The previous night, a witness's post on the USaviation.com forum had already noted that "John Edwards vp (vice-president) decals were being put on (the) engine cowlings and upper fuselage (of Kerry's campaign plane)". By the time the first story appeared on NBC, the news had already invited considerable cheers and doubts about the presidential pair's future on the forum.

The most successful collaborative news venture so far is probably the South Korea-based *OhmyNews*, a collaborative news service operating with the motto: "Every citizen is a reporter". Within only three years since its launch on 22/02/2000, it had become the country's most influential news site – a national forum attracting around two million readers a day, with 40,000 citizen-journalists (from housewives and schoolkids to professors) posting stories and comments on a given day and contributing 70% of its total content. In the summer of 2002, two Korean schoolgirls were run down to death by a US Army armoured vehicle on patrol, an incident that the conservative mainstream Korean media never wanted to question. *OhmyNews*, however, treated it so harshly and aggressively that mainstream outlets finally had no choice but to pay close attention. As a result, for the first time, a huge movement against the American military presence was organised around the country in the subsequent months, boosting the presidential candidacy of the then little-known reformist Roh Moo Hyun, who later granted his first interview as president to *OhmyNews*. As of May 2006, the news site remained a strong leader, with 95 full-time staffers and 42,000 citizen contributors publishing 160 articles per day. Since July 2005, it has been running an international English-language version which, by May 2006, had attracted 850 contributors from 85 countries. There is now also a Japanese version of *OhmyNews* and online news ventures modeling after it have appeared in other countries (e.g. flix.dk in Denmark).

PP is not a phenomenon found only in the developed world. A visit to LiveJournal, a popular blogging service, on October 30, 2003 revealed that it had more than 1.4 million registered users from over 220 countries. In China, Baidu – the country's most popular search engine – reported that there were about 37 million blogs, with over 16 million bloggers, supplied by 658 blogging services by the end of 2005. During the recent earthquake in Sichuan, blog postings, Twitter messages, photos and video clips by witnesses, victims and other involved parties became a major source of information for the global media, including big names such as BBC, CNN or *New York Times*. In Vietnam, an unidentifiable Internet-savvy music fan recently shook the mainstream press after conducting an online investigation to break on an online forum that a very famous song of Bao Chan, one of the country's most established pop music composers, was totally copied from a Japanese album. The initially stubborn plagiarist eventually had to publicly apologise and withdraw his name from the song's credits. This was the beginning of subsequent exposures of some other pop-music plagiarists, also by online community members, which continued for a few months in 2004 (Nguyen, 2006).

An internationally renowned case from the developing world is the story of the now well-known Salam Pax, a young Iraqi architect and blogger in Baghdad in the second Iraq war. He remained mysterious, even unreal, in the mind of many people, until after the bombings, when *The Guardian* tracked him down in a modest Baghdad suburban apartment. But despite his secret identity and his stubbornness in revealing it, which stirred up serious debates not only across the Internet community but also in many of the world's most respected publications, he struck a dramatic emotional chord with tens of thousands of people during the war through his musings, with a caustic sense of humour, about happenings around him before and during the war on his web diary (named "Where is Raed?"). Links to his heartening and acute accounts were passed over the web and xcerpts from his blog were redistributed into 14 languages (Gillin, 2003; Piller, 2003). *Guardian Unlimited* (2003) described his musings as the "most compelling", "most gripping" and "most vivid" account of life during the war in various articles, and finally hired him to write for its blog in June 2003. Meanwhile, Rebecca Blood, a most authoritative voice in the world of personal publishing, said he was "putting a human face on history" (quoted in Piller, 2003).

In short, by tapping the power of the web and other new media to transform itself from mere news consumers into "prosumers" (producers cum consumers), the global public as the traditional underdog in the news flow is creating a new information order that might reshape the communication of public affairs. This has many normative implications for the public sphere and journalism that will be further discussed in Chapter 8.

The need for more details: three basic questions on the uses and gratifications of online news

In retrospect, the impressive penetration of online news in the past dozen years could be considerably attributed to the enormous news demand generated by recent national and international crises, disasters and conflicts. In the 1990s, according to Stuart Allan (2005), three events could be seen as "tipping points" – points where "seemingly minor, insignificant changes can suddenly generate profound consequences" – in the emergence and rise of online news: the Oklahoma bombing in April 1995, the crash of the TWA flight 800 in July 1996, the tragic and horrific accident that killed Princess Dianna in August 1997. The new millennium unfolded with the controversial presidential election in the US in 2000, the September 11 attacks and the subsequent wars on Afghanistan and Iraq, the Bali and London bombings and the general "war on terrorism", plus natural disasters such as the South Asian tsunami and Hurricane Katrina. On September 11, for example, CNN.com alone had 162 million page views — nearly a dozen times higher than on a typical day of the site. In Australia, traffic on the day was 239% higher than that of an average August day at news.com.au, 47% at smh.com.au and 33% at theage.com.au – according to Nielsen//NetRatings (Bogle, 2001). The demand for online news in the subsequent days and weeks (with the anthrax attacks and the war on Afghanistan) remained very high. For instance, the proportion of Americans using the Internet as the primary news source jumped from only 3% on September 12 to 8% a few weeks later (Harris Interactive, 2001). Thus, just as television news had the Vietnam War as a catalyst for penetrating societies, online news has been driven substantially by the general "war on terrorism".

Research, mostly from the US, has also confirmed that online news attributes – especially its ease/convenience of use and its immediacy – play a key role in its adoption and use. Weir (1999) found that the availability of breaking news is a significant, although weak, predictor of online news adoption. Wu and Bechtel (2002) found that disruptiveness ("the timely, urgent, breaking characteristic of news") was positively correlated with traffic to *The New York Times* online. Studies by the Pew Internet & American Life Project (.http://pewinternet.org.) found updates, wider range of viewpoints and convenience among the most cited reasons for Americans to go online for news and information during "big times" such as the Iraq War and the 2004 election. In a Nielsen//NetRatings study (Washingtonpost.com, 2005), the Internet was reportedly chosen by Americans thanks to its 24/7 availability (83% of respondents), the ability to multitask (70%), breaking and up-to-the-minute news (66%), easy ways to get information (63%), no cost (63%), convenience of use (61%) and the availability of a wide variety of sources (55%).

In a more substantial study, Salwen et al (2005) reported the following reasons for Americans to use news online: ability to get news at any time one wants (agreed by 95%

of users); ability to go directly to news of interest (91%); keeping up with the news online being quick and easy (88%); convenience to receive (84%); ability to learn more about breaking stories (82%); getting news online being easier than getting conventional news (71%); online news reflecting one's interests (68%); finding interesting news stories by chance while doing some other things online (68%); ability to get different viewpoints (65%); online news items catching users' attention when logging on or logging off the computer (60%); finding unusual news stories online (60%); ability to get news not available elsewhere (60%); ability to get more news than from conventional sources (57%); and online news being more in-depth than conventional news (52%). The authors' factor analysis yielded four underlining groups of online news attributes: its use convenience, its quantity and quality, its difference from traditional news, and its serendipity (accidental exposure).

In a rare non-US study, Chan and Leung (2005) factor-analysed ten online news features as perceived reasons for using online news among a Hong Kong sample to find three key factors: convenience (the ability to access diverse and searchable sources of information quickly, easily and from home), interactivity (the ability to participate in opinion polls and chat forums as well as to send email to editors) and multimedia (the ability to read news with graphics, video and audio content). Their regression analyses show that after controlling for lifestyle, reliance on traditional news, mass media use and demographic variables, convenience was a strong positive predictor of online news adoption, time spent on online news and the use level of online financial news, whereas multimedia was significantly positive in predicting the former two and interactivity was not significant in any case. Other research (Abdulla et al, 2002; Johnson & Kaye, 2002; Nozato, 2002; Schweiger, 2000) have found the positive effect of some aforementioned attributes as an integral component of online news credibility.

So far as it goes, however, it might be noted that previous academic research has not touched many issues regarding what users have done with the much-touted features of online news. For instance, to what extent have different types of online news services (e.g. email newsletters, searchable archives etc.) been used by users? Of those features generating the six user-centric groups of online news advantages defined in the previous chapter, what are the most favoured ones? What types of sites do people get their news from? The rest of this chapter will use Australian data to address these issues and thereby to add more details to the global picture of online news development. Taking into account the strengths and weaknesses of online news, it seeks to answer the following questions:

RQ4.1: To what extent have users implemented and taken advantage of the much-touted features of online news?

RQ4.2: To what extent have users appreciated these online news features?

RQ4.3: What are the potential obstacles to online news adoption and use?

Methodological issues: the news use survey for this work

The data for this chapter and most of this book derive from a national postal mail survey about the uses of news and current affairs that I conducted in Australia in 2004. The major methodological issues of this survey are detailed below:

Data collection

A random sample of 2,500 residential addresses was initially selected from the Desktop Marketing System – a frequently updated database of Australian addresses based on Telstra's telephone directories. The questionnaire was sent out for the first time with a cover letter in early July 2004. The cover letter personally addressed the household's member who was listed on the database. After a month, 420 valid responses were received, with a total of 304 notices of invalid participants (wrong addresses, changes of residential addresses, deaths and so on) being returned. The questionnaire and a reminder letter were resent in early August 2004 to those who had not responded. By the time the survey period ended (October 2004), a total of 790 valid responses and 398 notices of invalid participants were received. This indicates a response rate of 38%, which is satisfactory, given that this is a postal survey with a rather long questionnaire form (extending 16 A4-size pages) and a limited research budget. By comparison, a leading academic postal mail survey, the Australian Social Attitudes Survey – 2003, achieved a response rate of only 42% despite a more extensive (and expensive) follow-up strategy (Gibson et al 2004).

At the time the data were collected, Australia had already enjoyed a fairly deep Internet penetration, with more than 50% of Australian households having access to the medium (ABS, 2004). Its growth was still continuing: at the end of March 2005, according to the Australian Bureau of Statistics (ABS, 2005a), there were 689 ISPs in Australia, providing Internet access to almost 6 million subscribers of all types, which represents an increase of 4% (240,000 subscribers) from September 2004 (the time the fieldwork of this survey ended). Meanwhile, the proportion of businesses with Internet connection surged from 69% in 2001-2002 to 74% in 2003-2004 and 77% in 2004-2005 (ABS, 2006). Broadband was also on the way up, with the proportion of non-dial-up subscribers increasing by 39% from 1.3 million to 1.8 million between September 2004 and March 2005 (ABS, 2005a). By June 2005, 63% of businesses with Internet use were broadband-connected – an increase from only 41% one year before that (ABS, 2006). Dial-up, however, was still the most dominant way to access the Internet at home, accounting for 69% of household subscribers by the end of 2005 (ABS, 2005b).

Questionnaire design

The questionnaire (see appendix on page 303) was extended from one used in a pilot study among Brisbane residents in 2001 by the author. A few items were borrowed from previous studies, especially the mentioned biannual surveys of media use by the Pew Research Centre for the People and the Press. Covering over 270 single items related to different aspects of news needs and uses (including the use of the Internet, newspapers, magazines, television and radio for news), the questionnaire was divided into three sections, using strategies such as contingent questions and filter questions. In Section A, all respondents answered a wide range of news-related needs, attitudes and behaviours. Near the end of this section, a filter question was asked to discriminate Internet users from non-users. Those who identified themselves as Internet users continued to answer a number of questions related to their Internet usage, after which those who did not use online news were instructed to go to Section C, where both they and Internet non-users were presented with questions about their uses, satisfactions and affiliation with traditional news products.

Those who reported online news use were directed to Section B, which contains most of the variables used in this book. This section presented an intensive and extensive range of questions involving online news uses and gratifications, including reasons for using online news (appreciation of online news attributes), general levels of online news usage, use of individual features of online news, satisfaction with online news, change in their news behaviours since online news adoption and some other related aspects. At the heart of the data for this chapter and the next chapter are three sets of variables:

The first indicates perceived reasons for using online news, operationalised in terms of the extent to which respondents agreed or disagreed on a five-point Likert scale to a range of statements starting with "I get online news..." and ending with the following: (1) "...because I don't pay for it"; (2) "... because I have more news choices on the Internet"; (3) "...because I can combine getting news with other purposes online"; (4) "... because I can look for in-depth and background information whenever I want"; (5) "... because I can check for updated news whenever I want"; (6) "... because I can get news tailored to my interest only"; (7) "... because I can have my say to the news media"; (8) "... because I can discuss news and current affairs with my peers"; and (9) "... because I can find different viewpoints on the Internet".

The second set consists of about 30 multiple questions about the use of online news, including specific uses related to the above perceived reasons (these questionnaire items would manifest in the data analysis below) as well as the general level of using and being affiliated with online news (e.g. the perceived importance of news in Internet usage).

The third set was designed to measure satisfaction with news across five media: the Internet, newspapers, magazines, radio and television. In particular, the survey addressed the gratifications associated with five important and often-sought attributes that are common across all the five sources: the way news is presented; diversity of content;

different perspectives; timeliness and updates; and depth of coverage. Also, satisfaction with the five media in terms of eight major news content categories – national/state politics; international affairs; economics (including business and finance); entertainment and sports; science, technology and health; social problems (crime/disasters/accidents); culture and the arts; and local community affairs – were also explored.

Common demographic and socio-economic items (sex, age, education, income, labour status, types of job and living areas) were included at the end of Section B and Section C.

A definition of news

One fundamental concern in designing the questionnaire was how to define news and non-news information. For a non-user of online news, things are less problematic as news is generally understood to be current information from the mainstream media. For an online news user, however, the wide variety of potential sources of current information (such as information-exchange sites, community publishing sites, corporate-information sites, or weblogs) blurs the line between what is news and what is not. But as seen above, recent developments indicate that these sources might play a considerable role. I thus decided to accept the loose notion of "informational news" – coined by Burnet and Marshall (2003, p. 160) to reflect the cultural shift from institutionalise news towards "much more raw and less edited versions of phenomena and events, rubbing shoulders with much more journalistically constructed stories of phenomena". In the questionnaire, therefore, online news users were first given a question on their general Internet usage, which distinguishes "getting news" and "searching non-news information". However, what is "news" and "non-news" information was left for the respondent to decide. In later questions, non-mainstream sites were included as possible sources of news online.

Data analysis for this chapter

The final sample displays some biases when compared with the Australian 2001 Census data. Table 4.1 shows that younger people were underrepresented while males were overrepresented. As these two demographics have a potentially critical effect on online news adoption/use, the sample was weighted according to the 2001 Census joint sex-by-

Table 4.1: Comparison between the 2004 sample and the 2001 Census data in terms of age and sex (by percentage)

Age	Male		Female		Total	
	Sample	Census	Sample	Census	Sample	Census
18-29	3.7	22.6	8.1	21.3	5.6	21.9
30-39	11.9	20.3	18.8	20.1	15.0	20.2
40-49	23.4	19.8	21.2	19.4	22.4	19.6
50-59	23.7	16.3	21.8	15.3	22.8	15.8
60-69	19.8	10.5	15.8	10.2	18.0	10.3
70+	17.5	10.5	14.3	13.7	16.2	15.2

age distributions before data analysis. The weights reproduce the population distribution on the two variables. All analyses in this and later chapters are weighted. To depict a general pattern of online news uses gratifications, this chapter will mostly use descriptive statistics. Two-way tables are included when necessary.

Results

75% of the sample identified themselves as Internet users. Nearly 46% of these (or about one third of the sample) were using the Internet for news. This was a greater penetration rate than pay television, which was subscribed by 22% of the same sample. 9% of those using online news had been doing this for one year or less and 57% had at least three years' experience with it. 66% of the users were males, 72% lived in a metropolitan area, 67% worked full-time, 63% were professionals, managers or white-collar workers, 72% held at least a TAFE/trade certificate (42% with a undergraduate/CAE or higher degree), and over 58% had a before-tax household income of $50,000 or more. In addition, 79% of online news users were between 18 and 49 years of age. The influence of these socio-economic factors will be explored in detail in Chapter 6.

The implementation of online news

As part of Internet use, news reception was a regular activity for 33% of Internet users, lagging behind personal contact (emailing/messaging – being used often or very often by 82% of the online group), searching non-news information both for work/study (59%), and for other purposes (63%), e-commerce ("purchasing goods and using services like finance and banking" – 39%). The prevalence of online news use (in terms of regular use), however, was greater than Internet use for entertainment/relaxation (29% doing this often or very often) and interaction with other users (attending chat rooms, online forums and the like – 17%). More than half of online news users reported news as an essential (18%) or important (38%) part of their Internet use. Furthermore, nearly two-thirds of users (or 21% of the whole sample) said that online news had "some" or "a great deal" of contribution in shaping their perception and understanding of public affairs. In addition, the amount of time spent on online news is relatively high: when asked about their most recent online session in which they got news, users reported a mean amount of almost 15 minutes spent on news, which accounted for over more than a quarter (27%) of the total time spent on that online session (55 minutes).

Table 4.2 shows where people go for news online and which sources they like the most. 78% of online news users flocked to newspapers' websites for news. Given that newspapers outnumber news outlets on the web, this is hardly surprising. It is interesting, however, to note that accumulated news websites (e.g. news.yahoo.com or news.com.au) had become very popular news sources (used by 64% of online users), bypassing traditional broadcasters' news sites (62%) and those owned by news agencies (21%). Also, non-mainstream sources (i.e. "news sites offered by individuals, groups or organisations outside the mainstream media") were visited for news by a quarter of users while information exchange sites were used as news sources by 9% of users.

The bottom part of the table tells a somewhat different story: although newspapers' sites and news aggregators were the most visited, broadcasters' sites dominated the list of "most favoured" news sites, with ninemsn.com.au being chosen by 19% of relevant respondents and abc.net.au by 14%. The major Fairfax newspapers' sites (theage.com.au

Table 4.2: Sources of news online: uses and preferences (% of online news users)

Where people go for news online (minimum n = 207)

Newspapers' sites	78
Magazines' sites	45
Broadcasters' sites	62
News agencies' sites	21
Accumulated news sites	64
Non-mainstream sources	25
News/information exchange sites	9
Other sources	<1

Top news sites (n=180)*

Ninemsn.com.au	19
abc.net.au	14
smh.com.au	12
news.com.au	8
theage.com.au	7
news.google.com	6
news.yahoo.com	4

* Sites identified as "most favoured" by at least 3% of users

and smh.com.au) were ranked the fourth and the sixth favourite news sites. Between them was the News Limited-owned news aggregator news.com.au (8%). The two well-known international news-aggregating sites of news.google.com (6%) and news.yahoo.com (4%) also joined this list. Below these were four news sites (bbc.co.uk, wired.com, blic.co.yu and rallysa.com.au) that were chosen by nearly 3% of users but were not included in the table because these were within the margin of sampling errors.

As for typical use, online news consumption seems to spread throughout the day: 44% reported using online news whenever convenient while 32% did this between 9am and 5pm, 10% before 9pm and 14% during 5pm-12am. Their most recent online news session took place mainly at home (60%), "just today" (42%) or "within the past few days" (40%). In the same session, the majority (56%) said they "went deliberately to a news site to check news of the day"; 15% "heard something of interest happened and visited a news site to check it"; 13% "happened to go across a news item when doing something else"; 10% "got some news from other sources and went online for more details"; 4% "got an interesting news item from an email news alert" and 2% "got an interesting news item from a friend via an email message". None reported being "linked to an interesting news item from a news/information trading network" or any other ways of starting the session. On average, they visited 1.8 news sites and four in ten were combining this with doing something else such as eating and/or drinking (63%), talking/chatting to others (25%) and a range of activities like telephoning, emailing, "assisting a colleague" and even "watching children in a library".

Table 4.3 presents how current users have taken advantage of some popular online news services, classified along the six user-centric dimensions discussed in Chapter 3[1]. As can be seen, features related to the web's rich content were very popular choices, with nearly three quarters of online news users having visited a number of sites for the same news item (26% doing so often or very often), nine in ten clicking on links to related stories for in-depth/background information (46% frequently), and 57% finding other perspectives from non-mainstream news sites (16% frequently). Substantial use of the immediacy of the medium has also been made: only 30% of online news users said they had never received up-to-the-minute news several times a day and more than a quarter did this frequently. When asked "If right now, you heard something of great interest had just happened, which medium would you go first to check it?", 47% chose the Internet – compared with 34% choosing television, 17% radio, 2% newspapers and nobody for magazines. This is important in the context that the questionnaire was likely to be filled at home where traditional immediate news media like radio and television are available.

In terms of services that make online news convenient to receive, 16% of the online news sample combined general news reception with emailing and nearly one-third made their favourite news homepage the default front page of their web browser. News via mobile devices had not enjoyed a deep diffusion, being used by only 6%. As for services that provide news on demand, search engines topped the list of popular offers (having been adopted by 88% of online news users and frequently used by 42%), followed by personalised email news alerts (24%) and personalised news pages such as My Yahoo! or My MSN (22%). Multimedia news content had been experienced by nearly half of users

Table 4.3: How users have taken advantage of exclusive online news features (by percentage of online news users, minimum n = 210)

	Yes	Frequently*
Convenience of use		
Subscribe to email news alerts of general news	16	N/A
Set favourite news home page as default front page of web browser	32	N/A
Get news via a mobile device	6	N/A
Content richness		
Visit a number of sites for the same news item	73	26
Click on links to related stories for in-depth information	90	46
Find other perspectives from non-mainstream news sites	57	16
Immediacy		
Get up-to-the-minute news several times a day	70	26
Use the Internet as the first medium to check something that has just happened	47	N/A
Multimedia		
Get audio news	48	15
Get video news	45	15
Scan/skim rather than read stories	88	66
Print out some news items for later usage	52	16
News on demand		
Use search tools to find news of your interest	88	42
Subscribe to email news alerts tailored to your interest	24	N/A
Set up a personalized news page	22	N/A
Participation opportunities		
Participate in online news polls	48	17
Go to an information exchange site to have your say	21	4
Receive links to news stories from peers	50	8
Send links to news stories to peers	40	6
Pass information you have just heard or witnessed	71	27
Have heard terms like "weblogs" or "blogs"	28	N/A
Read weblogs	11	4
Post comments on weblogs	4	<1

*"Often" or "very often"

but was substantially used by a relatively small proportion (15% in both cases of audio and video news). An interesting point is that even with the written news text, 66% said they frequently scanned or skimmed rather than read word by word. Over half (52%) printed stories for later references, with 16% doing so frequently.

Participation opportunities, arguably the unique feature of online news, had been taken to some extent. 71% had passed their first-hand information to other users with 27% doing so often or very often. News exchange among peers had become somewhat common – with four in ten having sent news links to peers and half having received news links from peers – but it was a frequent behaviour among only a small portion of online news users (8% or less). Online opinion polls, the simplest form of participation, had reached almost half of online news users and were being participated frequently by 17%. Interestingly, while only 9% reported receiving news from news/information-trading sites (mentioned above), more than twice as many (21%) had gone to these sites to have their say (4% did this often or very often). Finally, weblogs – the participatory publishing form that has been gaining prominence around the world – had been heard of by 28% of online news users but read by only 11% (and frequently read by 4%). In addition, only 4% had posted comments on weblogs and virtually none did this on a frequent basis.

The appreciation of online news

Table 4.4 shows the mean appreciation scores of the aforementioned nine online news attributes. As can be seen, immediacy seems to be the most important attribute that drives online news adoption, scoring a mean of 4.11 on a five-point Likert scale of agreement/disagreement with the provided statement ("I get news online because I can get updated news whenever I want"). This is followed by the multitasking nature of Internet news use, i.e. the ability to combine news consumption with other daily online activities (3.87). Two content richness-related elements were rated third and fourth: the availability of in-depth and background information (3.65) and "more news choices" (3.51). The fact that news can be consumed on demand ("because I can get news tailored to my interest only") was also highly appreciated (3.47). Although online news is offered largely free by providers, the cost benefit element was collectively given a mean of only

Table 4.4: Reasons for using online news (mean value)

Please respond to the statement starting with I get news online…	
… because I don't pay for it	3.15
… because I can combine getting news with other purposes online	3.87
… because I have more news choices on the Internet	3.51
… because I can look for in-depth and background information whenever I want	3.65
… because I can find different viewpoints on the Internet	3.15
… because I can check for updated news whenever I want	4.11
… because I can get news tailored to my interest only	3.47
… because I can have my say to the news media	2.45
… because I can discuss news and current affairs with my peers	2.64

1 = "Strongly disagree"; 3 = "Neutral"; 5 = "Strongly agree"

3.15. The same score was given to the presence of different viewpoints, which can be seen as a sub-dimension of content richness. At the bottom of the list are two features representing participation opportunities: being able to discuss news and current affairs with peers (2.64) and to "have my say to the news media" (2.45).

Table 4.5 shows the gratifications obtained from online news use in terms of major news content and news attributes[2]. It is clear that most of the listed news types are well served online. The medium, with its global nature, is most gratifying in its provision of international news (with a mean "helpfulness" score of 2.3 – out of 3)[3]. This is followed by news about entertainment/sports (2.22), science and medicine (2.07), national/state politics and social problems (both scoring 2.00), economics (1.95) and culture and the arts (1.70). Local news was the only category that received a below-average mean score (1.24). In terms of medium attributes, the Internet was fairly satisfactory in all the five categories with, again, "timeliness and updates" coming first (3.99 out of 5), followed by content diversity (3.81), depth of coverage (3.74), the way news is presented (3.71) and representation of different viewpoints (3.60).

Table 4.5: Obtained gratifications from online news in terms of news content and medium attributes (mean values)

To what extent do you find the web helpful to follow the news types listed below?[a]

National/state politics	2.01
International affairs	2.30
Economics (including business and finance news)	1.95
Entertainment/Sports	2.22
Science, technology and health	2.06
Social problems (crime/disasters/accidents)	2.00
Cultures and the arts	1.70
Local community affairs	1.24
Overall evaluation of online news content	1.94

To what extent are you satisfied with the Internet in terms of the following?[b]

The way news is presented	3.71
Timeliness and updates	3.99
Diversity of news content	3.81
Depth of coverage	3.74
Representation of different viewpoints	3.60
Overall evaluation of online news attributes	3.77

a) 0 = "Not at all helpful"; 1 = "Not very helpful"; 2 = "Helpful"; 3 = "Very helpful"
b) 1 = "Very unsatisfied"; 3 = "Neutral"; 5 = "Very satisfied"

Also taken into account were two indices indicating online news users' overall satisfaction with the medium in terms of news content and attributes, constructed by taking the mean gratification of all the single characteristics presented above. For instance, if an online news user gave two on "the way news is presented" on the web, three on "timeliness and updates", four on "depth of coverage", four on "representation of different perspectives" and two on "diversity of content", then his/her mean total satisfaction with the medium is $(2 + 3 + 4 + 4 + 2)/5 = 3$. Both indices are highly credible with Cronbach's alpha coefficients of .86 (news content) and .87 (news attributes)[4]. Overall, the medium was given a mean of 1.94 (out of three) for news content and 3.77 (out of five) for medium attributes. It must be noted that although satisfactory, these medium satisfaction scores of online news did not reach very high, being still more or less below the scores indicating the "helpful" level (2) and the "satisfied" level (4). This might suggest that the Internet as a news medium is not really perceived as "powerful" as many news practitioners and commentators would hope.

Despite this, a further exploration (tables not shown) suggests that online news users gave higher satisfaction ratings to the Internet than to all or most traditional news sources in both form and substance. Particularly, the Internet was considered second to newspapers in terms of the way news is presented (3.71 versus 3.79), depth of coverage (3.74 versus 3.86) and diversity of news content (3.81 versus 3.86); second to radio in terms of timeliness and updates (3.99 versus 4.08); and second to none in terms of the representation of different perspectives. As a whole, the 3.77 overall satisfaction score of the Internet was on top of the list of all news sources (the second highest mean score, 3.71, was given to newspapers; and the lowest, 3.25, to magazines).

Potential obstacles to online news adoption

As for the oft-mentioned potential problems of online news usage (Table 4.6), this survey finds that all of them had been experienced by the majority of online news users. While encountering false news items and being irritated/insulted in online news exchange were

Table 4.6: Responses to some common potential problems of online news usage (by percentage of online news users, minimum n = 206)

How often do you find yourself...	Never	Not very often	Often	Very often
... being lost among too much information on the Internet	6	56	27	11
... missing some important news that you should know after an online news session	17	67	16	<1
... being tired of getting news on the computer screen	12	57	28	3
... encountering false news online	27	60	13	<1
... being irritated or insulted in an online news/information exchange network	50	38	11	1
... being frustrated with advertising inserted in the body of online news stories	12	32	35	21

not substantial problems (being experienced often or very often by no more than 20% of online news users), the others were notable. In particular,

- o 38% of users frequently found themselves being lost among too much information on the Internet;
- o nearly a third (31%) were frequently tired from reading news onscreen; and
- o 56% frequently found it frustrating to encounter advertisements inserted in the body of news stories – a very common practice by online news providers.

In order to further explore some of these problems and other obstacles to online news adoption/use, the survey asked those who were using the Internet without adopting online news why they did not. The results (Table 4.7) reveal that credibility is not an issue – with only 6% of the relevant respondents saying they did not get news on the Internet because they did not trust information on it. The demanding effort of reading onscreen did have an effect but were still cited as a reason by a minority (32%) of these Internet users. The overwhelming reason was that they found the news they received from other sources was already enough (77%). Other problems include the lack of time resources (47%) and, rather interestingly, inconvenience of use (32%).

Of those who chose "other reasons" with a specification, there were some noteworthy points for future research into online news. Nine respondents did not want online news because it would alter their established media routines/tastes, namely their "old" ways of using news. Their responses range from simple statements such as "I enjoy reading" to rather complex comments:

Table 4.7: Reasons for using the Internet without adopting online news (by percentage of Internet users who do not use online news, minimum n = 304)

Online news not convenient to use	32
Not enough time for news when online	47
Other news sources already enough	77
Don't trust information on the web	6
Find it tiresome reading on computer screen	32
Other reasons	5

o "(I) prefer to hear (*sic*) news while driving or see nightly news on TV or browse the newspaper."

o "I prefer the feel, look, smell and sense of (reading) a newspaper and discussing its content."

o (I) prefer to have the whole article in front of me rather than have to scroll through all the time."

o "I 'edit' my news: I am selective. This is easier with paper news. (Also,) car radio news is 'compacted' by the medium."

o "(I) never thought about using the Internet to gain access to the news. It would be a waste of download when the news is on TV every hour or half hour at night."

o "(I) prefer to watch TV with other family members. % usage is anti-social in some respects."

o "Because I get news in my relaxation time – i.e. casually reading the Sunday paper, watching at night after housework/children bed time, (or) listening to the radio whole working outside in my garden. Why would I strain my eyes, sit at a computer in a stuffy room to get the news? Get a real life please."

Four other people said they simply had no interest in receiving online news – quotes including "Not interested"; "(I) really don't care. I subscribe to the notion that no news is good news"; "I'm just not interested. Most of it is too depressing"; and "I'm not interested in searching for news when I could be doing other things". Bandwidth was a matter for three people. A 50-year-old female in a large town specified that she did not access the Internet regularly (therefore did not get news) because "I only have dial-up connection". A 41-year-old male professional was even more "bitter" in his tone: "For what it's worth, I would be very interested in using the Internet as a primary news source. However, our exchange is not ADSL-enabled and we only have dial-up." The third, a narrowband Internet user, simply cited the "cost factor".

Another (a 32-year-old female respondent doing home duties and living in a small town) cited a combination of cost and Internet accessibility as the reason: "I use Internet cafes to access the Internet. Too expensive to stay on to read news. I can't afford to have connection at home. Would love to but (it's) not a financial priority at the moment." The last respondent with a specific answer was trying to reduce the amount of time spent on the computer: "I hadn't thought about getting the news online – as I limit my time at a computer screen and generally when I finish working on a computer, I don't want to start hooking up the news".

Further analysis and primary conclusion: the potential development of online news in the years ahead

The primary and secondary data advanced in this chapter provide a clear answer to the second RQ of this book on current patterns of online news uses and gratifications inside and outside Australia. All over the world, online news has quickly penetrated into daily life, gaining the status of a major news source within less than a decade and contributing considerably to the diffusion of the Internet in general. This is not different in Australia: by September 2004, the Internet as a news medium had gained a considerable prevalence in Australian daily life and much of its touted technical capacity – including its immediacy, content richness as well as the availability of on-demand news services and participation opportunities – has been experienced in one way or another by the majority of online news users (and frequently taken advantage of by a substantial proportion of them). Specifically, hypertextual links to related information, the availability of a limitless range of news services, continuous updates, searchability and email-enabled news/information exchange and dissemination are the most used features. Although services that make news consumption easy and convenient online (e.g. email news alerts) have not been resorted to by the majority of online news users, the ability to combine news use with other purposes was reported as an important reason for online news consumption. To a lesser extent, the no-cost factor of online news is also seen as an advantage. Collectively, these features substantially contribute to keeping adopters with the new news medium. For the most part, these findings are in line with the above literature on the effect of online news attributes on its adoption/use.

Another noteworthy finding is that a large majority of online news users often or very often scan/skim stories rather than read them word by word. This is consistent with Jacob

Nielsen's 1997 survey which found that 79% of Internet users scan rather than read (see Chapter 3). While this is indeed no different from the way people read newspapers, more research into why this continues to happen on the web is worth doing. For now, four tentative reasons offered by Nielsen (1997) are notable. Accordingly, people scan on the web because (1) onscreen reading is tiring for the eyes and about 25% slower than print reading; (2) the nature of the web as a user-driven medium makes users feel that they have to move on and click on things; (3) users' attention is simultaneously drawn to hundreds of millions of competing pages; and (4) users do not have enough time to work too hard for their information.

However, some of the findings might not please some online news advocates. For example, multimedia content – one widely touted technical attribute of web news, had not been experienced to a considerable extent. This, however, is understandable, given the sluggish uptake of broadband technology in Australia and the general shortage of investment in multimedia ventures by the news industry both inside and outside Australia (see Chapter 2). Also, apart from news communication and sharing via email, other forms of participation enabled by the interactive nature of the web such as weblogs did not seem to have reached a critical mass. It must be noted, however, that participation means something very active on part of the user; therefore a small percentage on some of the variables related to this might be able to be considered significant by some observers. Also, by the time the survey was conducted, online participation opportunities remained limited in Australia because Australian mainstream news sites were slow in catching the wave while there were very few readable and high-quality participatory non-mainstream outlets (Bruns, 2005; Cook, 2005; Nguyen, 2006; Ward & Cahill, 2007).

All in all, while there are some considerable problems associated with online news usage (the physical demand of onscreen reading, information overload and embedded ads), the Internet has shown itself to be a relatively compelling news medium. Not only its major attributes are appreciated but also traditional news needs (except local news) are well-served on the web. With an overall satisfaction mean of 3.77 (out of five) in relation to its major news attributes, however, the medium might not be seen as powerful as it is widely assumed from a technology-determinist point of view. Despite this, the satisfactoriness of the Internet was on top of the list of all news sources. In order to explore the result of experiencing online news at a more intimate level, the survey also asked respondents some items indicating their enthusiasm about online news. The results are as follow:

o Half of users identified themselves as fans of online news. Given its early stage of development, this is a significant proportion although it is still lower than affiliation with most traditional news media (60% being fans of television news, 56% of newspapers, 53% of radio news and 18% of news magazines).

o More than a quarter (27%) chose the web as the best medium to serve their news needs – compared with 27% for newspapers, 28% for television, 18% for radio and virtually none for magazines.

o More than three quarters had some (46%) or a great deal of belief (31%) that the Internet would become the most important news source in the future.

In addition, more than six in ten online news users in the sample had often or sometimes shared their online news experience with peers. More importantly, two-way tables show that

o 66% of these people also identified themselves as online news fans;

o 89% had some or a great deal of belief that the Internet will become the most important news medium of the future; and

o nearly a third picked up the Internet as their best news medium – compared with only 25% choosing TV and around 21% for both newspapers and radio.

Thus, if innovation diffusion can be understood as a communication process in which people create and share information of an innovation in order to reach a mutual understanding of this new idea/technology (Rogers, 2003), it appears from the data that online news has a notable potential to foster wider adoption in the years ahead. But whether current Internet users who have not adopted online news are persuaded by those who have adopted, used and enjoyed it is another matter that needs further exploration at deeper levels. This will involve investigating the diverse effect of socio-structural factors (such as socio-economic backgrounds and Internet accessibility) as well as their communication needs and behaviours (such as attitudes to and needs for the news, habits of news usage, attitudes to new media technology, Internet experience and so on). Some of the factors cited above by those using the Internet without online news might not only affect adoption but also the level of online news use. These dynamics of online news adoption/use will be investigated in detail in Chapter 6. For now, it must be noted that while the data in this chapter show an important effect of online news attributes on its adoption/use, the process underlining this effect is still not well understood. How do the use and appreciation of online news attributes shape the way people use and depend on it? Which features have the strongest effect on these aspects of online news use? Having insights into this process will provide more crucial information on the role of the online news features in its future diffusion. The next chapter will explore these issues.

Notes

1. This list is not at all comprehensive. It comprises only those services that are popular on news sites inside and outside Australia by the time of the survey (based on my observations during 2001-2004). Promising but still new services such as RSS were not included.

2. I would have liked to include some other important news categories (such as education) but for practical reasons and for the purpose of exploring general satisfaction with online news content, this list was decided to be adequate. Also, although there are other factors that might have a direct influence on medium choice, only five attributes were chosen because of questionnaire length restraints.

3. Perceived helpfulness is a classic indicator of obtained gratifications from media consumption in uses and gratifications research (see Katz et al, 1973).

4. Cronbach's alpha is a coefficient indicating the internal consistency of an index, running from a low of zero to a high of one.

Chapter 5

The underlining adoption/use process: the effect of online news attributes on its use and attachment

Going beyond the mere descriptive statistics in Chapter 4, this chapter develops a theoretical model for investigating the effect of online news attributes on the way people use and integrate it into daily life. It starts with an examination of the famous five-stage innovation-decision process in diffusion theory (knowledge-persuasion-decision-implementation-confirmation) to point out that it is insufficient when applied to online news adoption. The main point of this part is that because of its diverse nature, its ubiquity and its high level of trialability, the decision to adopt online news does not necessarily lead to some substantial implementation as in the case of hardware innovations. Rather than focusing on a one-off adoption decision that follows persuasion and precedes implementation, it is needed to place the online news adoption/use process in a continually progressive model in which knowledge, persuasion, adoption decision, implementation and confirmation are temporally intermingled and interact with each other. From this, the chapter draws on expectancy-value theory in the uses and gratifications tradition to address this theoretical requirement. After a review of the strengths and weaknesses of this theory, the chapter integrates it with the diffusion perspective to propose a theoretical model for different pathways of online news adoption/use. This model provides the basis for the author to then use the 2004 data to explore the contribution of online news attributes to its adoption/use.

The effect of online news attributes on its adoption/use: the need for a continually self-reflexive model

As has been clear by now, however appealing an innovation is, it cannot be adopted in the same manner and/or at the same time by every member of the social system.

Innovation attributes are not something intrinsic but are a product of subjective evaluation by members of the social system. This is because underlining the macro-level (societal) S-curve diffusion process is the micro-level (individual) adoption process which "is essentially an information-seeking and information-processing activity in which an individual is motivated to reduce uncertainty about the advantages and disadvantages of the innovation" (Rogers, 2003, p. 172). To forecast the future of online news, therefore, there is a need to look at the importance of the subjective evaluation of innovation attributes throughout this micro-individual adoption process. According to Rogers (2003), the adoption process involves five stages, depicted in Figure 5.1 and summarised below:

o *The knowledge stage* is one in which an individual becomes aware of the existence of the innovation (awareness knowledge) either passively (by accident) or actively and then understands how it functions (how-to knowledge) and possibly why it functions so (principle knowledge). This active information-seeking behaviour is often affected by selective exposure (an individual's tendency to attend to communication messages that are consistent with his/her existing attitudes and beliefs) and selective perception (his/her tendency to interpret innovation messages in terms of these attitudes and beliefs).

o *The persuasion stage* takes place when one forms an affectively favourable or unfavourable attitude to the innovation after some initial contact with it. With selective exposure to and selective perception of different messages about the innovation, an individual mentally applies what he/she hears/reads about it to anticipated future situations to decide whether to try it or not. The major purpose of this forward planning is to reduce uncertainty about the expected consequences of the innovation, assessing the innovation's potential advantages and disadvantages in one's situation.

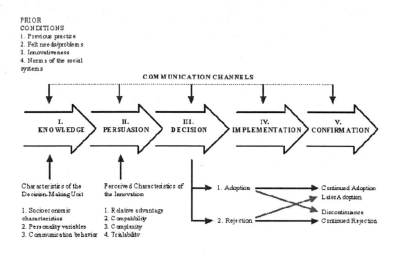

Figure 5.1: Rogers's (2003) five-stage innovation adoption process

o *The decision stage* takes place after an individual has some vicarious experience with the innovation (via direct trials or demonstration sessions held by change agents). When a level of certainty about the relative advantages of the innovation is obtained, the individual will decide to adopt (i.e. to make full use of an innovation). If not, rejection or delayed adoption will occur. In practice, rejection can happen at any stage in the innovation-decision process – one might hear something good about an innovation but never considers adopting it simply because he/she has forgotten about it.

o *The implementation stage* usually goes on immediately after the adoption-decision stage, involving overt behaviour change as the innovation is put into use. This could last for a lengthy period – until a point that the innovation is no longer a new idea/practice/object and becomes an "institutionalised" part of an adopter's daily life.

o *The confirmation stage* does not happen to every adopter. For many, the implementation process is the end of the innovation-decision process. For some others, however, something unfavourable happening during the implementation stage might cause a state of "internal dissonance" – the feeling that they should not have adopted the innovation. Thus they are motivated to try to reduce or eliminate this dissonance in the confirmation stage, in which they usually seek exposure to only messages consistent with their beliefs and values to support that their decision to adopt is correct. But not all information reaching them is good (because of misuse, for example) and unsupportive messages might lead to discontinuance – the decision to reject an innovation after having adopted it.

Although receiving some support from previous research, this five-stage model has to be treated with care in studying the diffusion of new media, especially the many free and ubiquitous online services such as online news. One way to see this is to discuss online news adoption in the light of what economists call "sunk" costs – costs that incur after the decision to adopt an innovation. For example, the fixed costs of purchasing a new technology cannot be recovered after it has been put into use – a substantial part of that cost has been "sunk" (Hall, 2003). Thus, from the economist's point of view, adoption is usually an "absorbing state" – a new product is hardly abandoned in favour of an old one after being adopted. Once deciding to buy a computer, for example, one is likely to implement it (i.e. put it into substantial use) – at least for the original purposes for which it is purchased. This is because the sunk cost after adoption is substantial – if for some reason, the user is disappointed that the new computer does not work as expected and wants to buy a better alternative, he/she has to sell the former at a lower price (i.e. accepting a cost for nothing). Because of this high level of sunk-cost risks, the adopter usually takes a serious pre-decision evaluation process, constantly weighting the computer's nontrivial cost against its perceived function and capacity and his/her related needs until uncertainties are minimised. This progress could be lengthened due to the fact that the machine is trialable only on a limited basis.

In contrast, online news is associated with almost no financial risk, and thus with much less chance for an "absorbing state". This is because online news is a ubiquitous service that is, for the most part, offered with no charge on existing technological platforms. With no further purchase of any device and almost no upfront cost (only a negligible Internet service fee paid to ISPs), Internet users could visit as many websites as they wish to try online news before deciding whether to make substantial use of it. That is, the sunk cost involved is trivial and not very tangible. The adoption of online news is, therefore, not necessarily in any absorbing state. As much as it is easy to try and adopt, online news can be as easily abandoned any time. This is especially likely in the context that there is a range of established and highly accessible news sources that can substantially serve the functions of online news. Thus, when a survey respondent reports that he/she is using online news, it does not necessarily mean that he/she has substantially integrated it into his/her daily routines[1]. He/she might be just in the trial step of the persuasion stage.

In other words, there is no clear distinction between trial, persuasion, determined adoption, implementation and confirmation in the case of online news: the adoption sequence might well be knowledge-decision-persuasion-implementation-confirmation to some people or even knowledge-decision-implementation-persuasion-confirmation to others. This is an ongoing and intermingled process in which different attitudes and behaviours modify each other and covary. Therefore, to understand the contribution of online news attributes to the way it is adopted, used and integrated into daily life requires a continually cycled and self-reflexive model rather than Rogers's linearly progressive and close-ended five-stage model. One approach that can fulfil this requirement is the popular expectancy-value theory in the uses and gratifications tradition.

An expectancy-value approach to media use

Founded by Martin Fishbein, expectancy-value theory is a social-psychology approach widely applied to explaining behavioural outcomes in a range of disciplines. According to this theory, an object (e.g. a computer, an online news site, or a philosophy) has many attributes, to each of which an individual develops an evaluative response called an attitude. This attitude is a *multiplicative product* of the individual's belief about the object's possession of this attribute *and* his/her affective evaluation of it (Fishbein, 1967; Fishbein, 1968; Fishbein & Ajzen, 1975). As this expectancy-value approach develops into the theory of reasoned action, attitudes are seen as the direct driver of an individual's intention, which in turn is the direct driver of behaviours (Ajzen, 1991; Fishbein & Ajzen,

1975; Malhotra & Galetta, 1999). In other words, individuals behave in a specific manner because they have had the intention to do so; and this intention is formed on their attitude to that behaviour, which in turn derives from their subjective belief in and evaluation of the potential outcomes of the behaviour. When a range of possible alternative behaviours are available, the one chosen will be the largest multiplicative product of expected success and value (Fishbein & Ajzen, 1975).

Applied to media uses, expectancy-value theory helps clarify the concept of expectation, a central element of U&G research since its inception. Galloway and Meek (1981) used expectancy-value theory to propose a process-oriented and path-goal perspective on media choice. At the heart of this proposal is that one seeks to satisfy some felt needs via exposure to a medium or content type, whose resulting gratifications will then modify later expectations of the potential outcomes of exposure to that medium/content type and thus affect subsequent exposure levels within and between media. In a more specific way, Palmgreen (1983), Palmgreen, Wenner and Rayburn (1980), Palmgreen and Rayburn (1985) and Rayburn and Palmgreen (1984) proposed a process depicted in Figure 5.2.

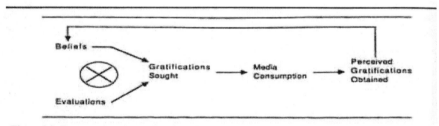

Figure 5.2: Expectancy-value model of media consumption – Source: Palmgreen & Rayburn (1985)

Accordingly, any media experience (including use behaviour, behavioural intention or attitudes) is a function of *expectancy* – or belief, formally defined as "the perceived probability that (a media) object possesses a particular attribute or that a behaviour will have a particular consequence", and *evaluation*, "the degree of affect, positive or negative, toward an attribute or behavioural outcome" (Palmgreen & Rayburn, 1985, p. 62). This is an ongoing process: the multiplicative product of beliefs and evaluations generates some to-be-sought gratifications (GSs), leading to media consumption. The gratifications obtained from this consumption (GOs) then feedback to the initial beliefs about the consumed medium or content type. In formula terms:

$$GS_i = b_i e_i$$

where

GS_i = the ith gratification sought from media object X
b_i = the belief that X possesses some attribute or an X-related behaviour
e_i = the affective evaluation of that particular attribute or outcome

From this model, Palmgreen and Rayburn (1985) developed a typology of media motivations with four joint products of beliefs and expectations (Table 5.1). First, if a medium, program or content type is believed to possess some negatively valued attribute, then true avoidance occurs. Second, if the media object is believed to possess a positively valued attribute, a positive approach (seeking positive gratifications) will take place. Third, if the media object is believed not to possess a positively valued attribute, then an individual will seek alternatives that do. Fourth, if the media object is believed *not* to possess a negative attribute, there is no true seeking of positive gratifications but one might still be motivated to use the source simply because it does not have that negatively valued characteristic. For example, one might watch television or surf the Internet because "at least it's not boring". This "negative approach" is especially likely to happen in situations where available alternatives are perceived to be "boring". It must be noted that there is no binary opposition here – "not boring" does not equal "exciting".

Table 5.1: A typology of media motivations leading to different media behaviours

		Evaluation of attribute	
		Negative	Positive
Belief in possession of attribute	No	Negative approach	Seeking of alternatives
	Yes	True avoidance	Positive approach

Source: Palmgreen & Rayburn (1985)

Expectancy-value theory also provides a specific explanation of the belief formation process, i.e. the constitution of "the primary information components determining the seeking of gratifications". In particular, Palmgreen (1983) and Palmgreen and Rayburn (1985) recognised three ways of belief formation:

o *Information beliefs* are formed via outside information sources (friends, relatives, mass media content), especially when there is little direct experience with the media object.

o *Inferential beliefs* are formed for objects not yet observed directly or unobservable, based on formal logic, personal theories of implicit personality, causal attributions and stereotyping. For example, a "police show" will stir up some typical attributes in one's expectation of the show.

o *Descriptive beliefs* are formed from direct observation of an object – i.e. exposure to a medium or content choice leads to the formation and modification of beliefs concerning attributes of the medium, as discussed above. Accordingly, beliefs in, and thus gratifications sought from, a positively valued media object are accumulated from gratifications obtained from actual use *over time*.

As will be seen shortly, all the three pathways of belief formation are quite important in the case of online news.

In relation to the concept of descriptive beliefs, it must also be noted that one can learn unexpected valuable attributes while seeking some other attributes through exposure to a media object. This exposure-learning process (McLeod, Bybee & Durall, 1982) happens in circumstances where one does not receive what is originally sought from a source but unexpectedly finds another valuable thing during the exposure process. Put simply, an individual uses a media object to seek a highly valued X attribute but during exposure, he/she does not find X but Y, an attribute that he/she also highly values but is not aware of initially; and thus instead of abandoning the content or medium because its lack of X-related gratifications, the individual still continues to use it for Y-related gratifications. Obviously, this exposure-learning process is very important for the success of any online news service, which tends to be offered with a combination and integration of several attributes. For example, during an election campaign, an individual logs on a news site with the motive to enhance or reinforce his/her judgement of candidates' stand on social issues but then finds that the medium is not as helpful as expected in this regard. This, however, does not necessarily stop him/her from continuing to use the medium because throughout his/her contact with the site, he/she increasingly enjoys, for example, the immediacy-enabled speedy coverage of election-related events and developments.

Unlike the linear process in diffusion theory, expectancy-value provides a continual and circular mechanism to explore how the expectation, persuasion and implementation of new media like online news services intermingle and affect each other in the progress toward full adoption and substantial use. It has been successfully applied in numerous studies of media uses, especially television use. However, the theory is not without limitations. One fundamental problem is Palmgreen and Rayburn's conceptual treatment of GSs as equivalent to attitudes. They argued (with no explanation) that both the seeking of gratifications and attitudes – originally defined by Fishbein and Ajzen (1975) as "generalised predisposition(s) to act in a consistently favourable or unfavourable manner toward an object" – could be predicted independently by the $b_i e_i$ product. This "is a logical impossibility", according to Stanford (1983, p. 248), who viewed GSs as not equivalent to attitudes but as something "approximating Fishbein and Ajzen's behaviour intentions", i.e. the model should go more like this: attitudes (sum of $b_i e_i$) → GSs → exposure. In this light, the sum of $b_i e_i$ (attitudes) is more like the concept of perceived attributes in innovation-diffusion theory than GSs in expectancy-value theory. This distinction between attitudes and GSs will be considered later in building a theoretical model of the online news adoption/use process.

Another potential problem is that expectancy-value theory ignores the fact that exposure is not always a logical outcome of gratifications-seeking. Media use can be unintentional in many circumstances. This might take the form of *passive use* due to the structure of media provision. For instance, there is a high chance for being exposed to unwanted content – e.g. when following the TV news bulletin. Unintentional use could also take the form of *ritualised, convenience-based use* of media services, especially those services being placed a neutral value on. An individual who neither likes nor dislikes a talk show might well watch it if it is convenient to use, although he/she would not care much if the show is not on at the time he/she available for consumption. Expectancy-value theory addresses values in a negative/positive dichotomy with deliberate attitudinal and behavioural outcomes and largely ignores these neutral values. In sum, actual media use is a combination of three use forms – active, passive and ritualised – i.e. it is not only a product of active gratification-seeking as expectancy-value theory posits. For the same individual, media use might be active (motivated), passive or convenience-based, depending on particular circumstances. Thus, media exposure and gratifications sought are not always complementary; sometimes they can even form a negative relationship – e.g. when one becomes dissatisfied with being exposed to too many unwanted items in a TV news bulletin.

These issues play a certain role in online news consumption. It is quite likely that a lot of ritualised use can result from surfing news websites. For instance, when a person visits a news site to check the main news of the day, it is likely that participation opportunities are available for him/her somewhere on the home page. After checking the main issues of the day, if the user still has some free time, he/she might not mind clicking through to read fellow users' responses to the news of the day and/or to express his/her views, although these are not really what he/she wants in the first instance. Also, although online news services give users substantial control over what to consume, structural provision problems still exist and could lead to passive use. For example, some news sites automatically turn on audio or video clips when a user arrives at their sites/pages, which can cause a lot of frustration and annoyance among many users, especially those who visit the sites for some very different and specific purposes or who are not in a mood to tolerate any unwanted and unexpected noise.

A suggested model of the online news adoption/use process

Based on the above, a more specific model to explain the micro adoption/use[2] process of online news has been built as a theoretical basis to explore the influence of online news attributes on the way it is adopted, used and integrated into daily life can be explored.

The model adopts the aforementioned strengths and avoids the weaknesses of both expectancy-value and innovation diffusion theory. The starting point here is that online news as a whole is diverse set of many separate services – e.g. breaking news email or mobile phone alerts, general email newsletters, customised email or RSS news bulletins, in-depth sections, searchable news archives and so forth. Each of these service packages can based primarily on only one online news feature but, as noted above, often combines and integrates several different features. With a high level of control over online content, the user is usually able to use or avoid any of these attributes at their wish, although passive use can happen in some cases. The adoption/use process of each attribute (Figure 5.3) goes as follows:

In the first instance, online news is believed or known to possess a particular attribute called X. This belief or knowledge can come from all the three sources mentioned by Palmgreen and Rayburn (1985), with each having a distinctive potential to boost the uptake of online news:

First, an individual might hear about X from someone in his/her social networks (friends, families, work colleagues etc.) or from the mass media (step 1a). Online news has an enormous advantage in relation to this belief formation, thanks both to the traditional news media's widespread self-promotion of their online operations in their offline versions and to the way peer networks can communicate about online news via online news delivery platforms.

Second, one might infer something about online news from other non-news Internet uses (1b). For instance, after a sufficient time of exposure to hypertextual links in using non-news information, a potential user might assume that online news could be provided with great depth via similar links. Given the Internet's multipurpose nature, this sort of inferential information – although requiring a certain level of cognitive intelligence – is a considerable potential driver of online news adoption.

Third, a substantial proportion of knowledge about X can be gained from unexpected exposure to it when using another online feature or service called Y (1c). Y can be a non-

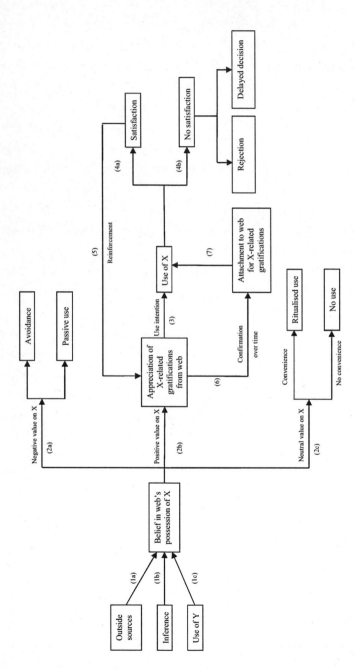

Figure 5.3: A suggested model for the micro-process of online news adoption/use

news service of the Internet: for example, while a user is searching for some specific information related to work or study, a news item of interest comes up, compelling him/her to click through. After this unexpected consumption, he/she discovers that this news item was posted on the web within only, say, two hours of the reported event. Y, however, is more likely to be another online news attribute thanks to the aforementioned convergence of attributes in online news packages. That is, the descriptive belief in one online news attribute is very likely to be formed during the use of another attribute. An example of this attribute convergence might be that when reading a story for updated details (Y), a user might be urged to click on the links to related stories in the body or at the end of the story – and becomes aware of the in-depth coverage of online news (X). That is, his/her initial belief in online news's depth is descriptive in nature, deriving from unexpectedly using it.

After the belief/knowledge formation stage, there are three possible outcomes:

First, if the individual has long been placing a negative value on X (step 2a), the outcome is likely true avoidance or rejection of X. However, in a limited number of cases, he/she might have to passively use it. In this case, a user might display a negative relationship between the use and appreciation of an online news attribute (see the example on the automatic audio/video clip on a news page mentioned above).

Second, if the existing value system of the individual neither favours nor disfavours X, the outcome is more a matter of convenience and availability (step 2c). If X is readily available for use at a time the individual does not have any situational restraint, then he/she uses it in a ritualised way – maybe to pass time or to avoid boredom. If X is not convenient for use OR if the individual is not available, then he/she does not use X without any real dissonance. See the above example on the ritual use of interactive participation facilities after checking the news of the day. In this case, the user might be substantially exposed to the X without appreciating it very much.

Third, and most importantly, if X is attractive to the potential adopter, he/she will develop a positive appreciation of the Internet in terms of X-related gratifications (step 2b), which can be seen as roughly equivalent to attitudes in Fishbein and Ajzen's (1972) original expectancy-value theory or perception of relative advantages in Rogers's (2003) innovation diffusion theory. Appreciation here is not the direct driver of exposure to X like GSs but takes the form of *a general reason* for which intentional use of X takes place on a daily basis. More precisely, as a result of this general appreciation, when an individual feels the need for X-related gratifications, he/she will develop a use intention that leads to exposure to X (step 3). For example, an individual with a strong belief in the immediacy of the Internet might think of the Internet immediately when he/she feels the need for updated details on some events, which then is likely to lead to exposure to online breaking news. This has two alternative products:

o If the individual is satisfied with what is received from this exposure (i.e. obtaining positive gratifications), he/she will then reinforce the initial belief, and thus the initial appreciation, that online news, for example, is timely and updated (4a). The level of this subsequent appreciation depends on the extent to which he/she is satisfied after previous exposure as well as the general subjective value he/she places on X. Over time, if the user is continuously satisfied with X, his/her belief in X is continually reinforced (step 5), leading to increasing appreciation of the Internet in terms of X-related gratifications and thus an increasing attachment to this medium in seeking these gratifications (step 6), which in turn translates into a more substantial use of online news to obtain them (step 7).

Attachment is understood here in a broad sense – as the degree to which an individual is cognitively and affectively affiliated with and/or dependent on the medium for X-related gratifications. It takes the form of a range of behaviours such as dependence on the medium for X-related needs or enthusiasm about it. In general, the use of and attachment to online news features are in a *mutually causal* relationship over time – i.e. they covary, especially during the early stages of the medium. However, it is believed here that at some point, use becomes a function of attachment – i.e. after a substantial period of additive appreciation and confirmation, the user will develop some degree of attachment to some specific online news features and then plan his/her news use on this cognitive/affective background, which ultimately results in a distinctive use pattern of these features.

o   If the outcome of X use is negative right from the first few trials, then online news might be no longer sought to gratify X-related needs (step 4b). To continue the example above, if the potential adopter/user cannot find enough updated news from news sites after several visits, he/she might generalise that the online news environment is not immediate, leading to either an abandonment of using online news for immediacy or a delayed decision (until he/she – via some communication channels "renews" the initial belief and starts the seeking process over again). That a user finds or does not find satisfaction with online news performance in terms of this particular attribute, however, has only a partial role in his/her adoption/use of the whole medium. The individual does not necessarily abandon online news right away just because it does not have X. As noted, while seeking gratifications associated with X, he/she might – either via accidental exposure, inferences, or outside information sources – develop awareness of some other valued features not expected in the first instance. The end of X-seeking might be the beginning of Z-seeking.

It must be noted that the adoption/use "mini-processes" of different attributes need not be separated in time – they can and are likely to be temporally intermingled. Over a sufficient period, these mini-processes result in a certain set of online news appreciation – and thus a set of well-articulated needs for the whole medium. While some initially sought gratifications might not be provided, there are others well supplied during the process. When these gratifying factors are taken together, they gradually form a distinctive image of online news in the user's recognition system, leading to a certain level of attachment to it, which in turn leads him/her to integrate it into daily news consumption. Again, it is believed that while overall attachment to and overall use of the online news medium covary, use will become the outcome of attachment at some point in time.

Research questions

It is, however, beyond the scope of this study to test this whole proposed model. In conceptualising the whole process in that way, I aim at designing a theoretically sound model to explore the way in which online news attributes shape its adoption/use and thereby to explore the extent to which the much-touted features of online news contribute to its diffusion. To arrive at a conclusion about this, the model suggests three questions concerning three specific relationships:

At the least abstract level, the model posits that the overall use of the Internet as a news medium is the summative product of individual feature uses. While this sounds trivial, this is an important basis to explore what, among the plethora of online news features, are actually generating traffic on online news sites. It might well be that the use of only one or a few features contribute substantially to overall use. At one extreme, for example, an individual might mostly receive breaking news online but devotes so much time to it that he/she displays a higher level of general online news use than one who uses many features in a less substantial way. This raises the first research question:

RQ5.1: Which *used* features of online news contribute to its overall use level?

At a more abstract level, the model posits that while an appreciated online news feature (X) is likely to be used, a used feature is not necessarily an appreciated one. There is a high chance that some people use X substantially without appreciating it as a reason for their online news use because it is just an unintentional by-product of some other intentional use. Also, there is a chance for negative relationships between the use and appreciation of the same attribute. The second research question derives from this:

RQ5.2: To what extent are online news features being used because they are appreciated?

Beyond the relationship between the appreciation of a particular feature X and its corresponding use is that between the appreciation of X and the use of and attachment to online news as a whole. The model implies that due to the convergence of attributes in online news services, the use-use relationships underlining the first research question, although explaining what drives traffic to news sites, might say little about why online news is used. In other words, the most important features of online news might not be those that drive traffic to news sites but those whose appreciation serves as a statistically significant driver of its overall attachment and use. Also, the appreciation of one feature might underline that of some, or maybe all, other features. It is quite likely, for example, that an individual cites in-depth coverage and/or immediacy as their reasons for using online news only in the context that he/she has taken it primarily as being convenient to use. In other words, convenience might be the primary reason and immediacy and in-depth coverage are, although important, only secondary reasons. This can be likened to the fact that a car user with a general priority for safety appreciates speed and comfort as reasons for using a car brand on the underlying evaluation that it has satisfactory safety-related features. This forms the basis for the third research question:

RQ5.3: Which *appreciated* features of online news drive its overall attachment and use levels?

Data analysis methods

To answer the above research questions, this chapter continues to utilise the 2004 news use survey data, using logistic regression for a range of dependent variables indicating online news attachment and use on three sets of independent variables indicating the use and appreciation of different online news attributes.

Dependent variables

Online news use levels are represented by (1) its general use frequency; and (2) the amount of time spent on online news in the most recent session. The most recent online news session was treated as a typical one because the 2004 survey was conducted during a period in which there was no event of widespread interest to attract an unusual audience size and time spending (e.g. a national election or the Olympic Games) and thus can reflect the effect of general news orientation to online news. However, care was taken during the data interpretation process because an individual's day-to-day media use, as will be discussed in the next chapter, can be strongly determined by many situational factors (e.g. his/her immediate use context, or timetable of the day) (McQuail, 1997; Weibull, 1985). Indicators of attachment to online news include (1) the perceived importance of online news in Internet usage; (2) self-identification as a fan of online news (yes/no); (3) perception of the Internet as "the best news medium to serve your news need" (yes/no).

Independent variables

There are two main sets of independent variables. The first includes 16 use behaviours corresponding to 16 popular news features on the web, measured in terms of either yes/no questions or frequency questions (very often/often/not very often/never). These are used as predictors of overall online news use to answer RQ5.1. These variables were introduced in Table 4.3 in the previous chapter and will self-manifest again in Table 5.2 of this chapter. The second set of independent variables consists of the appreciation of nine commonly touted features of online news, operationalised as perceived reasons for using online news as seen in Chapter 3. For the purpose of table presentation, these are condensed as follows: no cost ("because I don't pay for it"); more news choices ("because I have more news choices on the Internet'); multitasking ("because I can combine getting news with other purposes online"); in-depth/background information ("because I can look for in-depth and background information whenever I want"); 24/7 updates ("because I can check for updated news whenever I want"); customised news ("because I can get news tailored to my interest only"); "have my say" ("because I can have my say to the news media"); discussing news with peers ("because I can discuss news and current affairs with my peers"); and different viewpoints ("because I can find different viewpoints on the Internet"). Unfortunately, multimedia as another exclusive feature of online news was accidentally omitted from the questionnaire due to a technical error during the printing process.

Statistical procedures

For RQ5.2, pairwise correlations were calculated with consideration of their statistical significance. This allows us not only to see the strength of relationship between the appreciation of one online news feature and its corresponding use (e.g. the appreciation of online immediacy and the use of online breaking news) but also to compare this association with the cross-feature use-appreciation associations (e.g. the appreciation of online immediacy with the use of, say, hypertextual links for in-depth information; or the use of immediacy with the appreciation of online depth of coverage). Some composite variables were constructed during this process and will be introduced when they first appear.

For RQ5.1 and RQ5.3, logistic regression models were employed. Logistic regression is a variation of the usual linear regression and is used for dichotomous response variables, i.e. the occurrence and non-occurrence of some outcome event (e.g. adoption versus non-adoption, frequent versus infrequent use). It is different from linear regression in that the dependent variable is not measured in terms of its mean value but in terms of the logarithm of the odds (called the log odds or logit) of a particular outcome. More particularly, it is based on a linear function for the logarithm of p/(1-p), with p denoting the probability (proportion) of one of the dependent variable's two outcomes – e.g. the log odds of being an adopter or a frequent user. Despite this difference, logistic regression is similar to linear regression analyses in the sense that it is a joint test that indicates (1) whether at least one of the covariates has a statistically significant relationship with the dependent variable (i.e. whether all the independent covariates form a good set of predictors for the dependent variable) and (2) which of the covariates is/are statistically significantly associated with the dependent variable.

Logistic regression is used for this chapter because it allows for uniform tests for all five dependent variables. Two of these variables (e.g. online news fans and perception of the Internet as the best news medium) were originally dichotomous (yes/no). The other three dependent variables were recoded from their original categories as follows: use frequency was binary-recoded as frequent (every day or several times a week) versus infrequent (several times a month or less often); time spending as "above average" (spending more than the mean time, 14.9 minutes, in that session) versus "below average" (less than 14.9 minutes); and perceived importance as "an important part" and "an essential part" versus "not an important part" of Internet use.

As logistic regression analysis is possibly an unfamiliar technique, I will present the first logistic model with all essential information about coefficients and p-values both in the table (Table 5.2) and the analysis text. For the purpose of condensed and concise data interpretation, however, later models will be presented using the familiar star-system (*) to indicate statistical significance and will be analysed with regard only to key information about statistical significance. The actual p-values associated with coefficients will not be presented in tables but will be mentioned in the analysis text.

Results

This section presents the findings in three sub-sections, each for one of the three sub-RQs espoused earlier. Further methodological issues will also be discussed when necessary.

Relationship between the use of different online news services and its overall use

Table 5.2 shows the logistic regression model that answers RQ5.1 on the relationship between the uses of different online news services and its overall use. It provides the following information:

- o The likelihood-ratio chi-square statistic with 16 degrees of freedom is 57.9 and has an associated p-value of less than .001, meaning that collectively, the 16 variables indicating uses of specific online news services formed a very good set of predictors of overall use frequency.

- o Two of the 16 services were significant positive predictors of overall use frequency: receiving up-to-the-minute news several times a day (coefficient = 1.41, $p < .001$) and subscription to general news mail alerts (coefficient = 1.75, $p = .02$). This means that when controlled for other uses, subscription to general email news alerts and using the Internet to check updated news throughout the day improved overall frequency of online news use. More specifically, the log odds of being frequent online news users increased with using the Internet to check up-to-the-minute news throughout the day and with subscription to general news alerts. For instance, other uses being equal, the log odds of being a frequent online news user was 1.75 greater for subscribers of general email news alerts

146

Table 5.2: Logistic regression analysis for the effect of the use of different online news services on general online news use (n = 194)[a]

	Coefficient	p-value
Subscribe to free email alerts of general news[b]	1.75	.02
Subscribe to free email news alerts tailored to your own interests only	-1.21	.03
Set up a personalised page offered by Internet services and online news providers	-0.72	.13
Set your favourite news home page as the default front page of your web browser	-0.32	.46
Use search tools to find news of your interest[c]	-0.31	.19
Get up-to-the-minute news several times a day	1.41	< .001
Visit a number of sites for the same news item	-0.15	.65
Get audio news in addition to reading	0.21	.49
Get video news in addition to reading	0.19	.56
Click on links to related stories for in-depth coverage (including background information)	0.32	.28
Participate in online news polls	0.69	.08
Find other perspectives from sources outside the news mainstream media	0.12	.69
Go to an information exchange site to express your opinions	-1.05	.06
Send links to news stories to your peers	0.10	.85
Receive links to news stories from your peers	-0.32	.48
Read weblogs	0.22	.71
LR chi2 (df 16)[d]	57.90	<.001

(a) For frequency of online news use with 1 = Frequent use ("every day" or "several times a week") and 0 = Infrequent use ("several times a month" or "less often"); from (b) to before (c): dummy variables with 1 = "Yes" and 0 = "No"; from (b) to before (d): all variables with the same categories; 0 = "Never"; 1 = "Not very often"; 2 = "Often"; 3 = "Very often"; (d) Likelihood Ratio Chi-squared Test with 16 degrees of freedom.

than non-subscribers. In more concrete terms, the odds of being a frequent online news user was $e^{1.75} = 5.75$ times higher among subscribers to general news alerts than among non-subscribers, other things being equal.

o Subscription to customised email news alerts was a significant negative predictor (coefficient = -1.21, p = .03) – that is, if other specific uses are held constant, subscribers to customised news alerts were less likely to be frequent users of online news.

Some plausible explanations could be found for this effect pattern. The positive effect of continuous use of updates on general use frequency is easy to make sense of: getting up-to-the-minute news several times a day apparently contributes substantially to the number of times news is received from the Internet in an average week. Similarly, the positive effect of subscription to general email news alerts is not surprising because email is the most prevailing application of the Internet so far. Meanwhile, the negative coefficient of subscription to customised news alerts does not mean that this use has a negative effect on general use. Rather, it suggests that there might be people who use online news only infrequently because this use is tied with seeking some specialised news categories that are delivered to the email box on an infrequent basis. For example, one might subscribe to customised news services on a weekly or monthly basis and only (or mostly) visits an online news site when these specialised news alerts arrive at his/her mailbox.

Relationships between the appreciation of online news features and their corresponding use

As demonstrated before RQ5.2 was raised, the use and appreciation of an online news feature can be unassociated or even negatively associated because, due to the convergent nature of online news features, it can be used in a passive or ritualised manner. Thus a feature can only be seen as a driver of its use when it satisfies two statistical conditions: (1) its use and appreciation must be at least moderately correlated; and (2) this correlation must be higher than that between the appreciation of this feature and the use of any other feature. In order to explore this, pair-wise correlations between perceived reasons for online news use and the use frequencies of different online news features were constructed in Table 5.3. Several methodological points need to be mentioned before analysing this table. First, of the nine reasons introduced above, the cost factor was eliminated from this table because there is no real corresponding behaviour to explore. Second, the table contains a few composite variables that were created from original use variables to simplify the data:

- o An index of overall non-news Internet use variable was constructed by taking the mean of six variables indicating using the Internet for entertainment and relaxation, e-commerce, personal contact, interaction with other online users (via forums, chat rooms), searching non-news information for work/study, and searching non-news information for other purposes. The six original variables had four values (0 = "Never", 1 = "Not very often"; 2 = "Often" and 3 = "Very often") and generated an index with a reliability coefficient (alpha) of .65. This composite variable was included because prima facie, it seems to correspond best to the appreciation of the ability to do multitask while consuming news online.

o A second mean index (exchanging news and current affairs with peers online) was constructed in the same way on frequencies of sending links to news stories to peers, receiving links to news stories from peers, and passing some heard/witnessed information to others, with a reasonably high Cronbach alpha coefficient of .81.

o Other composite variables include the use of customised services (sum of subscription to customised news email alerts and setting up a personalised news page) and the use of multimedia content (mean frequency of getting audio news and getting video news).

Now, looking at Table 5.3, it can be first noted that every correlation coefficient between the use of an online news feature and its corresponding appreciation (bolded in Table 5.3) is statistically significantly positive. Although none of the coefficients exceeds .48, most showed moderately positive relationships. More importantly, there is quite consistent evidence to infer that the appreciation of a specific feature does explain its corresponding use. Reading the table horizontally, it can be seen that the highest correlation coefficient in each row is almost always found between the appreciation of one feature and its corresponding use behaviour(s). In particular, the strongest association across the rows was found between:

o "because I can combine getting news with other purposes online" and the frequency of using non-news Internet services (.36);

o "because I can find different viewpoints on the Internet" and frequency of finding views from non-mainstream news sites (.35);

o "because I can have my say to the news media" with frequency of going to a news and information exchange site to express opinions (.39);

Table 5.3: Pair-wise correlations between the appreciation of different online news attributes and their corresponding uses

	Use online non-news services	Use customised news services	Get updates several times/day	Visit many sites for same news item	Click on links to related stories	Find views from non-mainstream sites	Use multimedia content	Express opinions on a news-trading site	Exchange news with peers
Multitasking	**.36**	Ns	.31	.33	.25	.17	.19	.18	.16
More news choices	--	.15	.44	**.48**	.26	.20	.27	.18	.23
In-depth and background information	--	Ns	.23	**.33**	.23	.19	Ns	Ns	Ns
Different viewpoints	--	Ns	.16	.29	.17	**.35**	.23	.23	.21
24/7 updates	--	Ns	**.42**	.43	.35	.17	.29	Ns	.19
Customised news	--	**.15**	.26	.29	.24	.20	Ns	.24	Ns
"Have my say" to the news media	--	.12	.17	.32	.22	.21	.20	**.39**	Ns
Discussing news with peers	--	.22	Ns	.14	Ns	**.28**	.16	.21	**.28**

Coefficients between the appreciation of each online attribute and its corresponding use are bolded; -- Not explored because there are no prima-facie relationships between these variables; ns = not significant

- o "because I can discuss news and current affairs with my peers" and two closely related behaviours: exchanging news with peers and with finding non-mainstream perspectives (both at .28);
- o "because I have more news choices on the Internet" and frequency of visiting many sites for the same news item (.48); and
- o "because I can look for in-depth and background information whenever I want" and frequency of visiting many sites for the same news items (.33).

A slight deviation from this pattern is that the appreciated immediacy of online news ("because I can check for updated news whenever I want") has its strongest correlation with visiting many sites for the same news items (.43), rather than with getting updated news several times a day (.42). However, these correlation coefficients are almost identical, allowing us to tentatively conclude that online news updates are used because they are appreciated. Indeed, the data show that more news choices and immediacy tend to vary with each other. This is confirmed by two other facts: (1) the appreciated ability to have more news choices was found to form its second strongest correlation with getting updated news several times a day (.44); and (2) the appreciated ability to find in-depth and background information had the second strongest association with the same behaviour (.23). This is not difficult to understand because when people look for immediacy, they might tend to (and sometimes have to) visit many news sites because (a) not all sites are continuously updated and (b) developing stories are usually short of details that stimulate further exploration.

Customisation is the only feature that deviated from the above pattern of correlation strengths. The appreciation of the ability to "get news tailored to my interest only" had a fairly weak, although significant, association with its corresponding use of customised news services (.15). It was also the weakest significant correlation across its row.

Relationships between the appreciation of different online news features and its overall attachment and use levels

As bolstered for RQ5.3, the defining features of online news – those that serve as a benchmark to compare different online news use and attachment levels and to explain the primary reasons for online news to be chosen among others – are not necessarily those that are significant in the above use-use relationships but are those whose appreciations survive as significant predictors of online news attachment and use after all appreciated features are controlled for each other. Tables 5.4 and 5.5 provide insights into this.

Table 5.4 contains three logistic regression models for the effect of appreciated online news features on three aspects of online news attachment: perceived importance of online news in Internet use, perception of the Internet as "the best medium to serve your news needs", and self-identification as an online news fan. As for the perceived importance of online news in Internet usage, the logistic model was a good fit with LR chi2 = 84.8 (p < .001) and yielded three significant positive predictors: 24/7 updates (coefficient = .95, p < .01), in-depth/background information (coefficient = .66, p = .02) and more news choices (coefficient = .47, p = .05). That is to say, as the whole, online news was perceived as an important or essential part of daily Internet use thanks more to its appreciated provision of some traditionally upheld news qualities – its immediacy as well as its content depth and diversity – than to any innovative utilities that are unique to online news (such as customisation, interaction with peers or feedback to the news providers).

Table 5.4: Logistic regression analyses for the effect of the appreciation of online news attributes on online news attachment (regression coefficients)

	Importance[a] (n = 199)	Best medium[b] (n = 164)	Fandom[c] (n = 200)
No cost	0.17	0.28	0.34*
More news choices	0.47*	0.34	0.24
Multitasking	-0.04	0.47	-0.21
In-depth/background information	0.66*	-0.10	-0.05
24/7 updates	0.95**	1.66***	0.76**
Customised news	0.29	-0.17	0.48**
"Have my say" to the news media	0.04	-0.04	0.21
Discussing news with peers	-0.06	0.03	-0.09
Different viewpoints	-0.01	0.31	0.12
LR chi2(9)[d]	84.81***	62.22***	53.83***

*(a) Perceived importance of online news in Internet use (1 =" Essential" or "Important"; 0 = "Not Important"); (b) Choosing the Internet as "the best medium to serve your news needs" (1 = Yes; 0 = No); (c) Self-identifying as an online news fan (1 = Yes; 0 = No); (d) Likelihood Ratio Chi-squared Tests with nine degrees of freedom; * p ≤ .05; ** p ≤ .01; *** p ≤ .001*

As for the perception of the Internet as "the best medium to serve your news needs" (LR chi2 = 62.2, p < .001), immediacy was the only significant predictor (coefficient = 1.66, p = .001). Meanwhile, online news fandom (LR chi2 = 53.8, p < .001) was the outcome primarily of the appreciation of its immediacy (coefficient =.76, p = .005), its ability to get news tailored to one's interests (coefficient = .48, p = .01) and its lack of cost (coefficient = .34, p = .03). Compared across all three dimensions of online news attachment, the common predictor is the appreciated immediacy of online news.

Table 5.5 moves beyond indicators of online news attachment, displaying the effect of the appreciation of online news features on its use levels. As for use frequency (LR chi2 = 46.9, p < .001), three of the nine appreciated features serve as significant positive predictors: the non-cost factor (coefficient = .41, p = .01), the ability to do to multitask (coefficient = .62, p = .01) and immediacy (coefficient = .74, p < .01). The first two are explainable: the more activities people conduct online, the more frequently they use the Internet, which in turn leads to more chance to intentionally or accidentally use online news. And of course, this use would be much more limited if online news is available

Table 5.5: Logistic regression analyses for the effect of the appreciation of online news attributes on general online news use (regression coefficients)

	Use frequency (n = 200)[a]	Time spending in most recent session (n = 191)[b]
No cost	0.41**	0.15
More news choices	-0.12	0.41*
Multitasking	0.62**	-0.50*
In-depth/background information	0.08	-0.12
24/7 updates	0.74**	0.64*
Customised news	-0.09	0.02
"Have my say" to the news media	-0.19	-0.05
Discussing news with peers	0.21	0.48*
Different viewpoints	0.06	-0.11
LR chi2(9)[c]	46.94***	28.15***

(a) 1 = Frequent use ("every day" or "several times a week") and 0 = Infrequent use ("several times a month" or "less often"); (b) 1 = Above average and 0 = Below average; (a) Likelihood Ratio Chi-squared Tests with nine degrees of freedom; * p ≤ .05; ** p ≤ .01; *** p ≤ .001

with some charge. The third significant contributor is also easy to understand: the more people expect the Internet to be a good source of breaking news, the more likely people are to go online for it frequently.

As for the amount of time spending in news in the most recent session (LR chi2 = 28.2, p < .001), four variables remain as significant predictors: more news choices (coefficient = .41, p = .05), multitasking (coefficient = -.50, p < .05), 24/7 updates (coefficient = .64, p < .05) and the ability to discuss news with peers (coefficient = .48, p = .02). The three significant positive predictors in the model can be explained as "qualitative" use reasons that tend to consume time. In other words, people spend more time on news in a typical session because (1) they receive more news from more sources; or (2) they consume more breaking stories; or (3) passing news of interest to peers is often accompanied with expressing ideas and writing comments, which certainly take more time than merely reading the news.

Meanwhile, the negative contributor – the web's multipurpose nature – can be seen as a "quantitative" element for several possible reasons. First, it might be the case that while the ability to do multitask contributes significantly to the density of online news usage (i.e. use frequency), it also reduces the time spending on news in any specific session. In other words, as people do many things frequently on the web and get news according to this frequent use, there is less news suiting their interests each time they log on news sites, resulting in less time spending than that of less frequent visitors to these sites. Second, it could be because those who combine news with their Internet uses might be too busy and cannot spend much time on news in each section. The reason for these people to get news on the Internet might well be just to save time. The third possibility is the same as what Jacob Nielsen (1997) said about why people often scan/skim online news rather than read it word by word: because the web is a "compulsive" environment, people usually do something online with the feeling that they need to move on because there are millions of other things out there. That is, as users get news because it is combinable with other activities, their news use might be restrained by the drive to do other non-news activities.

Before reaching a conclusion about the effect of online news features on online news use, there remains another task. The model in Figure 5.3 suggests that over a certain amount of time, the appreciation of online news features does not directly affect its use but indirectly affects online news attachment that leads to its use. Is it supported by the 2004 survey data? In order to explore this, two more logistic models were regressed for online news use frequency and time spending on the nine appreciation variables, controlling for the above three dimensions of attachment. The results are shown in Table 5.6. As can be seen, in both models, none of the appreciated attributes was a significant predictor and neither was online news fandom. The significant effect of perceived importance of news in Internet use and the view on the Internet as the best news source suggests that the appreciation of online news features affects its use level indirectly through its attachment levels. The result also shows that only more or less cognitive attachment to online news (not totally affective attachment like fandom) influences its use levels. The effect of this cognitive attachment should be further explored future research.

Table 5.6: Logistic regression analyses for the effect of the appreciation of online news attributes on its overall use, controlling for attachment levels (regression coefficients)

	Use frequency (n = 196)[a]	Time spending in most recent session (n = 196)[b]
No cost	0.27	0.11
More news choices	-0.38	0.47
Multitasking	0.39	-0.41
In-depth/background information	-0.16	-0.52
24/7 updates	0.43	0.61
Customised news	-0.24	-0.03
"Have my say" to the news media	-0.15	-0.17
Discussing news with peers	-0.52	0.39
Different viewpoints	0.01	0.00
Being an online news fan	0.60	-0.11
News important or essential in Internet use	1.63**	1.69***
Internet as best medium to serve news needs	2.50*	-1.06*
LR chi2(11)[c]	65.36***	36.65***

*(a) 1 = Frequent use ("every day" or "several times a week") and 0 = Infrequent use ("several times a month" or "less often"); (b) 1 = Above average and 0 = Below average; (c) Likelihood Ratio Chi-squared Tests with 11 degrees of freedom; * p ≤ .05; ** p ≤ .01; *** p ≤ .001*

It must be noted, however, that while perceived importance was a significant positive contributor in both cases (coefficient = 1.63 with p = .002 in the case of use frequency and coefficient = 1.69 with p = .001 in the case of time spending), the best-medium perception was only positive for use frequency (coefficient = 2.50, p = .03) and is significantly negative in the case of time spending (coefficient = -1.06, p = .03). While this seems contradictory to common sense, it might happen because those who see the Internet as the best news medium are compelled to use it much more frequently and thus spend less time in each specific session than those who do not. But, again, this tentative explanation needs to be further explored.

Conclusion: online news attributes and its future diffusion

Based on the above suggested theoretical model of the online news adoption/use process, the empirical data in this chapter, plus the data in the previous chapter, provide in-depth information to answer the RQ3 of this book ("To what extent and in what way do the much-touted attributes of online news contribute to the way users adopt, use and integrate it into daily life?"). First, although online news packages are often delivered with an integration of several features, there is convincing evidence that all the online news features explored in this study (except customisation) are not used passively or unintentionally as a by-product of using another (Table 5.3). Second, the data reveal that most of the examined online news attributes are important contributors to the overall online news experience in one way or another. In particular:

o   The capacity for continuous updates is probably the most crucial feature of online news. After being controlled for other medium factors, the appreciated immediacy of online news sustains its significant effect on all of the five use and attachment variables. They contributed not only to the cognitive and affective affiliation with online news (the perceived importance of online news, the chance for it to be thought of as the best news medium and the chance for it to be affiliated with in a fandom-like manner) (Table 5.4) but also to actual use behaviours (online news use frequency and the amount of time spent on it in a specific session) (Table 5.5). In addition, getting updated news is a primary positive contributor to online news use frequency (Table 5.2).

o The ability to multitask – one important aspect of the use convenience of online news – also seems to be a crucial tool for news sites to sustain visitors. This is well reflected by the fact that subscription to general email news alerts – a most common service that offers the combination of news and other online uses – is one of the only two primary positive contributors to online news use frequency (Table 5.2). Also, the appreciated ability to combine news with other online purposes is a determinant of online news adoption in general but also a primary positive contributor to its use frequency (Table 5.5). However, this appreciated ability is also negatively associated with time spent on online news in a specific session (Table 5.5).

o The availability of more news choices and in-depth/background information – two of the most important content-richness features – has also shown a crucial effect. These are two of the three key drivers of the perceived importance of online news (Table 5.4). This is important in the context that perceived importance is the only attachment variable that has a positive effect on both online news use frequency and time spending on it (Table 5.6). In addition, the data show that the appreciation of these two content-richness features and that of immediacy tend to be clustered together, suggesting that the use of immediacy and rich content usually complement each other. However, the appreciated availability of different viewpoints, which can be seen as a dimension of content richness, does not have a significant contribution to any use and attachment aspect of online news.

o The appreciation of the no-cost factor is a significant positive contributor to online news use frequency (Table 5.5). This suggests that free access seems to be a condition for online news to be used more frequently. If providers want online news to continue its uptake in the years ahead, the paid-content model will probably not work well. In addition, the no-cost factor has a significant effect on self-identification as online news fans (Table 5.4).

o The appreciated ability to get news tailored to one's interest only has a significant positive effect on online news fandom (Table 5.5). It either does not have an association or does have a negative association with other online news use/attachment variables. In addition, those who use customised email newsletters tend to be less frequent online news users (Table 5.2).

o The two variables representing interactive participation – the appreciated ability to "have my say to the media" and to discuss news and current affairs with peers – are not significant in determining most of the five attachment and use variables, except for the fact that the appreciation of the capacity for news exchange does have a positive effect on time spending on online news in a specific session (Table 5.5). Also, the actual uses of these two features are not significant contributor to online news use frequency.

The general conclusion is that although online news has many unique attributes such as customisation and interactive participation opportunities, it is still the same established attributes such as immediacy, content richness and use convenience that are likely to be the major drivers of its development in the future.

So far as it goes, however, the effect of online news attributes have been assessed and explored out of the socio-psychological context of its users. As has been reiterated several times, because online news must find its way into established media use patterns of its potential adopters, the process from being aware of online news to adopting and substantially using it is influenced by many factors beyond its technical power. Indeed, these factors "superimposed" on every step in the online news adoption/use model in Figure 5.3. For instance, one with high education or more Internet experience might be more likely to be able to infer about online news attributes from other Internet uses than one with limited education or less Internet experience. The next chapter will chart the effect of possible non-medium determinants on different aspects of online news adoption/use, including the appreciation of online news attributes.

Notes

1. In reality, the nexus between the adoption decision and the actual use level is applied to any innovation, including hardware innovation. As Steinfield et al (1989, p. 61) argued in the case of the computer: "Despite continually optimistic forecasts of adoption and evidence of steady computer sales, data are sparse concerning what actually happens after a family acquires a personal computer. Does it entertain in the living room, facilitate work in the study room, or gather dust in the closest?" The point here is that online news, as a free and ubiquitous product online, has much more chance than a computer to be adopted without being substantially used.

2. Because of the blur line between adoption and use, from this point onward, I tend to use "adoption/use" rather than "adoption and use", except when there is a need to separate the two terms.

Chapter 6

Beyond the technology: socio-structural determinants of online news adoption/use

---

The previous chapters show that online news attributes have substantially been used and appreciated, playing an important role in different aspects of its adoption/use. With the improvement of online news technologies and their associated services still on the way, this suggests that online news has a substantial potential to continue to grow. This chapter explores who are likely to be the next adopters and substantial users of online news by answering the fourth research question of this book on the social correlates of public adoption and use of online news. Seeing online news both as an innovation and a media service, the chapter merges diffusion theory (Rogers, 2003) with the structural approach to media audience formation and other uses and gratifications perspectives (McQuail, 1997; McQuail, 2000; Weibull, 1985) to develop a theoretical framework for investigating the effect of non-medium factors on online news adoption/use. In general, the formation of online news audiences is characterised by different aggregates of individuals, whose different socio-psychological characteristics imply different needs for and perceptions of online news, resulting in different ways of adopting and implementing the news medium. Drawing from the work by the above authors and previous studies of news uses and new media adoption, I will identify three major sets of socio-structural determinants of online news adoption/use: social locators; news orientation/behaviours; and Internet experience. I will then use the 2004 survey data to examine this, finding strong influences of these three determinants on the adoption likelihood, use frequency and perceived importance of online news.

Social determinants of innovation adoption: a brief review

As noted in Chapter 5, the innovation-decision process is in essence an information-seeking process to reduce uncertainty about the innovation, through which an individual continuously asks questions concerning how it works, what it works for, why it should be adopted and how it could be fitted in his/her own life (Rogers, 2003). The answers to these questions are subjective, depending on the characteristics of the potential adopter. In particular, for the same innovation, different individuals, because of their different socio-economic and psychological resources and different socio-cultural communication situations, may experience different contact with, exposure to and perception of an innovation, which result in different innovation decisions. Some people try the innovation and delay their adoption decision until an adequate number of people in society, especially those in their near-peer networks, have adopted the innovation; others would be more enthusiastic to quickly integrate it into their existing life. In reality, since the technical features of an innovation are usually subjectively evaluated and thus vary across individuals, some scholars have argued that innovation attributes can be conceptualised as personal background variables indicating beliefs and attitudes about innovations (Covvey & McAllister, 1982; Steinfield, Dutton & Kovaric, 1989).

A major task in predicting the future of online news development, therefore, is to ask who current adopters are and how they differ from non-adopters in their socio-psychological background and their attitudes to online news attributes. Regarding this, the diffusion literature has asserted that the key determinant of the innovation adoption behaviour is innovativeness – the willingness to try a new idea/practice/object, formally defined as "the degree to which an individual or other unit of adoption is relatively earlier in adopting new ideas than other members of the system" (Rogers, 2003, p. 280). Throughout the diffusion process, there are five groups of adopters: (1) innovators (earliest adopters, who make up 2.5% of the total number of individuals adopting an innovation); (2) early adopters (the next 13.5%), (3) early majority (34%); (4) late majority (34%); and (5) laggards (the last 16%). When plotted over time, these groups follow a normally distributed, bell-shaped curve as seen in Figure 6.1. According to Rogers (2003, pp. 282-285), the different levels of innovativeness among these five groups of adopters are reflected in their distinct characteristics as follow:

o *Innovators* are venturesome. With a strong interest in and "a desire for the rash, the daring, and the risky" (Rogers, 2003, p. 283), they are eager to try new ideas. To cope with a high degree of uncertainty, they are usually able to understand and apply complex technical knowledge, capable of absorb substantial financial and social losses from unprofitable innovations, and often reach out of a local circle of peer networks and into more cosmopolite social relationships with other innovators for references.

o *Early adopters* are more likely to be localites and are respectable as opinion leaders or role models for their local reference groups. These people make judicious innovation decisions – i.e. they are willing to take a calculated risk but with concern for failure. The information they pass to their peers about the innovation is a means for them to gain respect and remain respected.

o *Early-majority adopters* usually deliberate for some time before a complete adoption and thus seldom lead in their peer network. Their thinking fits into what Alexander Pope said in 1711: "Be not the first by which the new is tried, nor the last to lay the old aside" (Rogers, 2003, p. 284).

o *Late-majority adopters* are sceptical and cautious about innovations, adopting them either out of an economic necessity or as a response to increased peer pressures.

o *Laggards* are the most localite with almost no opinion leadership. They hold traditional values and primarily interact with those holding these same values in making a decision as to whether to adopt the innovation or not. They have limited resources and are thus generally resistant to or suspicious of the new.

Although there is no consensus about whether innovativeness should be seen as a personality trait, consistent evidence has emerged to ensure that the degree to which one is early in adopting innovations is a function of at least three groups of variables: socio-economic status, personality values and communication behaviours. Rogers (2003, pp. 280-291) has generalised the operation of these variables as follows:

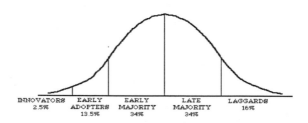

Figure 6.1: Categories of innovation adopters over time (Rogers, 2003)

o *Socio-economic status:* Earlier adopters are likely to have more education, higher literacy levels, higher social status, a greater degree of upward social mobility and larger-sized units (farms, schools, companies etc.) than later adopters. Age and sex, however, do not have enough consistent effect to be generalised in adoption research.

o *Personality:* Compared with later adopters, earlier adopters have greater empathy (the ability to project oneself into the role of another person), less dogmatism (the degree to which an individual has a relatively closed belief system), greater ability to deal with abstraction, greater rationality (the ability to use the most effective means to reach a given end), more intelligence, a more favourable attitude towards change, greater ability to cope with uncertainty and risk, more favourable attitude toward science, less fatalism (the degree to which an individual perceives a lack of ability to control his/her future) and more aspirations (for formal education, higher status, occupations and so on).

o *Communication behaviours:* Earlier adopters are likely to have more social participation, be more highly interconnected through interpersonal networks, be more cosmopolite (oriented outside a social system), have more contact with change agents, greater exposure to mass communication channels, seek information about innovations more actively, have greater knowledge of innovations, and have a higher degree of opinion leadership.

These three groups of variables, along with the nature of the innovation (its perceived attributes, as explored in the previous chapters), constitute the four groups of primary determinants of innovation adoption. However, the diffusion tradition has been criticised for being too descriptive and atheoretical (Williams, Strover & Grant, 1994). Indeed, in the 551-page fifth edition of his seminal work, *Diffusion of Innovations* (with the first edition being published in 1962), Rogers (2003) still provided little theoretical link between these determinants and the way one behaves in each stage of the innovation-decision process – i.e. it remains largely unclear what roles these factors, especially socio-economic status, play in each of the five stages of the innovation-decision process.

Despite the adoption process being undertheorised, intensive and extensive evidence of the effect of these factors has been found in past studies of the adoption of different new media technologies since the early 1980s. As Steinfield et al (1989, p. 77) summarised in the case of home computing adoption:

> The existence of a favourable economic, social, and educational background, the existence (and increase) of particularly 'friendly' system features, the existence and increase of both a broadly and narrowly conceived social environment that supports the development of computing use and skills, and the existence and increase of personal reasons for use, skill at use, and positive attitudes toward the technology are believed to operate together to shape the amount, regularity, and diversity of use over time.

The remainder of this chapter will integrate this body of knowledge with the socio-structural approach to media audience formation and other empirical research on media use to identify three groups of determinants of online news adoption/use: general news orientation and behaviours, socio-economic status and Internet experience. A range of research questions will be posed throughout this discussion.

The potential effect of news orientation and its associated behaviours on online news adoption/use

As noted above, innovation diffusion research has generalised that earlier adopters tend to have a higher level of exposure to mass media content. Much research into new media adoption has shown that early adopters tend to use more available media. Cable television subscription, for example, was found to be associated with more newspaper and magazine reading and radio listening (Rothe et al, 1983; Becker, Dunwoody & Rafaeli, 1983). Lin and Jeffres (1998) discovered a positive correlation between interest in adoption of multimedia cable television and the amount of newspaper reading and radio listening. In Belgium, those intending to adopt HDTV reported watching more television, listening to more radio, and reading more newspapers than those who did not (Dupagne & Agostino, 1991). In Hong Kong, the intention to subscribe to interactive TV was positively associated with newspaper and magazine consumption (Leung & Wei, 1998). Traditional media use has also been found to be the most powerful predictor of audio information service adoption (Neuendorf et al, 1998). In the case of Internet adoption, evidence about the importance of traditional media use is mixed: while some research produced little or mixed support (Brusselle et al, 1999; Jeffres & Atkin, 1996; Lin, 1994; Lin 1998; Rhee & Kim, 2004), a number of studies found more media exposure among early adopters (see, for example, Robinson et al, 2000 and Stempel et al, 2000). A more detailed discussion of this will be presented in the next chapter.

For now, despite the contradictory picture about the role of media exposure in Internet adoption, under the concept of compatibility in diffusion theory, it could be expected that online news adopters are likely to be heavier news users than nonadopters. This is because people tend to evaluate innovations according to their existing needs and values and adopt those that are compatible to these needs and values (Rogers, 2003; Steinfield et al, 1989). In other words, online news would have been likely to be less appealing to and thus to have been rejected/delayed by people with, for instance, lower news need. This becomes even more likely because the Internet is a much more information-intensive news medium than traditional media, and, according to Lin (2001), until recently remained largely text-based. Indeed, this might well be the reason why, as the rich body of Internet use research mentioned in previous chapters and many other studies (Atkin, Jeffres & Neuendorf, 1998; Lin, 2001; LaRose & Eastin, 2004; Nguyen, 2003; Nguyen & Western, 2006; Nguyen & Western, 2007), news and non-news information have been among the most valued and utilised functionalities of the Internet. Atkin et al (1998) and Lin (2001) contended that information utilities are likely to remain the *raison d'être* for the Internet – at least until more web-streaming content for entertainment is in place.

Beyond the idea of need and taste compatibility, this prediction about more news (and non-news information) use among online news adopters is further substantiated by a media use perspective called the structural approach to media audience formation, which is briefly introduced below:

Originally developed by Weibull (1985) and later adapted by McQuail (1997, 2000), the structural – or more exactly, socio-structural – approach distinguishes two central concepts relating to media use: *media exposure* and *media orientation*. The former is actual media use under a certain circumstance, which dynamically changes from one particular point in time to another, while the latter is fairly stable, being accumulated over time and representing general patterns of media use. Media orientation "takes the form of an affinity for certain media, specific preferences and interests, habits of use, expectations of what the media are good for", which will affect situational use (McQuail, 2000, p. 386).

On a day-to-day basis, what an individual chooses to consume from the media options available to him/her is based largely on his/her general media orientation, although this is also subject to a range of situational (and relatively unpredictable) factors such as his/her individual circumstances, use contexts and available content at the time of consumption. In other words, news orientation and its associated news use pattern, can serve as good predictors of daily news use. Apart from problems associated with structural provision that might lead to passive or unintentional uses at some particular point in time (Chapter 5), a user generally seeks news or a specific type of news only when he/she has an interest in and a need for it. Thus, an individual with a strong interest in sports news will likely to read sports pages even if he/she does not have much time for serious news at a particular time of disposal (Weibull, 1985) – he/she might probably read these pages before reading other news sections, which might be omitted if no more time is available.

Media orientation applies to the choice across content categories or media, too. Someone interested in news and current affairs, for instance, would be likely to watch news bulletins than entertainment programs on television if his/her time budget of the day does not allow him/her to attend to everything. Eijck and Rees (2000) found from longitudinal Dutch data between 1975 and 1995 that newspaper non-readers and heavy readers of entertainment content in newspapers watched television (an entertainment-oriented medium) the most, whereas those reading newspapers for serious information were the least likely to watch television. Based on this observation, it is sensible to expect that because the Internet is a multimodal and multipurpose medium that facilitates many essential daily tasks, a user with a weak orientation to news might be less likely to go online for news than for other purposes – he/she might be more interested in online gaming or chatting or non-news information, for example. In other words, it is those with a more pronounced orientation to and more use of news and current affairs information who are more likely to adopt online news earlier and to use it more substantially.

This argument can be extended to argue that earlier adopters or heavier users of online news might have a higher level of news exchange within peer networks than their counterparts. This is because a user with a stronger orientation to news is more likely to be motivated to discuss news and current affairs – via face-to-face communication or on the telephone – with people in his/her interpersonal network such as family members, friends, relatives, neighbours and work colleagues. As elaborated in Chapter 3, uses and gratifications research has shown that people use news partly because it is a social utility for them to gain social status, to enhance their work efficiency or to obtain something else in their near-peer networks. In the study by Salwen, Driscoll and Garrison (2005), web news users discussed news with others 5.58 days a week – significantly higher than web users (4.74) and web non-users (4.52). This argument also corresponds well with the diffusion perspective that earlier adopters usually have a higher level of opinion leadership and are more willing to communicate with their peers about issues of their interest – whether it is about a technological innovation, a recently introduced service, or an emerging public issue. This kind of informal exchange is especially important in the interactive web environment, where people sharing the same interest can find a wide range of easy ways to pass on their news and views.

All this literature suggests that there should be some effect of different aspects of news orientation/behaviour – including general news use levels, news needs, news attachment and news exchange behaviours – on online news adoption, use and attachment. This facilitates asking the following question:

RQ6.1: To what extent do news orientation and its associated behaviours affect online news adoption, attachment and use?

The potential effect of social locators on online news adoption/use

As briefly mentioned above, diffusion research from different disciplines has found that earlier adopters of innovations are likely to be of higher socio-economic status (SES). Wealthier and more educated individuals have been argued to be likely to be more ready to take up new media technologies because they are more able to afford them and because many technologies have become a status (Reagan, 2003; Rogers, 1986; Rogers,

2003). Empirical support for this argument is not difficult to find from around the world: the married, more educated, higher-income profile of adopters or potential adopters has been consistent in the case of multimedia cable television (Lin & Jeffres, 1998), interactive television (Leung & Wei, 1998), computers (Lin, 1998), wireless technologies (Wareham, Levy & Shi, 2004), and Internet services (Atkin et al, 1998; Cameron, 2004; Davison & Cotten, 2003; Federal Communications Commission, 2000; Hellwig & Lloyd, 2002; Horrigan & Rainie, 2004; National Office of the Information Economy, 2003; Rhee & Kim, 2004; Rice & Katz, 2003; Rogers, 2004; Zhou & He, 2002c). Although age and sex have no consistent effect in innovation diffusion theory, they have been found to be significant predictors in most of these studies, with the younger male being the typical image of earlier new media adopters.

With all this compelling evidence from new media adoption, it could be predicted with some confidence that SES and other social locators such as sex and age have a considerable effect on how online news is adopted and used. This is consistent with the so-called knowledge gap between people with high and low SES, which was discovered in the late 1960s by Tichenor, Donohue and Olien (1970, pp. 159-160), who summarised it as follows:

> As the infusion of mass media information into a social system increases, segments of the population with higher socio-economic status tend to acquire this information at a faster rate than the lower status segments, so that the gap in knowledge between these segments tends to increase rather than decrease.

While there are some disputes and empirical inconsistencies concerning this gap, a review of over 90 research articles on the issue shows that this is an enduring social phenomenon (cited in Mason & Hacker, 2003).

But how do social locators affect the adoption/use of online news? Again, this can be theoretically elaborated from a socio-structural point of view. As demonstrated above, general media orientation/behaviour is a set of good predictors of media audience formation. But not only are media orientation/behaviour patterns *per se* crucial; so are the factors that shape this pattern. According to McQuail (2000), media orientation is a joint outcome of social background and past media experience, being shaped by two largely constant elements of the social structure: (1) an individual's social situation and his/her associated media-related needs; and (2) the media structure, i.e. the media options that are available and accessible to an individual, given his/her socio-economic situation (McQuail, 2000). In this light, whether an individual is likely to adopt and use online news depends on (1) who he/she is in the social structure and (2) whether online news is accessible and/or available to him/her. The role of online news accessibility/availability will be tackled in the next section. For now, the focus will be on social situations.

Under the socio-structural approach, which derives from uses and gratifications research, social situations generate media-related needs that motivate people to seek some gratifications from the media structure (McQuail, 2000; Weibull, 1985). According to Katz et al (1974), social situations are the source of

o   tensions and conflicts that can be eased via media usage;

o   awareness of problems via mass media exposure;

o   needs derived from impoverished real-life opportunities that can be satisfied via media use;

o   certain values that can be affirmed and reinforced via media use; and

o   the need for sustaining membership of a valued social grouping by being familiar with certain media materials.

For example, people with higher socio-economic statuses tend to use more news and information from the media because their jobs require much information processing and because their network requires them to master certain kinds of professional and social knowledge. In contrast, soap operas are often sought and used by those lacking a real social contact with the outside world such as older people or housewives (McQuail, 1997; McQuail, 2000).

In addition to formulating media-related needs, social locations also link to cognitive capacity and other environmental factors that facilitate information processing. The information gap can be partly explained by "deficits" caused by lack of psychological and social use resources, especially education and education-related matters. More particularly, Tichenor et al (1970) suggested five reasons for the knowledge-gap hypothesis: (1) higher SES people are better in their communication skills, education and the ability to read and comprehend information; (2) higher SES people can find it easier to store information and recognise the topic from background knowledge because of their better education; (3) higher SES people are better in their selective exposure, acceptance and retention; (4) higher SES people have a social context, especially interpersonal networks, that tends to facilitate their information acquisition; and (5) mass media content itself, especially newspaper content, tends to be geared towards middle-class people (see also Ettema & Kline, 1997). Genova and Greenberg (1979) also explained the knowledge gap in terms of differences between interests in news among different SES groups.

Research since then has confirmed these explanations. Graber (1989) noted a trend that people usually expect serious news/information from print media and entertainment content from broadcast sources – and one major difference between the two choices lies in demographic attributes. In the above-cited Dutch study, newspaper entertainment content readers were found to have less education than those reading newspapers for information (Eijck & Rees, 2000). Similarly, Guo (2000) discovered a strong demographic influence on media users' emphasis on comprehensiveness of media coverage. In another study (Hagen, 1994), the well-educated were also found to take television much less seriously than newspapers as an important news source. Meanwhile, information services that require less cognitive skills have been associated with a different picture. For example, Atkin and LaRose (1994) found that phone polling services were more likely to be adopted by lower SES segments of the American public and Neuendorf et al (1998) found that SES did not discriminate between users and non-users of audiotext polling.

Thus, given that the Internet is an information-intensive medium that tends to attract news/information-oriented people with more cognitive capacity, online news adopters can be expected to display a higher SES profile than those using the Internet without adopting online news. There is emerging evidence to support this. Li (2003), for example, found that education and personal income were among the factors that formed the most powerful set of predictors of the adoption likelihood of the electronic newspaper in Taiwan. Weir (1999) found the seven demographic variables of his online sample, including education, race, job and home ownership, were significant predictors of online news usage although they accounted for only 1.5% of total variance in the adoption likelihood of online news among Internet users. Conway (2001) found that the percentage of heavy online news users increased monotonically with educational levels (43% of those with high school completion, 47% of these with some college education, 47% of those with completed college education, and 57% of graduate school experience). In their series of national surveys, Salwen et al (2005) also discovered the same thing: the average amount of formal education and the household income of online news users were significantly higher than that of both Internet users and Internet non-users.

Apart from SES variables, there has been evidence of the significant effect of two other important social locators – age and sex – on online news adoption and use. For age, Li (2003) found that Taiwanese adopters of electronic newspapers were younger than likely adopters, who were in turn younger than non-adopters. None of the relevant studies reported in a review of online news development around the world by Nguyen (2003) contradicts the trend that young people are turning to the web for news and, in some cases, at the expense of traditional news media uses. A similar trend was found in a more recent study by Horrigan (2006). In terms of sex, the body of evidence is "thinner" but does exist. Conway (2001), for example, found that men were much more likely than women to be "cybernewsers" (70% versus 48% of the sample) and were almost twice as likely to use online news more heavily (63% versus 32%). The Pew Research Centre (2004, 2005) also found males were much more likely than females to be online news users. In another study, 49% of male Internet users read news online at least five days a week, compared with only 31% of their female counterpart and the real reason for this gender gap was Internet experience (Weiss et al, 2003). On the basis of this literature, the second research question is raised:

RQ6.2: To what extent do social locators affect online news adoption, attachment and use?

The potential effect of Internet experience on online news adoption/use

Moving beyond the social structure, this section continues to draw on both the socio-structural approach and diffusion theory to argue that experience with the Internet forms another potential powerful set of predictors of online news adoption/use.

The influence of Internet experience can again initially be seen from the diffusion perspective. As noted earlier, the innovation-decision process is a cumulative learning process, in which the perceived relative advantage (benefits) of an innovation is often very small during the initial phase. The willingness to adopt an innovation depends much on how a user experiences it. More exactly, the perceived attributes of an innovation are "likely to be a function of an individual's experience and expertise, which in turn can be a function of social background" (Steinfield et al, 1989, p. 76). In the case of online news, two things can be inferred from this. First, the perceived compatibility, complexity and observability of online news might increase as one becomes more familiar with, more competent in and more exposed to the Internet. This is partly because, as Eastin and LaRose (2000) argued from a Social Cognitive Theory perspective, increased self-efficacy – i.e. "belief in one's capability to organise and execute a particular course of action" (p. 361) – in the use of Internet technologies is causally preceded by prior experience. Second, experience with, and thus potential appreciation of, many relative advantages of online news might be different from one Internet user to another because of differences in their general experience with the Internet. The more ability and knowledge a consumer has acquired to predict the outcome of closely related products, the more likely he/she is to detect superior new products in the same class and thus more likely to adopt it (Hui & Wan, 2004).

In the case of online news, there are many scenarios related to these two points. For instance, an Internet veteran might find it more comfortable and easier to read online news than an Internet novice because the former has more understanding of how the Internet works, is more used to reading onscreen, or simply is more appreciative of its information quality. In another case, some users or potential users, especially those using dial-up Internet services, might consider online news not free at all as they still have to pay for Internet downloads. Slow Internet connections could also contribute to shaping a negative view of online news, or at least a less enjoyable experience with multimedia content. Or because of their immature Internet usage, many people are simply unaware of a wide range of options like RSS feeds or weblogs and so on. To take another example, some people might only find it time-efficient and convenient to combine news reception with other purposes if they already used the Internet substantially for other purposes.

Thus, from the innovation diffusion perspective, Internet experience – broadly understood here as the extent to which an individual can access, uses, masters, enjoys, and depends on the Internet for daily activities – plays a very crucial role in determining online news adoption and the extent to which it is put into full use.

Exactly the same conclusion can be reached from the socio-structural perspective on media use. In this approach, media orientation is formed on the basis of past media experience, which is in turn determined by the media structure. The media structure, according to Weibull (1985), encompasses two components: media institutions and media output. At the quantitative level of analysis, the media structure includes the number of media institutions and the volume of their produced content. At the qualitative level, it consists of the type of media and the type of produced media content. An individual makes two choices – a choice of media institutions and a subsequent choice of content within these institutions' output, both of which must satisfy his/her media-related needs. Because of this choice, the relationship between the media structure and individual users is "a matter of availability or accessibility" (Weibull, 1985, p. 130). This role of media accessibility, however, might be cancelled out to a substantial extent in the case of online news for at least four reasons: (1) the web is a multimedia environment where any type of traditional news/information formats is available; (2) the Internet is space-independent in the sense that news/information from any corner in the world could be approached only after one or a few clicks; (3) as a result of this spatial independence, the Internet is also temporally independent: media content is available for the user to use whenever they want; and (4) most of this content is offered free of charge.

In other words, having Internet access now equals having the power to access the whole global media structure to achieve as much news and information as desired. As Nguyen and Western (2007) argue: "While the free diversity of content/media options will force Internet users to make choices suitable to their social/psychological situations, one could even argue that the media structure no longer plays an important role in determining an Internet user's entry into the world of online news/information". What matters, again, appears to be Internet experience. It is logical to expect that the more Internet access one has and/or the more he/she understands, uses and depends on the Internet, the more likely he/she is to encounter and try online news and thereby to adopt it or use it more substantially. This might happen both intentionally – e.g. a user with more Internet access and use is more likely to think of this medium right away when he/she wants some news – or unintentionally, e.g. a user with more Internet access and use is more likely to be "accidentally informed" by some news items during their Internet usage (via a link to a news story in a friend's email message, or via an unintentionally searched item).

Supportive evidence for this has emerged. Research around the world has shown that people with Internet connection both at work and at home are more likely to use online news more frequently (Nguyen, 2003). In a Swedish study, about 40% of experienced users (4.5 years or more) but only 20% of beginners (less than 1.5 years) read news on the web (Findahl, 2001). In the US, a 2,000-respondent survey by MORI Research in early 2002 found that while only 41% of the general Internet community had been online for at least four years, 62% of online newspaper readers were so (Coats, 2002). Indeed, the effect of Internet experience is not specific to the adoption and use of online news but can be found in the case of many other online services. Hui and Wan (2004), for example, found a positive relationship between online shopping adoption and non-shopping Internet uses – particularly the use of communication and search tools for work and entertainment – in Singapore. Similarly, Howard et al (2001) discovered that veteran Internet users (those with more than three years of Internet experience) behaved significantly differently from less mature users.

One particularly important dimension of Internet experience is bandwidth (broadband versus dial-up connection). Characteristically, broadband means not only a permanent connection but also high speed of data transfer. It saves much surfing time and makes the web truly accessible at any time as the need to dial up through a telephone modem has been eliminated. The high speed also facilitates downloading big files (such as video clips), making web content much more enjoyable and compelling to users, who might quickly embrace the multimedia advantage of the web as the result. In other words, broadband connection substantially improves the willingness to use and attach to the Internet via improving accessibility to the Internet as well as the enjoyability of their Internet usage. Broadband, therefore, has a potentially huge impact on the use frequency and time budget for online activities in general and online news in particular (Nguyen, 2003).

A Pew Research Centre survey of the difference between broadband and dial-up users (Horrigan & Rainie, 2002) unveils this close relationship: (1) high-speed users expanded their online activities to a large extent, doing seven things online (compared with three by dial-up users) on a typical day; and (2) high-speed users are much more active in using the Internet — not only as receivers but also as creators and manipulators of online content (almost six in ten had created or shared files with others on the web and 26% did this on an average day). Other research consolidates these findings. The MORI research cited above discovered that broadband users spend much more time on the Web than dial-up users and indeed go online much more frequently from home (Coats, 2002). In the Swedish study, Internet users with permanent and high-speed connection (1) found fewer technical problems; (2) were more pleased with the availability of online goods and services; (3) felt the web had more to offer them; (4) felt more involved in discussion about information technology; and, (5) did more things than dial-up users (Findahl, 2001). In Australia, broadband users spent 16.3 hours online per week, compared with 10.2 hours among dial-up users, according to Nielsen/NetRatings's Australian Internet and Technology 2004-2005 Report (cited in Sinclair, 2004). Figures from the Australian Bureau of Statistics show that while the amount of downloads among dial-up subscribers remained flat at around 1500 million megabytes from the 2003 September quarter to the March 2005 quarter, its counterpart among non-dial-up users increased steeply from 3000 to over 11 million megabytes during the same period (ABS, 2005a).

The link between news consumption and broadband connection has also been established. In 2001, Market Facts conducted a nation-wide study to discover that American broadband users were much more likely to take advantage of the multimedia nature of the Internet to optimise coverage of breaking news and live events. Accordingly, 23% of the broadband audience relied on the web as a primary source of breaking news while only 6% of dial-up users did so (MSNBC, 2001). The MORI research reveals the link in the other way: readers of online newspapers are more likely to have a home broadband connection than the general Internet user — 37% compared with 25%. In terms of news consumption, these users are three to four times more likely to go online for local and national/world news than the average Internet user (Coats, 2002). The PRC's broadband-difference survey results in an even more striking fact: on any given day 46% of broadband users received their news online while only 40% read newspapers (Horrigan and Rainie, 2002). During the first six days of the 2003 Iraq War, broadband users (and Internet veterans) got more online news than any other group. In particular, nearly half of broadband users got war news online (Rainie et al, 2003). Also within the Pew Internet & American Life Project, a recent substantial study on the effect of broadband on online news consumption (Horrigan, 2006) found the following:

- o 43% of broadband users got online news "yesterday", compared with 26% of dial-up users.

- o The increase in home broadband connections accounted for about 25% of the increase in the growth in daily online news consumption between 2002 and 2005.

- o Young broadband users (in the under-36 age group) are likely to consult more news sources online than their dial-up counterpart.

The third research question arises from all this body of research:

RQ6.3: To what extent do different aspects of Internet experience affect online news adoption, attachment and use?

Data analysis methods

To answer the above research questions, this chapter continues to employ a wide range of dependent and independent variables from the 2004 survey, briefly described below:

Independent variables

- o Social locators include age, sex, and five SES variables: education, household income, job types and employment status, and the nature of residence areas (rural areas, small towns, large towns and metropolitan areas). To simplify the data analysis, the initial nine categories of job types were recoded into active professionals (including professionals and administrators/managers who were still in the labour force); active white-collar workers (working clerical/sales and services personnel); active blue-collar workers (working tradesperson/skilled worker, agriculture worker, and labourer) and those not in the labour force (including unemployed or retired people, students and home-duties workers).

o News orientation/behaviour was represented by four main groups: (1) general news usage (time spending and frequency); (2) the perceived need to follow eight different types of news content (national/state politics; international affairs; economics, including business and finance; sports and entertainment; science, technology and health; social problems such as crime, disasters and accidents; culture and the arts; and local community affairs); (3) other psychological indicators of news orientation (the degree of enjoying keeping up with the news; self-identification as news junkies; and the degree of agreement/disagreement with two statements: "News is not as important as it once was" and "I wish I had more time to follow the news"); and (4) news exchange behaviours (frequency of discussing news with peers via the telephone and when meeting them). A mean index of overall news need was constructed based on the eight news-need variables, with a Cronbach alpha of .67. A composite variable for news exchange combining face-to-face and telephone news discussion was also created to simplify the data in multivariate models.

o Experience with the Internet was measured by Internet accessibility (work only, home only, other place only or a combination of some or all of these); broadband accessibility; years of Internet usage; perceived levels of understanding the Internet; perceived importance of the Internet in daily life; frequency of Internet usage; frequency of using the Internet for six non-news purposes (entertainment and relaxation; e-commerce; personal contact; interaction with other online users via forums or chat rooms etc; searching non-news information for work/study; and searching non-news information for other purposes). Within these, two indices were created: (1) a mean index of overall non-news Internet usage based on the six non-news variables (alpha = .65); and (2) a standardised mean index for most of the above variables (alpha = .81). The latter was standardised because its individual components had different response categories.

Dependent variables

The response variables chosen for this analysis only include adoption, use frequency and perceived importance of online news in Internet usage. These are the central cognitive and behavioural indicators of online news attachment and use. The other three aspects of attachment and use considered in the previous chapter (being a fan of online news, perception of the Internet as the best medium, and time spending on online news in the most recent session) were left out to avoid a cumbersome analysis. At the end of the analysis, the appreciation of online news features – based on a mean index of the appreciation of the nine online news features explored in the previous chapter – were explored again in relation to the investigated socio-structural variables.

Statistical procedures

The data analysis was conducted in two steps. In the first step, hypothesis testing for means and proportions was performed for each of the socio-structural variables to explore its bivariate relationship with the dependent variable. Although bivariate relationships between socio-structural factors and the above three aspects of online news adoption/use might reflect the existence of other correlated variables, I still like to provide them here as they might have important implications for many readers of this book. In the second step, all relevant variables were included in multivariate logistic regression models to explore the unique contribution of each relevant independent variable to the response variable after relevant statistical control. This will help to find out the primary socio-structural factors that contribute to the three mentioned dimensions of online news adoption/use. As the index indicating the appreciation of online news features is a continuous variable, the multivariate relationships between it and socio-structural factors were examined with linear regression.

During data analysis, most of the social-locator variables were dichotomised to allow proportion difference tests or dummy-coded for logistic and linear regression models. Some other original variables were recoded to allow some numerical measures (e.g. "daily" = 30 times/month; "several times a week" = 15 times/month; "several times/month" = 4 times/month; and "less often" = 1 time/month). All recoded variables will be explained in the bottom of their tables.

Results

As in Chapter 5, this section will present the findings in relation to the three sub-RQs raised above. Wherever necessary, additional details on statistical measures in the tables will be provided.

News orientation/behaviour and online news adoption

Table 6.1 shows the bivariate relationships between different aspects of news orientation/behaviour and the adoption likelihood of online news. The entries for users and non-users of online news are typically mean scores on a particular response variable, except for the variables measuring self-identification of as a "news junkie" and news use over 30 minutes per day. The entries of these variables are proportions. The significance tests are two-sample z-tests for differences in means and proportions.

Table 6.1: Bivariate relationships between news orientation/behaviour and online news adoption among Internet adopters (z-tests for differences in means and proportions)

	Non-users	Users	p-value
Specific news needs[a]			
National/state politics	1.38	1.60	.002
International affairs	1.67	1.91	<.001
Economics (including business/finance)	1.25	1.38	.09
Sports and entertainment	1.64	1.68	.71
Science/technology and health	1.66	1.68	.80
Social problems (crime/disasters/accidents)	1.76	1.71	.52
Culture and the arts	1.33	1.16	.02
Local community affairs	1.91	1.66	<.001
Overall news need[b]	1.57	1.60	.54
Other news orientation indicators			
Enjoying keeping up with the news[c]	2.43	2.64	<.001
Self-identifying as news junkies (proportions)	0.31	.45	.001
News is not as important as it once was[d]	2.23	2.16	.45
I wish I had more time to follow the news[d]	2.96	3.17	.01
News use levels			
Frequency of news usage (times/month)[e]	27.20	28.33	.03
Over 30 minutes/day on news (proportions)	0.55	0.56	.74
News discussion with peers			
On the phone[f]	1.59	1.76	.01
When meeting them[f]	1.70	1.86	.02

(a) 0 = "Not at all strong"; 2 = "Not very strong"; 3 = "Strong"; 4 = "Very strong"; (b) Mean index of needs for all the eight news categories; alpha = .67; (c) 0 = "Not at all"; 1 = "Not much"; 2 = "Some"; 3 = "A good deal"; (d) 1 = "Strongly disagree"; 2 = "Disagree"; 3 = "Neutral"; 4 = "Agree"; 5 = "Strongly agree"; (e) "Every day" = 30 times/month; "Several times a week" = 15 times/month; "Several times a month" = 4 times/month; "Less often" = 1 time/month; (f) 0 = "Never"; 1 = "Not very often"; 2 = "Often"; 3 = "Very often"; 420 ≤ n ≤ 528

The picture is quite mixed, with some news orientation/behaviour variables appearing to have a significant positive effect and quite a few others being insignificant or significantly negative predictors. Regarding the needs to follow specific categories of news, while there was no statistically significant difference between online news adopters and those using the Internet without adopting online news (hereinafter referred to as non-adopters or non-users) in their overall news need (1.60 versus 1.57, $p = .54$), individual news categories show different patterns. While adopters were not significantly different from non-adopters in their need to follow economic news (1.38 versus 1.25 on a 0-4 scale; $p = .09$), sports and entertainment news (1.68 versus 1.64; $p = .71$), science/technology and health (1.68 versus 1.66; $p = .80$) and social problems (1.71 versus 1.76; $p = .52$), the former reported

o a significantly stronger need for news about national/state politics (1.60 versus 1.37; $p < .001$) and international affairs (1.91 versus 1.67; $p < .001$); and

o a significantly weaker need for news about local community affairs (1.66 versus 1.91; $p < .001$) and culture and the arts (1.16 versus 1.33; $p = .02$).

This mixed picture of news needs makes sense, given the information-intensive nature of online news. More particularly, given the long-observed trend that people tend to use information-intensive sources like newspapers for serious news and information (Graber, 1989), it is understandable that online news, which is at least as information-intensive as newspapers, among those with a stronger need for hard news types like national/state politics and international affairs and with less interest in "softer" news like culture and the arts. This pattern is consistent with innovation diffusion research, which has shown that earlier adopters of innovations are more cosmopolite – i.e. they tend to be more oriented to the outside world (Rogers, 2003). As can be seen from Table 6.1, the highest news need score in the case of non-users was 1.91 for local community affairs while its counterpart among users (also 1.91, coincidentally) was given to international affairs. Conversely, while nonusers scored 1.67 on international affairs, users scored 1.66 (virtually the same value) on local affairs. Regarding the other psychological aspects of news orientation, we can see the following:

o 45% of users – compared with 31% of nonusers ($p < .001$) – identified themselves as "news junkies" (defined in the questionnaire as those "who would miss the news very much if [they] couldn't get it for a substantial time").

o Users reported a higher mean level of enjoying keeping up with the news (2.64 versus 2.43 out of three, p < .001).

o Users tended to feel more restrained by their time budget for news consumption, scoring a mean of 3.17 (versus 2.96) on a five-point Likert scale of agreement/disagreement in response to the statement "I wish I had more time to follow the news".

o Users were less likely to agree that "news is not important as it once was" (2.16 versus 2.23) but this difference was not significant (p = .45).

In terms of news use behaviours, while users received news more frequently (28.3 times/month versus 27.2 times/month, p = .03), there was no statistically significant difference in the amount of time the two groups spent on news consumption: 55% of non-users and 56% of users spent more than half an hour a day on news (p = .74). As for news exchange, users discussed news and current affairs with their peers more often than non-users, either when talking on the phone (1.76 versus 1.59, p = .01) or when meeting them (1.86 versus 1.70, p =.02).

When all these news orientation/behaviour factors are controlled in a multivariate model (shown in the second column in Table 6.4), enjoying keeping up with the news was the only significant unique contributor to adoption (coefficient = .43, p = .03). Being a news junkie almost reached the conventional significance level (coefficient = .41, p = .06). Collectively, these variables form a good set of predictors, with a LR chi2 statistic value of 27.2 and an associated p of less than .001.

News orientation/behaviour and online news use frequency

As can be seen from Table 6.2, there was, again, no significant difference in overall news need between frequent and infrequent users but a stronger pattern of serious news needs was found among frequent users: 1.68 versus 1.42 (p < .05) in the need for news about international affairs; .99 versus 1.73 (p = .03) for national/state politics news; and 1.52 versus 1.24 (p = .03) for economic news, which was not a significant discriminator in the case of adoption likelihood. Meanwhile, the need for news about culture and the arts remained as a negative predictor of online news use frequency, being significantly weaker among the frequent users than their counterpart (1.05 versus 1.33, p = .01). No significant difference was found in the news categories of sports and entertainment; science, technology and health; social problems; and local community affairs. The no longer significant effect of the need for local news on online news frequency is understandable because the level of being oriented to wider community (cosmopoliteness) can affect online news adoption in diffusion theory but is not necessarily a discriminator of the use level among those who already adopt it.

Table 6.2: Bivariate relationships between news orientation/behaviour and frequency of online news usage (z-tests for differences in means and proportions)

	Infrequent users	Frequent users	p-value
Specific news needs[a]			
National/state politics	1.42	1.68	<.05
International affairs	1.73	1.99	.03
Economics (including business/finance)	1.24	1.52	.02
Sports and entertainment	1.70	1.61	.54
Science/technology and health	1.75	1.64	.33
Social problems (crime/disasters/accidents)	1.78	1.71	.58
Culture and the arts	1.33	1.05	.01
Local community affairs	1.75	1.59	.20
Overall news need[b]	1.59	1.60	.84
Other news orientation indicators			
Enjoying keeping up with the news[c]	2.43	2.72	.001
Self-identifying as news junkies (proportions)	0.37	0.51	.06
News is not as important as it once was[d]	2.36	2.15	.19
I wish I had more time to follow the news[d]	3.12	3.26	.30
News use levels			
Frequency of news usage (times/month)[e]	27.40	28.60	.10
Over 30 minutes/day on news (proportions)	0.64	0.56	.25
News discussions with peers			
On the phone[f]	1.64	1.84	.09
When meeting them[f]	1.54	2.00	<.001

(a) 0 = "Not at all strong"; 2 = "Not very strong"; 3 = "Strong"; 4 = "Very strong"; (b) Mean index of needs for all the eight news categories; alpha = .67; (c) 0 = "Not at all"; 1 = "Not much"; 2 = "Some"; 3 = "A good deal"; (d) 1 = "Strongly disagree"; 2 = "Disagree"; 3 = "Neutral"; 4 = "Agree"; 5 = "Strongly agree"; (e) "Every day" = 30 times/month; "Several times a week" = 15 times/month; "Several times a month" = 4 times/month; "Less often" = 1 time/month; (f) 0 = "Never"; 1 = "Not very often"; 2 = "Often"; 3 = "Very often"; $177 \leq n \leq 211$

In terms of general news use, both time spending on news per day and its use frequency were not significant predictors of online news frequency. As for news exchange behaviours, face-to-face discussion of news and current affairs with peers was still a significant distinguisher between infrequent and frequent online news users (1.54 versus 2.00) but phone discussion was not (1.64 versus 1.84, p = .09). Of the other four indicators of news orientation, enjoying keeping up with the news was the only significant predictor of online news use frequency (2.43 among infrequent users and 2.72 among the others, p = .001). Although not significant, being a news junkie was quite an important factor: 37% of infrequent users identified themselves as news fans while 51% of the other group did so (with a near-significance p-value of .06). Unlike adopters and non-adopters, frequent and infrequent users were not distinguished in terms of their feeling of not having enough time for news consumption (3.26 versus 3.12, p = .30). Finally, while frequent users were less likely to agree that "news is not important as it once was" (2.15 versus 2.36), this difference was not significant (p = .19).

In the multivariate model (the third column in Table 6.4), news orientation/behaviour again formed a distinctive set of predictors of online news use frequency, as shown by the statistically significant likelihood-ratio chi-squared statistic (26.5 with eight degrees of freedom and p < .001). Enjoying keeping up with the news continued to be a significant predictor after being controlled for the other variables (coefficient = .82, p = .02). Unlike in the case of adoption likelihood, the level of news exchange with peers was now a significant contributor (coefficient = .87, p = .008). Interestingly, however, time spending on news per day was significantly negatively associated with online news frequency (coefficient = -.76, p = .05).

News orientation/behaviour and perceived importance of online news

As for the perceived importance of online news (Table 6.3), the needs for news about national/state politics, international affairs and economics were again positive predictors, scoring respectively 1.79, 2.10 and 1.53 among those who saw online news as an important or essential part of the Internet use, compared respectively with 1.31 (p < .001), 1.65 (p < .001) and 1.20 (p = .005) among those who did not. In addition, the need for science, technology and health news was now significantly stronger (1.77) among the former group than the latter (1.50, p = .01). As a result, despite the fact that there was no significant difference in the needs for the other news categories, the overall news need (not significant in the cases of adoption and use frequency) was now a significant positive predictor of perceived importance of online news (1.48 versus 1.66, p = .001).

This finding is understandable: perceived importance is a cognitive dimension of online news attachment and is not necessarily reflected in overt use behaviours. It is rather a

Table 6.3: Bivariate relationships between news orientation/behaviour and perceived importance of online news in Internet use (z-tests for differences in means and proportions)

	Not important	Important	p-value
Specific news needs[a]			
National/state politics	1.31	1.79	<.001
International affairs	1.65	2.10	<.001
Economics (including business/finance)	1.20	1.53	.005
Sports and entertainment	1.65	1.65	1.00
Science/technology and health	1.50	1.77	.01
Social problems (crime/disasters/accidents)	1.62	1.78	.14
Culture and the arts	1.20	1.13	.56
Local community affairs	1.76	1.56	.08
Overall news need[b]	1.48	1.66	.001
Other news orientation indicators			
Enjoying keeping up with the news[c]	2.56	2.69	.12
Self-identifying as news junkies (proportions)	0.29	0.56	<.001
News is not as important as it once was[d]	2.26	2.11	.36
I wish I had more time to follow the news[d]	3.03	3.25	.09
News use levels			
Frequency of news usage (times/month)[e]	26.90	29.40	<.001
Over 30 minutes/day on news (proportions)	0.54	0.58	.55
News discussions with peers			
On the phone[f]	1.52	1.89	<.001
When meeting them[f]	1.57	2.04	<.001

(a) 0 = "Not at all strong"; 2 = "Not very strong"; 3 = "Strong"; 4 = "Very strong"; (b) Mean index of needs for all the eight news categories; alpha = .67; (c) 0 = "Not at all"; 1 = "Not much"; 2 = "Some"; 3 = "A good deal"; (d) 1 = "Strongly disagree"; 2 = "Disagree"; 3 = "Neutral"; 4 = "Agree"; 5 = "Strongly agree"; (e) "Every day" = 30 times/month; "Several times a week" = 15 times/month; "Several times a month" = 4 times/month; "Less often" = 1 time/month; (f) 0 = "Never"; 1 = "Not very often"; 2 = "Often"; 3 = "Very often"; $179 \leq n \leq 213$

result of an internal psychological process in which, for some background reasons, people feel the need to follow the news is somewhat indispensable. This suggests that those seeing online news as important or essential in their Internet use are serious news users, looking for serious news from a "serious" news medium. It is not a matter of enjoyment but of something like a "moral imperative". This seems to be confirmed by the fact that while there was no difference in the mean levels of enjoying keeping up with the news between those who attached an importance to online news and those who did not, the former were twice more likely than the latter (57% versus 29%, p < .001) to "miss the news" if they could not get it for a substantial time.

As for news behaviours, frequency of news usage was a significant positive predictor of perceived importance (26.9 versus 29.4 times/month, p < .001) but time spending was not, further affirming the "moral imperative" to follow the news regularly (albeit with less time) among those who see online news as an important/essential part of their

Table 6.4: Multivariate logistic regression analyses for the effect of news orientation/behaviour on the adoption, use and perceived importance of online news (regression coefficients)

	Adoption (n = 514)	Use frequency (n = 205)	Perceived importance (n = 207)
Overall news need[a]	-0.45	-0.94$^{\neq}$	0.48
Enjoying keeping up with the news	0.43*	0.82*	-0.68
Being a "news junkie"	0.41$^{\neq}$	0.14	0.80*
News is not as important as it once was	0.03	-0.12	-0.05
I wish I had more time to follow the news	0.15	-0.02	0.23
News usage frequency	0.02	0.02	0.12**
Spending over 30 minutes/day on news	-0.32	-0.76*	-0.54
Discuss news & current affairs with peers[b]	0.23	0.87**	0.78**
LR chi2 (8)[c]	27.20***	26.54***	39.74***

(a) Mean index of needs for all the eight news categories; alpha = .67; (b) Composite variable of discussing news and current affairs via the telephone and face-to-face; (c) Likelihood Ratio Chi-squared Tests with 8 degrees of freedom, categories for dependent variables as in Chapter 5; * p ≤.05; ** p ≤ .01; *** p ≤ .001; $^{\neq}$ p-value marginally significant.

Internet use. Indeed, these people scored higher than their counterpart in their response to "I wish I had more time to follow the news" (3.25 versus 3.03), although this difference is only marginally significant (p = .09). The two variables indicating news exchange also came as significant predictors (1.52 versus 1.89 and 1.57 versus 2.04, both at p < .001).

When all news orientation/behaviours variables were examined together (the fourth column in Table 6.4), there were three significant positive predictors of perceived importance of online news, with general frequency of news use being the most significant (coefficient = .12, p = .007), followed by news exchange (coefficient = .78, p = .01) and being a news junkie (coefficient = .80, p = .02). Collectively, the logistic regression model was a good fit, with a likelihood-ratio chi-square (8df) of 39.7 (p < .001).

Social locators and online news adoption

Table 6.5 shows a strong pattern of socio-economic differences between online news adopters and those using the Internet without adopting online news. It is clear that online news is still mainly used by socio-economically advantaged segments of the population. Of the relevant SES variables, household income was the only one that did not statistically significantly discriminate the two groups: 54% of nonusers and 58% of users having a before-tax household income of over $50,000 per year (p = .28). The patterns for the other SES variables are as follows:

- Nearly three quarters (72%) of users and only more than half (55%) of nonusers were living in a metropolitan area (p < .001). In more detail, 12% of users living in a large town, 7% in a small town and 9% in a rural area – their respective counterpart in the non-user groups were 17%, 9% and 19% (data not shown).

- 67% of users were working full-time, compared with 51% of nonusers doing so (p < .001). In total, 84% of users were active in labour force, compared with 74% of the other group (data not shown).

- 63% of users identified themselves as either professionals (including administrators) or white-collar workers (i.e. those in clerical/sales and services occupations) – compared with 52% of nonusers doing so (p = .01).

- 42% of users held a university/CAE or postgraduate degree while 34% of nonusers did so; but this difference only approached conventional significance level (p < .06).

Table 6.5: Bivariate relationships between social locators and online news adoption among Internet adopters (z-tests for proportion differences)

	Non-users	Users	p-value
Personal background			
Being a male	.49	.66	<.001
Being less than 50 years of age	.68	.79	<.001
Socio-economic status			
Living in a metropolitan area	.55	.72	<.001
Working full-time	.51	.67	<.001
Being an active white-collar or professional	.52	.63	.01
Having a university degree (graduate or postgraduate)	.34	.42	.06
Having household income of over $50,000/year	.54	.58	.28

501 ≤ n ≤ 519

As for the last two demographic variables, the online news world seems to be dominated by younger people and males. In particular, 66% of users and 49% of non-users were males, ($p < .001$); and 79% of users were from 18 to 49 years of age – compared with 68% of the other group were ($p < .001$). Indeed, when the users were split into age groups, there was a clear linear downward trend of online news adoption likelihood along the increase of age: 32% in the 18-29 age range; 24% in their 30s; 21% in their 40s; 14% in their 50s; 5% in their 60s; and 4% being 70 or over (these data are not shown).

To explore the multivariate relationship between social locators and online news adoption, a number of dummy variables for social location were created. For living areas, three variables indicating a small town, a large town and a metropolitan area were used with living in a rural area as the reference category. For job types, absence from the labour force was the baseline with dummy variables for blue-collars, white-collars and professionals. In terms of educational levels, no completion of year-12 education was the reference category, with dummy variables for year 12, certificate, graduate degree and postgraduate degree. Finally, household incomes in the ranges of $20K-$50K, over $50K-$75K, over $75K-$100K and over $100K were compared with less than $20K. The multivariate results (first column in Table 6.8) show that the model is a good fit (LR chi2 df[16] = 19.1, p < .001), with four significant individual predictors of the adoption likelihood of online news: age (coefficient = -.03, p < .001), sex (coefficient = .77, p < .001), living areas (coefficient for metropolitan = .85, p < .01) and job types (coefficient for professionals = .63, p < .03). None of the dummy variables indicating education and household incomes had a statistically significant effect.

Social locators and online news use frequency

The above effect of social locators, however, largely disappears in the case of use frequency (Table 6.6). Of the seven variables, sex was the only significant predictor of online news use frequency, with 53% of infrequent users and 70% of frequent users being males (p = .02). The p-values associated with the other variables are very high, ranging from .32 to .80. In the multivariate model (second column in Table 6.8), these variables did not collectively form a good model to predict use frequency (LR chi2 [16 df] = 22.7, p = .12), although sex and education were marginally significant predictors with p-values on the verge of the conventional significance level of .05.

Table 6.6: Bivariate relationships between social locators and frequency of online news usage (z-tests for proportion differences)

	Infrequent users	Frequent users	p-value
Personal background			
Being a male	.53	.70	.02
Being less than 50 years of age	.77	.81	.55
Socio-economic status			
Living in a metropolitan area	.67	.73	.32
Working full-time	.85	.87	.80
Being an active white-collar or professional	.67	.65	.74
Having at least a university degree	.39	.40	.84
Having household income of over $50,000/year	.55	.59	.60

202 ≤ n ≤ 212

Social locators and perceived importance of online news

Turning to the perceived importance of online news, a fairly similar pattern was found as in the case of use frequency (Table 6.7). Regional location was the only significant predictor of perceived importance (77% of those saying news is an important or essential part of their Internet usage were living in a metropolitan area – compared with 64% of their counterpart).

In the multivariate model, the significant effect of living areas in the bivariate relationship disappeared while education and incomes became significant, with none of their relevant dummy variables being associated with an insignificant p-value. The model is a good fit, with LR chi2 df(16) = 37.7 and p < .01, allowing us to conclude that the typical user who sees online news as an important/essential part of his/her Internet use is likely to be one with at least year-12 education or a smaller household income. The second finding is counter-intuitive but may reflect a strong commitment to online news among a small subsample of low-income earners in this dataset.

Table 6.7: Bivariate relationships between social locators and perceived importance of online news in Internet usage (z-tests for proportion differences)

	Not important	Important	p-value
Personal background			
Being a male	.67	.65	.74
Being less than 50 years of age	.81	.78	.60
Socio-economic status			
Living in a metropolitan area	.64	.77	.04
Working full-time	.84	.83	.93
Being an active white-collar or professional	.63	.62	.95
Having a university degree (graduate or postgraduate)	.37	.46	.20
Having household income of over $50,000/year	.63	.54	.21

203 ≤ n ≤ 213

Table 6.8: Multivariate logistic regression analyses for the effect of social locators on the adoption, use and perceived importance of online news (regression coefficients)

	Adoption (n = 509)	Use frequency (n = 205)	Perceived importance (n = 206)
Sex	0.77***	0.73≠	-1.12
Age	-0.03***	0.00	0.02
Small town	0.56	0.59	-0.01
Large town	0.43	-0.07	0.08
Metropolitan area	0.85**	0.41	0.72
Blue-collars	-0.28	-0.29	-0.27
White-collars	0.26	-0.01	0.78
Professionals	0.63*	0.17	0.29
Year 12	0.26	1.12	1.78*
Certificate	0.38	1.14	1.33*
Graduate degree	0.41	0.98	1.91**
Postgraduate degree	0.52	1.52≠	2.38**
$20K-$50K	0.14	-1.29	-2.20**
Over $50K-$75K	-0.32	-0.57	-2.38***
Over $75K-$100K	-0.20	1.22	-2.58***
Over $100K	0.08	-1.02	-2.43**
LR Chi2 (16)	69.13***	22.74	37.70**

*Likelihood Ratio Chi-squared Tests with 16 degrees of freedom, categories for dependent variables as in Chapter 5; all independent variables were dummy-coded, except age; * $p \leq .05$; ** $p \leq .01$; *** $p \leq .001$, ≠ p approaching .05.*

Experience with the Internet and online news adoption

Table 6.9 presents the bivariate relationships between online news adoption and different aspects of Internet experience. None of the presented tests resulted in a p-value of .001 or higher, suggesting an extremely strong pattern of effect of all the Internet experience-related variables on online news the likelihood of online news adoption. More importantly, the values (means or proportions) in the column representing non-users were consistently smaller than their corresponding values in the users' column – i.e. online news adoption likelihood increased along with higher scores in every aspect of Internet experience. The particular differences are as follows:

  o   46% of nonusers versus 75% of users had Internet access at more than one place.

Table 6.9: Bivariate relationships between Internet experience and online news adoption (z-tests for differences in means and proportions)

	Nonusers	Users	p-value
Internet access at more than one place (proportions)	0.46	0.75	<.001
Having broadband access (proportions)	0.47	0.70	<.001
Broadband access at more than one place (proportions)	0.09	0.22	<.001
Years of Internet usage[a]	4.01	5.24	<.001
Perceived level of understanding the Internet[b]	2.12	2.67	<.001
Perceived importance of the Internet in daily life[c]	2.53	3.26	<.001
Frequency of Internet usage (times/month)[d]	17.46	25.00	<.001
Using Internet for entertainment and relaxation[e]	0.83	1.29	<.001
Using Internet for e-commerce	1.18	1.68	<.001
Using Internet for personal contact (emailing/messaging etc.)	2.03	2.53	<.001
Using the Internet for interaction with other online users (attending forums, chat rooms etc.)	0.47	0.78	<.001
Using the Internet to search non-news information for work and study	1.48	2.15	<.001
Using Internet to search non-news information for other purposes	1.52	2.05	<.001
Overall use of online non-news services[f]	1.08	1.53	<.001
Overall experience with the Internet[g]	-0.17	0.40	<.001

(a) "One year or less" = .5 year; "Over 1-2 years" = 1.5 years; "Over 2-3 years" = 2.5 years; "Over 3-5 years" = 4 years; "Over 5 years" = 7.5 years; (b) 1 = "Not very much"; 2 = "Some"; 3 = "A good deal" (c) 1 = "Unlikely to become an essential part of my life"; 2 = "Might become an essential part of my life"; 3 = "Will become an essential part of my life"; 4 = "Is an essential part of my life"; (d) "Every day" = 30 times/month; "Several times a week" = 15 times/month; "Several times a month" = 4 times/month; "Less often" = 1 time/month; From (e) to before (f): 0 = "Never"; 1= "Not very often"; 2 = "Often"; 3 = "Very often" (f) Mean index for frequencies of using the above six non-news services; alpha = .65; (g) Standardised mean index of all the above variables, except broadband accessibility; alpha = .81; 501 ≤ n ≤ 522

o Seven in ten users had broadband access – compared with less than half of users (47%) doing so. In addition, the former were twice more likely to have broadband access at more than one place than the later (22% versus 9%).

o Users had been online for an average of 63 months (5.24 years) and non-users 48 months (4 years).

o Users used the Internet much more frequently than non-users (25 times/month versus 17.45 times/month).

o Users utilised any non-news function of the Internet on more regular basis than non-users. As a result, the overall use of non-news Internet services was higher among users (1.53) than non-users (1.08). It is worth noting here that the net differences in the means were greater in the case of the two non-news information functions than in any other (a difference of .67 for "searching non-news information for work and study" and .53 for "searching non-news information for other purposes" – compared with a net difference between users and non-users of .50 in the case of using the Internet for personal contact, which is the highest of all the non-information functions). This suggests that online news adopters are not only news-oriented as shown above but are more information-oriented in general.

o Users reported more Internet expertise (2.67 out of three with three indicating understanding the Internet "a good deal") than non-users (2.12)

o Users attached more importance to the Internet in their daily life (3.26 versus 2.53).

o Users reported more self-efficacy (perceived levels of understanding the Internet) than nonusers (2.67 versus 2.12).

As the result of these findings, users scored much higher in overall experience with the Internet than non users. The standardised score of overall Internet experience was negative (-.17) for non-users and positive (.40) for users – i.e. non-users' overall Internet experience was below the mean (zero) while that of users was fairly high above it.

Again, all the variables were included in a logistic regression model (shown in second column in Table 6.12). To simplify the data, the non-news Internet use index was used instead of its individual components and to avoid overlapping effect, having broadband access at more than one place is not included. Two factors came out as significant predictors of adoption: perceived understanding of the Internet (coefficient = .58, p = .006) and the non-news Internet usage index (coefficient = 2.71, p < .001). Together, all these aspects of Internet experience forms a good model to predict online news adoption (p < .001).

Experience with the Internet and online news use frequency

Table 6.10 shows that although frequent users of online news scored higher than infrequent users in all of the above Internet-experience indicators. The effect on use frequency of a substantial number of these indicators, however, is not statistically

Table 6.10: Bivariate relationships between Internet experience and frequency of online news usage (z-tests for differences in means and proportions)

	Infrequent users	Frequent users	p-value
Internet access at more than one place (proportions)	0.71	0.75	.47
Broadband access (proportions)	0.60	0.74	<.05
Broadband access at more than one place (proportions)	0.13	0.25	.06
Years of Internet usage[a]	4.74	5.66	.008
Perceived level of understanding the Internet[b]	2.40	2.78	<.001
Perceived importance of the Internet in daily life[c]	3.11	3.31	.21
Frequency of Internet usage (times/month)[d]	19.60	27.10	<.001
Using Internet for entertainment and relaxation[e]	1.18	1.36	.24
Using Internet for e-commerce	1.68	1.69	.98
Using Internet for personal contact (emailing/messaging etc.)	2.45	2.63	.06
Using the Internet for interaction with other online users (attending forums, chat rooms etc.)	0.74	0.76	.90
Using the Internet to search non-news information for work and study	1.87	2.31	.001
Using Internet to search non-news information for other purposes	1.79	2.24	<.001
Overall use of online non-news services[f]	1.44	1.58	.10
Overall experience with the Internet[g]	0.21	0.51	<.001

(a) "One year or less" = .5 year; "Over 1-2 years" = 1.5 years; "Over 2-3 years" = 2.5 years; "Over 3-5 years" = 4 years; "Over 5 years" = 7.5 years; (b) 1 = "Not very much"; 2 = "Some"; 3 = "A good deal" (c) 1 = "Unlikely to become an essential part of my life"; 2 = "Might become an essential part of my life"; 3 = "Will become an essential part of my life"; 4 = "Is an essential part of my life"; (d) "Every day" = 30 times/month; "Several times a week" = 15 times/month; "Several times a month" = 4 times/month; "Less often" = 1 time/month; From (e) to before (f): 0 = "Never"; 1= "Not very often"; 2 = "Often"; 3 = "Very often" (f) Mean index for frequencies of using the above six non-news services; alpha = .65; (g)Standardised mean index of all the above variables, except broadband accessibility; alpha = .81; 209≤ n ≤211

significant. These are having Internet access at more than one place (71% versus 75%, p = .47); having broadband access at more than one place (13% versus 25%, p < .06); perceived importance of the Internet (3.11 versus 3.31, p = .21); using the Internet for entertainment and relaxation (1.18 versus 1.36, p = .24); using the Internet for e-commerce services (almost identical); using the Internet for personal contact (2.45 versus 2.63, p = .06); using the Internet for interaction with other online news users (.74 versus .76, p = .90); and overall non-news Internet usage (1.44 versus 1.58, p = .10). However, strong relationships existed between use frequency and the other variables. In particular, frequent users

- o were more likely to have broadband access (74% versus 60%, p < .05);
- o had more years of Internet usage (5.66 versus 4.74 years, p < .01);
- o had more perceived understanding of the Internet (2.40 versus 2.78, p < .001);
- o used the Internet more often (27.1 versus 19.6 times/month, p < .001); and
- o used the Internet more often to search non-news information for work/study (2.31 versus 1.87, p = .001) as well as for other purposes (2.24 versus 1.79, p < .001).

Overall, frequent users had significantly more experience with the Internet than infrequent users, scoring .51 and .21 respectively on the overall Internet experience index (p < .001). However, the gap is narrowed down when compared with its counterpart in the case of adoption likelihood. It is also worth noting that unlike non-adopters, infrequent users scored a positive value on the standardised index.

In the multivariate model for use frequency (third column, Table 6.12), there are three notable findings. First, despite being insignificant in the bivariate relationship, non-news Internet usage was a significant positive predictor in the multivariate model (coefficient = .94, p = .02). Second, again, perceived level of understanding the Internet had a significant contribution with (coefficient = .86, p = .01). The third factor, frequency of Internet usage, was the most significant, with coefficient = .10 and p < .001. Together, the model is a good fit, with a likelihood ratio chi-square value with seven degrees of freedom of 57.7 and a p-value of less than .001.

Experience with the Internet and perceived importance of online news
Table 6.11 displays the individual effect of the above variables on perceived importance of online news in Internet usage. Of the 15 relevant variables, six were not significant: having broadband access, perceived level of understanding the Internet, perceived importance of the Internet in daily life, using the Internet for ecommerce, for personal contact and for interaction with other users. Compared with their counterpart, those who perceived online news as an important or essential part of their Internet usage

- o were more likely to have Internet access at more than one place (.66 versus .45, p < .001);

Table 6.11: Bivariate relationships between Internet experience and frequency of online news usage (z-tests for differences in means and proportions)

	Not important	Important	p-value
Internet access at more than one place (proportions)	0.45	0.66	<.001
Having broadband access (proportions)	0.63	0.74	.07
Broadband access at more than one place (proportions)	0.10	0.30	.001
Years of Internet usage[a]	4.93	5.60	.04
Perceived level of understanding the Internet[b]	2.58	2.72	.07
Perceived importance of the Internet in daily life[c]	3.14	3.32	.21
Frequency of Internet usage (times/month)[d]	23.03	26.17	.004
Using Internet for entertainment and relaxation[e]	1.02	1.44	.002
Using Internet for e-commerce	1.62	1.71	.48
Using Internet for personal contact (emailing/messaging etc.)	2.45	2.61	.08
Using the Internet for interaction with other online users (attending forums, chat rooms etc.)	0.66	0.86	.16
Using the Internet to search non-news information for work and study	1.67	2.46	<.001
Using Internet to search non-news information for other purposes	1.66	2.30	<.001
Overall use of online non-news services[f]	1.35	1.66	<.001
Overall experience with the Internet[g]	0.21	0.53	<.001

(a) "One year or less" = .5 year; "Over 1-2 years" = 1.5 years; "Over 2-3 years" = 2.5 years; "Over 3-5 years" = 4 years; "Over 5 years" = 7.5 years; (b) 1 = "Not very much"; 2 = "Some"; 3 = "A good deal" (c) 1 = "Unlikely to become an essential part of my life"; 2 = "Might become an essential part of my life"; 3 = "Will become an essential part of my life"; 4 = "Is an essential part of my life"; (d) "Every day" = 30 times/month; "Several times a week" = 15 times/month; "Several times a month" = 4 times/month; "Less often" = 1 time/month; From (e) to before (f): 0 = "Never"; 1= "Not very often"; 2 = "Often"; 3 = "Very often" (f) Mean index for frequencies of using the above six non-news services; alpha = .65; (g) Standardised mean index of all the above variables, except broadband accessibility; alpha = .81; 208≤ n ≤210

- o were more likely to have broadband access at more than one place (.30 versus .10, p = .001);
- o had more years of Internet experience (5.6 years versus 4.9 years, p = .04);
- o used the Internet more frequently (26.2 versus 23 times/month, p = .004);
- o used the Internet for entertainment and relaxation more frequently (1.44 versus 1.02, p = .002);
- o used the Internet to search work/study-related non-news information more frequently (2.46 versus 1.67, p < .001);

o   used the Internet for to search non-news information for other purposes more frequently (2.30 versus 1.66, p < .001);

and therefore,

o   had more overall online non-news usage (1.66 versus 1.35, p < .001); and

o   had more overall experience with the Internet (.53 versus .21, p < .001).

In the multivariate model (fourth column, Table 6.12), only one aspect of Internet experience was significant: overall non-news usage (coefficient = 2.38, p < .001). The collective effect was significant at p < .001.

Table 6.12: Multivariate logistic regression analyses for the effect of Internet experience on the adoption, use and perceived importance of online news (regression coefficients)

	Adoption (n = 489)	Use frequency (n = 205)	Importance (n = 212)
Having Internet access at more than one place	0.25	-0.78	-0.77
Having broadband access	0.43	0.55	0.47
Years of Internet usage[a]	-0.03	0.08	0.05
Perceived level of understanding the Internet[b]	0.58**	0.86**	-0.05
Perceived importance of the Internet in daily life[c]	-0.09	-0.26	-0.02
Frequency of Internet usage (times/month)[d]	0.01	0.10***	0.03
Non-news Internet use[e]	2.71***	0.94*	2.38***
LR chi2 (7)[f]	221.49***	57.74***	60.23***

*(a) "One year or less" = .5 year; "Over 1-2 years" = 1.5 years; "Over 2-3 years" = 2.5 years; "Over 3-5 years" = 4 years; "Over 5 years" = 7.5 years; (b) 1 = "Not very much"; 2 = "Some"; 3 = "A good deal" (c) 1 = "Unlikely to become an essential part of my life"; 2 = "Might become an essential part of my life"; 3 = "Will become an essential part of my life"; 4 = "Is an essential part of my life"; (d) "Every day" = 30 times/month; "Several times a week" = 15 times/month; "Several times a month" = 4 times/month; "Less often" = 1 time/month; (e) Mean index for frequencies of using the above six non-news services; Cronbach alpha = .65; (f) Likelihood Ratio Chi-squared Tests with seven degrees of freedom, categories for dependent variables as in Chapter 5; * p ≤ .05; ** p ≤ .01; *** p ≤ .001.*

Further analysis: online news attributes in their social context

Although this chapter has considered the impact of socio-structural factors the adoption, use frequency and perceived importance of online news, there is still no exploration of how these socio-structural factors influence the way online news is appreciated. As discussed above, social locators, general news orientation and Internet experience might mediate the relationship between online news appreciation and its adoption, use frequency and dependency. To explore this, I carried out multivariate linear regression modelling of online news appreciation first on each of the three groups of socio-structural variables (Table 6.13) and then on all of them (Table 6.14). The appreciation variable was an index constructed from the nine identifying reasons for using online news explored in the previous chapter (no cost, more news choices, multitasking, in-depth and background information, immediacy, customisation, "have my say" to the media, news discussions in peer networks, and different viewpoints), with an alpha of .81.

As can be seen from the results presented in Table 6.13, social locators explained for 11.4% of the variance in online news appreciation, with age (coefficient = -.008, $p < .04$), living in a metropolitan area (coefficient = -.316, $p < .04$) and all dummy income variables except for the "over $75K to $100K" category (coefficient = -.367, $p = .06$) being negative significant predictors. The negative effect of age might not be surprising as the young is often more enthusiastic about and receptive to new media. But it is quite striking that people living in metropolitan areas and with higher incomes – i.e. those with more resources to use and enjoy online news – displayed a lower level of online news appreciation. In fact, all the three other living-area dummy categories were associated with negative coefficients, although they are not significant. Meanwhile, education, occupation and sex have no significant effect. In terms of news orientation, news use frequency (coefficient = .217, $p = .03$) and news exchange levels (coefficient = .194, $p < .02$) were significant positive predictors but time spending on news was significantly negative (coefficient = -.291, $p = .003$). Together, this group explains for about 9% of the variance in appreciation ($p = .001$). Where Internet experience was concerned, the only significant predictor in the multivariate model for appreciation was the non-news Internet use index (coefficient = .401, $p < .001$). Together, all aspects of Internet experience explain for 15% of the total variance in appreciation ($p < .001$).

Table 6.13: Multivariate linear regression analyses for the effect of different groups of socio-structural variables on the appreciation of online news attributes

	Coefficient	p-value
Model 1 (Social locators)		
Sex	-0.086	.35
Age	-0.008	<.04
Small town	-0.308	.15
Large town	-0.214	.25
Metropolitan area	-0.316	<.04
Blue-collars	-0.117	.54
White-collars	0.299	.10
Professionals	0.012	.94
Year 12	0.210	.27
Certificate	0.115	.49
Graduate degree	0.168	.37
Postgraduate degree	0.243	.23
$20K-$50K	-0.345	.05
Over $50K-$75K	-0.500	.009
Over $75K-$100K	-0.367	.06
Over $100K	-0.415	.04
Adjusted R-squared	0.114	.001
Model 2 (News orientation/behaviour)		
Overall news need	0.194	.15
Enjoying keeping up with the news	-0.164	.08
Being a "news junkie"	0.033	.74
News is not as important as it once was	-0.050	.18
I wish I had more time to follow the news	-0.010	.84
News usage frequency	0.217	.03
Spending more than 30 minutes on news per day	-0.291	.003
Discuss news & current affairs with peers	0.194	<.02
Adjusted R-squared	0.088	.001
Model 3 (Internet experience)		
Having Internet access at more than one place	0.059	.57
Having broadband access	0.165	.08
Years of Internet usage	-0.006	.74
Perceived level of understanding the Internet	-0.018	.84
Perceived importance of the Internet in daily life	0.002	.96
Frequency of Internet usage (times/month)	0.006	.27
Non-news Internet use	0.401	<.001
Adjusted R-squared	0.148	<.001

Table 6.14: Multivariate linear regression analyses for the effect of all socio-structural factors on the appreciation of online news attributes

	Coefficient	p-value
Sex	0.043	.66
Age	-0.002	.63
Small town	-0.156	.46
Large town	-0.100	.58
Metropolitan area	-0.267	.08
Blue-collars	-0.086	.66
White-collars	0.440	.02
Professionals	0.117	.43
Year 12	-0.037	.85
Certificate	-0.008	.96
Graduate degree	0.249	.90
Postgraduate degree	0.089	.67
$20K-$50K	-0.324	.07
Over $50K-$75K	-0.586	.002
Over $75K-$100K	-0.506	.009
Over $100K	-0.605	.003
Overall news need	0.055	.69
Enjoying keeping up with the news	-0.021	.83
Being a "news junkie"	0.069	.49
News is not as important as it once was	-0.054	.13
I wish I had more time to follow the news	0.84	.10
News usage frequency	0.013	.20
Spending more than 30 minutes on news per day	-0.229	.02
Discuss news & current affairs with peers	0.179	.04
Having Internet access at more than one place	0.000	1.00
Having broadband access	0.833	.42
Years of Internet usage	0.035	.11
Perceived level of understanding the Internet	0.030	.75
Perceived importance of the Internet in daily life	-0.054	.21
Frequency of Internet usage (times/month)	0.001	.91
Non-news Internet use	0.351	<.001
Adjusted R-squared	0.260	<.001

When all socio-structural variables were put together to explore their collective effect on online news appreciation (Table 6.14), they accounted for 26% of the total variance in appreciation. Of the social locator variables, occupation now turned out to be a significant predictor, with being working white-collars obtaining a coefficient of .44 (p = .02), while income remained a significantly negative one. Of the news orientation group, average time spending on news was again negatively associated with appreciation (coefficient = -.229, p = .02) and news change had a positive effect (coefficient = .179, p = .04). Of the Internet experience variables, non-news Internet usage was the only significant predictor, with coefficient = .351 and p < .001.

Conclusion: social determinants of online news adoption/use

The above data support the theoretical predictions elaborated for this chapter on socio-structural determinants of online news adoption/use. At this stage, the book's fourth research question ("What are the social determinants of public adoption and use of online news?") could be answered via the following answers to the three research questions raised in this chapter:

First, in relation to RQ6.1, general news orientation and its associated news behaviour pattern are a set of strong predictors of online news adoption, use and attachment. In terms of news need, an increase in the need to follow hard news – national/state politics, international affairs, economics, and to some extent, science, technology and health – has positive impact on the adoption likelihood, use frequency and perceived importance of online news. Meanwhile, the need to follow non-hard-news categories are typically almost the same or less strong among those who adopt or frequently use or attach an importance to online news, although the relevant relationships are not always statistically significant. It is probably because of the mutual compensation between the strong need for hard news and the weak one for "softer" news that the overall news need is normally not a significant contributor in the three dependent variables, both before and after controlling for other indicators of general news orientation/behaviour.

In addition to the need to follow hard news, attachment to the news (being a news junkie) is a significant or almost significant positive contributor to all the three response variables while the extent to which one enjoys keeping up with the news has a positive impact on adoption and use frequency. After controlling in multivariate models, enjoying keeping up with the news emerges as a defining contributor, with a significantly positive unique effect on both adoption and use frequency. Meanwhile, being a news junkie is a significant contributor to the perceived importance of online news but not to the two behavioural variables. As for general news behaviours, average daily time spending on news has no effect on all three response variables but frequency of news use does increase adoption likelihood and perceived importance. Indeed, after controlling for all the other variables, time spending has a marginally significant negative effect on the frequency of online news use. The use of news for socialisation (interpersonal discussion with peers either face-to-face or via the telephone) is a very consistent contributor, being significant in not only in most of the bivariate tests but also in the multivariate models for use frequency and perceived importance of online news.

Second, in relation to RQ6.2, social locators, when uncontrolled, are strong positive associations with entry into the online news world (except for household income) but do not have any substantial relationship with its use frequency. When the variables are controlled for each other, the following social locators continue to have a significant unique contribution to online news adoption: being a male, being a professional, being in the labour force and living in a metropolitan area. Probably because socio-economic differences level off among online news adopters, however, these variables do not lead to different use frequencies. As for attachment, most individual social locators (except living areas) do not predict the perceived importance of on online news in Internet usage; but when all are considered together, those with higher education and, quite strangely, lower household incomes are the most likely to see it as important or essential.

Third, in relation to RQ6.3, it can be concluded that when explored individually, every indicator of Internet experience entailed in this study has an effect on at least one aspect of online news adoption, use and dependency. When all Internet-experience variables are considered together, online news adoption is significantly predicted by perceived understanding of the Internet and non-news online use while its use frequency is uniquely contributed by not only these two factors but also general Internet use frequency. In terms of attachment, the perceived importance of online news is uniquely predicted only by non-news online use. All this suggests that online news adoption likelihood and its use and attachment levels are more a matter of Internet use and skills rather than accessibility or other factors. That is, as the Internet continues its development, those who use it more and/or have more skills to use it will be more likely to adopt, substantially use and depend on it for news.

Chapter 7

The complementary relationship between online news and information and traditional sources

With the unprecedented emergence of the Internet as a powerful news and information medium, as seen in Chapter 2, the fear of being driven out existence has been dominating traditional news industries, especially newspapers, since the 1990s. This chapter theoretically and empirically examines this issue from a user-centric approach, exploring whether there is a complementary relationship between online news and information and traditional sources. It starts with a detailed review of previous studies on the displacement and replacement effect of new media on old media, arguing that it might be misleading to place too much emphasis on the medium-centric assumption that new media will eventually drive old media out of existence because they all serve the same functions for users. Instead of this assumption, the chapter goes on to adopt a use-centric perspective, exploring a possible complementary relationship between old and new media, which is the fifth research question posed in Chapter 1. The key point here is that no medium can be seen as an absolute functional alternative to another: each medium has its distinctive features to serve different human beings in different contexts and thus complements other media in satisfying their diverse media-related needs. Therefore, even if people have to reduce some of their time and financial resources spent on the old after adopting the new, they do not necessarily abandon the former.

Using data from Australian Survey of Social Attitudes among 4270 Australians in 2003, this theoretical perspective will be tested within the specific domain of news and information use. The findings indicate a clear complementary effect of networked sources on traditional ones: despite the apparent "power" of the Internet in news and information capacity and quality, online news and information users at different use levels still use traditional sources substantially. In general, the more people use the Internet for news and information, the more they use other sources, especially those that are more information-intensive.

Medium-centric perspectives: the displacement/replacement effect of new media

Since the first empirical attempts to explore the potential effect of new media on old media in the 1940s, there have been two main approaches to the issue: one is centred on the medium and its attributes and supports a displacement and replacement (absolute displacement) hypothesis; the other is focused on users' needs and often results in proposing a complementary effect of the new on the old (Lee & Leung, 2004.). Both of these have been applied to investigating the impact of the Internet and will be reviewed below.

The most pronounced medium-centric approach so far is Maxwell McCombs' Principle of Relative Constancy. This principle was inspired by media owner Charles Scripps, who contended that mass communication products have become staples of consumption in our society (much like food, clothing and shelter) and thus, "in spite of the increasing complexity of mass communications with the advent of new media, the pattern of economic support has been relatively constant and more closely related to the general economy than to the various changes and trends taking place within the mass media field itself" (quoted in McCombs, 1972., p. 5). In other words, as staples, mass communication receives a constant share of the economic pie, or a relatively fixed proportion of all expenditures. Using aggregate data of consumers' and advertisers' spending on mass communication in the USA from 1929 through 1968, McCombs found strong support for this hypothesis: despite some short-term anomalies, the ratio of media spending to total consumer spending remained relatively fixed (around 3%) during the four decades (McCombs, 1972.). This media-spending share constancy hypothesis, which was so compelling that McCombs raised it to the status of a principle, was confirmed in a follow-up study for the 1968-1977 decade (McCombs & Eyal, 1980.).

The Principle of Relative Constancy has a dramatic implication for the fate of traditional media in a landscape marked by a rapid increase in the number of new media. When a new medium is introduced, money spent on it either comes from new money in the economy or must be diverted from existing media and non-media spending. During the 1948-1959 period, when television rapidly entered American households, McCombs tested these three possible sources to determine which accounted for television revenue. He discovered that the Principle of Relative Constancy also held for this shorter period of television penetration, which means television did not bring about any significant increase in total media spending (that is, it did not divert from non-media spending). It was new money in the economy and other media's losses that combined to finance television. In other words, despite economic growth, the intrusion of television took place during this decade at the expense of older media, especially those with a functional equivalence to television, such as movies. For example, five years after the introduction of television in the American market, the value of motion picture admissions plunged from $1.5 billion to $1.17 billion, a loss of $330 million (McCombs, 1972). In short, the Principle of Relative Constancy could be understood as a zero-sum game, in which value is neither created nor destroyed and, therefore, in the long run, new media would gradually displace and eventually replace old media with similar functions.

The Principle of Relative Constancy has also received support from aggregate data in other countries. For example, the change in the proportion of British spending on media was found to be statistically insignificant during the 1963-1990 period (Dupagne, 1994). For the 1987-1998 period, this accounted for around 4% of total consumer spending in Britain (Wollen, 2002). The book was later developed to incorporate time as an obstacle to new media adoption, as McCombs originally argued:

> For a time the consumer can increase the amount or number of goods enjoyed per time limit. He sips his martini, scans his newspaper and listens to the stereo simultaneously. But there must be some limit... The Principle of Relative Constancy describes a major economic constraint on the growth of the media in the marketplace over the past 40 years. But even with continued economic growth, mass media consumption may reach asymptote, with the ultimate constraint likely to be scarcity of time. For the immediate decades ahead, these two factors, time and money, will jointly constrain the growth of mass media in the marketplace (McCombs, 1972, p. 63)

The rationale is clear: there are only 24 hours a day; time spent on one activity cannot be spent on another. "Time is a zero-sum game phenomenon, like a hydraulic system – it can be reshaped and redistributed like a fluid, but it cannot be expanded like a gas" (Nie et al, 2002., p. 217).

This assertion has received considerable support from a number of industrial and academic studies on Internet impact. On the relationship between Internet usage and social activities, an innovative time-diary study by Nie et al (2002.) found a clear replacement effect: with common demographics (education, sex, marriage status, race, age, living alone, and being a single parent) being controlled, there were statistically significant negative relationships between time spent online and time spent with family, with friends, and with work colleagues. Meanwhile, the amount of time being alone significantly increased. When their sample was split by location of use, the effect became more obvious: home Internet use came directly out of interaction with family members while work Internet use was compensated by reduction in the amount of time spent face-to-face with co-workers. In addition, time spent using the Internet at both places concomitantly increased time alone, further substantiating that "Internet use, more than any other activity, isolates people from simultaneous active engagement with others" (Nie et al, 2002., p. 230). Finally, while the number of work-related e-mails showed no effect on time spending with family members, a one-minute decrease of the latter was found for each personal e-mail message sent or received.

As for the use of other media, a survey by Gomez Advisors and InterSurvey in December 1999 found 25% of its 4,600 American respondents reduced their time reading newspapers and 46% watched television less because of Internet usage (Lent, 2000.). Another by Gartner G2 found less use of postal mail (by over half of respondents), less long-distance telephone calls (one third), less television viewing (20%), less newspaper reading (20%) less movie going (18%), less video watching (15%) and less magazine reading (15%) (Saunders, 2002.). According to an Interactive Advertising Bureau study, a quarter of Internet users in its sample spent less time with television and over one in ten read less print media (cited in Lee & Leung, 2004.). Some academic studies have arrived at the same conclusion. A Stanford University survey discovered that 60% of regular Internet users decreased time watching television while one third did so to newspaper reading (O'Toole, 2000.). Kayany and Yelsma (2000.) found a clear gradual displacement process happening to traditional media (television, telephone, newspapers and domestic conversations) in Internet households, especially among heavy Internet users. Among them, again, television suffered from the most dramatic reduction, although not to a statistically significant level. It was also the first to be significantly reduced in a study on pre-Web electronic bulletin board usage and its impact by James, et al (1995.), followed by book reading, phone talking and letter writing in that order.

Studies in other countries also support this. 56% of European respondents in a recent survey by the UK-based research firm Strategy Analytics reported cutting down their television watching time since adopting broadband (*The Register*, 2004.). In Norway, less time reading newspapers was recorded with a growth in Internet usage from 2003 to 2004 (Statistics Norway, 2005.). In Hong Kong, Lee and Leung (2004.) reported reduced newspaper reading, radio listening and television watching by respectively 35%, 40% and 53% of Internet users in their sample. All of these studies suggest that as the Internet is displacing traditional media usage, the possibility for an absolute displacement (that is, replacement) in the long run is high.

Communication history, however, reveals a totally different picture. Predictions of the demise of old media are as old as mass communications themselves. During the early days of the telegraph, as seen in Chapter 2, publisher James Gordon Bennett was so overwhelmed by its immediacy that he contended: "The telegraph may not affect magazine literature but the mere newspapers must submit to destiny and go out of existence" (quoted in Standage, 1998., p. 149). It was also Bennett who was among the people who forcefully and scandalously declared the death of pre-newspaper media – the books, theatres and churches – in an 1836 article: "Books have had their day – the theatre have had their day – the temple of religion has had its days. A newspaper can be made to take the lead in all of these in the great movements of human thought and of human civilisation. A newspaper can send more souls to Heaven, and save more from Hell, than all the churches or chapels in New York – besides making money at the same time" (quoted in DeFleur & Ball-Rokeach, 1989, p. 54). More recently, in 1982, amidst the impressive emergence of electronic publishing and other new media ventures, journalist Steve Piacente bluntly told his colleagues that "as mullet-wrapper of the future, the newspaper is doomed" (quoted in Patten, 1986., p. 4). More examples can be found in Nguyen (2007) and Nguyen (2008).

As late as 2006, these prophecies of doom have turned out to be exaggerated: newspapers have adapted well in their competition with radio and television to remain a very important part of daily life, just as music recording survived radio and radio survived television. As Brown (1999) put it in an informal but concise way:

> What a buncha cards, those New Media kids! Or maybe they're just exasperated because the gray bears won't get out of the way. Pundits have been predicting the death of newspapers for more than 100 years. In 1880, the assassin was supposed to be photography. In the 1920s, newspapers were going to be destroyed by radio; in the 1950s, TV was going to destroy newspapers and radio. In the 1990s the Web was going to destroy . . . well, you get the idea, and it is a misleading one because the main theme of media history is not extirpation of one form by another, but mutual accommodation among forms. Old Media has *(sic)* shown a remarkable resilience.

This suggests that old and new media, including the Internet, might compete but do not kill each other: they coexist and complement each other. Why do the above studies contradict this mutual accommodation? The next sections will answer this question and will apply the theories underlining this answer to the specific case of online news and information.

User-centric perspectives: the complementary effect of new media

To answer the above question, it is necessary first to revisit the problems associated with the Principle of Relative Constancy and the subsequent studies of time displacement. First, the constancy concept developed by McCombs is potentially unreliable because of its many theoretical and methodological drawbacks. Extending McCombs's data to 1981, Wood (.1986.) revisited his methodological approach to discover that the Principle of Relative Constancy's inherent hypothesis of income-share constancy in mass media spending, although correct for the whole six-decade period, was not supported in short-run tests. In particular, mass media spending significantly fluctuated from one decade to another and decade-long increases in disposable income were associated with either drop or surge in media spending. Such short-run departures from constancy were found in later studies showing that mass media spending dramatically increased after the VCR penetrated daily life (Wood & O'Hare, 1991.; Dupagne, 1994.; Noh & Grant, 1997.). Son and McCombs (1993.) found that total mass media spending was up to 3.7% in 1987 from 2.2% in 1975 although they argued that this was a short-term exception rather than something to discredit the long-term Principle of Relative Constancy. The Principle of Relative Constancy, Wood argued, is therefore, "a correct long-term descriptive relationship with doubtful predictive values":

> To be sure, new forms of mass media can be expected to contend for consumers' time and money in the future, just as television did so successfully in the 1950s. But new technologies will not be shut out of the market, nor will existing technologies be doomed because of a historically descriptive constant share of income going to the media. The economic constraint the new and old technologies will face is that they will have to compete successfully for the consumer's time and money. This is the same constraint faced by producers of every consumer good and service. Useful as it is for summarizing past long-run trends, the Principle of Relative Constancy can say little about the future (Wood, 1986., p. 51)

Recent research has also called the constancy assumption into question in the light of demand theory. Noh and Grant (1997.) found the constancy assumption a biased adoption of consumer demand theory since it only takes income into account and leaves aside other possible explanations. For example, even if income remains constant, consumer spending on mass media will change as the result of a change in the price of a media good. Similarly, Dupagne (1997.) asserted that the proportional relationship in the Principle of Relative Constancy is inconsistent with the dominant, traditional, micro-economic model of consumer choice and that using different methodological factors might result in conflicting evidence about the Principle of Relative Constancy. Using empirical data from Belgium, the study explored five independent variables (income, price, population, unemployment and interest rate) to find that price and population were better predictors of consumer spending on mass media than income. See also Dupagne and Green (1996) for further details.

The second, and probably more important, problem of the displacement and replacement hypothesis is the associated technological-determinist assumption of functional equivalence. As it has become very clear by now, uses and gratifications research has intensively and extensively shown that individuals are consciously or subconsciously active before, during and after their media exposure; they generally select media channels and content that suit their situation, which encompasses a choice based not only on available resources and the medium's technological attributes but also on their needs and wants, their social and psychological origins, their past media experience, the socio-cultural settings of use and the availability of content.

In other words, there are many audiences or user groups with different sets of media preferences rather than only one audience or one user group with a relatively homogenous set of media preferences. Despite the many relative advantages of e-mail for distant communication, for example, some empirical research has found that the telephone is still used more for contacting far-away relatives while e-mail is used more for contacting far-away friends, suggesting that "the norms, demands and joys of kinship interaction are more apt than friendship to call forth the greater social presence of face-to-face or telephone conversations" (Chen, et al 2002, p. 96). Thus, by encompassing the audience as no more than a "lump of clay", easily moulded by media technologies, and media usage as a mere "give one, take one" process, the functional equivalence assumption is unnecessarily limited. In this light, it is urged that each medium should be recognised as having its own advantages and disadvantages and, thus, its own right to exist, to meet human beings' information and communication needs.

The crucial importance of media characteristics is widely recognised in past information behaviour models, although they are classified under different umbrellas and specified with different roles. In Johnson's model, for example, "information carrier factors" include information utilities and characteristics of different channels (see Case, 2002 and Wilson, 1999 for more detailed discussions of these). One model that has much to do with the above uses and gratifications perspective is Wilson's global model of information behaviour (Wilson & Walsh, 1996; Wilson, 1999; Niedźwiedzka, 2003). In this model, Wilson grouped source characteristics (e.g., currency, accessibility, reliability) into what he called "intervening variables", along with psychological characteristics (e.g., outlook on life, value system, knowledge, emotion, self-perception, prejudices, preferences etc.); demographic attributes (e.g., age, education, social status); social roles played by the individual; and environmental factors (e.g., legislation, degree of stabilisation).

All these variables, through activation mechanisms such as risk/reward weighing, could either support or hinder information behaviour, leading to preferences for some sources over others. Thus, the totality of information behaviour is submerged in a context of personal, role-related and environmental (including medium) factors (Niedzwiedzka, 2003.). From the uses and gratifications perspective, this can be understood in this way: source characteristics and other intervening variables interact with each other in formulating information behaviour. In reality, these intervening variables combine to form different dimensions of media orientation/behaviour discussed in Chapter 6. A person with limited education, for instance, might have limited cognitive capacity and, therefore, would not like reading, which leads him or her to preferring retrieving information from television and radio than from the more demanding newspapers and magazines. In a broader context, it could be then argued that different media as different content (information and/or entertainment) resources will coexist for a number of reasons:

First, *each medium serves its audiences in a different manner within different contexts*. Radio survived television at least partly because it can be combined with other daily activities to save time (e.g., listening to the news while driving to work or while conducting outdoor activities). Newspapers survived radio and television partly because they are portable, allow random access to content and offer a high degree of temporal freedom (Hsia, 1989.). Similarly, the book could survive electronic publishing thanks partly to what Wilson called 'informality of use':

> When I read a novel, I do so in all kinds of places – in bed, on the train, in the bath, by my plate in a restaurant. I've even seen some people reading when they walk down the street! Do I really want to drag out my notebook computer, attach it to my portable telephone, dial-up a Website and start reading (at some enormous cost in telecommunication charges) on all of these occasions? Of course not. This factor will apply to all those kinds of books that people read for

entertainment, creative stimulation, vicarious experience and 'escapism' – novels, poetry, travel books, history, biography, popular science, and so on. Again, the existence of a market will be the determining factor: if the market is there, it will be satisfied, and I cannot see the market declining in the face of competition from electronic products (.Wilson, 1997.).

Second, *each medium has a distinctive content profile.* Although all media provide information and entertainment-related content, newspapers, for example, are more information-intensive (that is, offering both broad and in-depth content), which has substantially contributed to their survival in coping with their more entertainment-oriented broadcasting competitors.

Third, and most importantly, because different media could serve the same media-related need in a different way within a different context, *all – or most – of them might be used by individuals who experience a high level of that need.* For example, people with a strong need for entertainment could seek entertainment content across all media, probably with television being the most frequently used medium for this purpose. A somewhat extreme scenario could be: an individual with a high orientation to entertainment content might listen to music on the radio while driving to work or jogging, switch on the television in the lounge at night for some movies or drama and log on the Internet for some gaming before going to bed.

These arguments are not new. As early as 1913, this fact that old media facing a new medium would be forced to restrict themselves to what they serve best had already been promoted as a "law" by German historian Riepl (cited in Becker & Schoenbach, 1989). It is partly on these bases that Dutta-Bergman recently contended that studies that found a more-less relationship are "a product of the preoccupation with selling the new and discarding the old on one hand... and nostalgic lamenting over the loss of the old at the footsteps of the new on the other hand". Accordingly, this "myopic vision of the medium as the driving force' is so dominant that it leads these studies to 'a reliance on biased research methodology that is created to detect competition, constraining the answers to respondents to a competing media framework" (.Dutta-Bergman 2004., p. 42). While these criticisms might appear excessive, it is true that most of the above-cited studies that found support for the displacement process of Internet usage do approach the issue in this competition-based framework, implicitly or explicitly assuming the Internet as a functional alternative to traditional media and thus asking respondents direct questions like "Decrease a lot" or "Increase a lot" or along a "More-About the same-Less" scale.

Meanwhile, a different picture emerges from those studies that investigate the impact of Internet usage on traditional media usage from a user-centric vantage point, comparing old media usage between users versus non-users or heavy versus light users of the Internet.. Arbitron NewMedia, for instance, found that that heavy users of the Internet were likely to report more radio listening and television watching and that the total time heavy users spent on television, radio, audio tapes and CDs, newspapers and magazines were higher than light users. Stempel et al (.2000.) compared their survey data between 1995 and 1999 to discover that although there was a considerable decline in regular traditional media usage, Internet adoption was not the cause of this change. In particular, they found not only that the Internet had no adverse effect on the use of traditional news products, but also that Internet users were more likely than non-users in all age, income, education and sex groups to read newspapers and listen to radio news.

The zero-sum hypothesis was also rejected by Robinson et al (.2000.), who employed the Pew Research Centre's annual surveys from 1994 to 1998 to find little change in the use of traditional news and entertainment media, despite a three-fold increase in Internet usage and a 25% increase in home computer usage. In terms of the absolute amount of time (measured by minutes a day), there was little monotonic relation in the 1998 data; that is, traditional media use was not found to be progressively less as Internet usage increased. Both Robinson et al (.2000.) and Stempel et al (.2000.) concluded that Internet and traditional media uses are supplemental or complementary. In other words, there is a more-more, rather than a more-less, relationship between old and new media. The more people use the Internet, the more they use traditional media. All this is well in line with a long-observed trend to the so-called "all-or-nothing" model of media exposure, which states that "those who are heavy users of one medium are also likely to use other mass media fairly regularly; and people who make light use of mass communication are likely to be restrictive to all the media" (.Wright, 1986., p. 114).

It must be cautioned, however, that these findings do not to totally discredit the displacement hypothesis. The fact that newspaper circulation numbers have been following a downward trend all over the world in the past four decades, a period in which a range of new media were introduced, suggests that a displacement process might well be under way. The user-centric, more-more relationship does not necessarily imply that people spend more time on media use after adopting a new technology. The 2004 data in Chapter 6, for example, show that average daily amount of time spending on news was not different between adopters or frequent users of online news and their counterparts. What is important here is that, as implied in the all-or-nothing model itself, people with stronger media-related needs would use all available media. Thus, it could be argued that online users might originally have a much higher time budget for total media usage than non-users; and therefore, a certain reduction in the former's use of existing media might not lead them to becoming lighter users of other media than the latter. In other words, even when an individual reduces old media time spending to compensate for the adoption of a new medium, s/he still could display a more-more profile of media usage across all sources because of an originally big gap in time budget between that individual and one with weak needs for media-related utilities. My argument here is that, even if heavy media users have to tip their traditional media budget to compensate for Internet usage, there must be a limit in their reduction – to the point that every available medium will be taken advantage of in the most effective and efficient way to serve their media-related needs.

The information-seeking pattern: three hypotheses

To sum up the above discussion, although the Internet appears superior to its print and broadcasting siblings in fulfilling their existing functions in a more efficient and effective way, it is not likely to drive the latter out of existence through a gradual displacement process. Because they serve human beings in different ways and different contexts, different media forms coexist and complement each other. It is, therefore, imperative to go beyond the medium-centric displacement/replacement perspective to explore the issue from a user-centric perspective, one that takes into account the interactions between media-related needs and the different levels of using available media to fulfil these needs. It is this complementary relationship that this chapter attempts to investigate.

In order to do this, however, this chapter goes beyond most previous research that has been exploring the complementary effect of general Internet use, rather than Internet news and information use, on traditional sources (Arbitron NewMedia, 1999; Stempel et al, 2000; Robinson et al, 2000). Since the Internet is a multipurpose medium, this might produce misleading findings about medium complementarity. Stempel et al (2000) inferred from their findings that Internet users might be information seekers, who either could listen to radio when surfing the net; or might turn to newspapers for more in-depth news than what was read on the net (or vice versa); or might see both the Internet and newspapers as useful information sources. But how can we ascertain this? Although the Internet is an information-intensive medium and although news and non-news information have been confirmed by surveys around the world to be an instrumental function of Internet usage (see Chapter 6), there is still a substantial number of people who use the Internet solely or mainly for non-information needs (such as entertainment and interpersonal communication).

Thus, general Internet usage might not be a good indicator to assess whether it is complementary to old media in terms of news and information utilities. In order to do so, the Internet should be seen primarily as a news and information medium (as opposed to the Internet as an interpersonal medium, or an entertainment medium and so on). If the complementarity hypothesis holds in the news and information market, it is then expected that online news and information users at different usage levels are likely to be news and information "junkies", receiving news and information frequently from traditional sources, especially from those information-rich sources like newspapers, as well as the Internet.

We have a range of sensible reasons to believe so. The Internet requires a high level of concentration on the screen content, which means that it certainly cannot be used for news and information while people do some other things (such as driving to work or doing gardening). Similarly, some Internet news and information users might still like watching the six-o'clock news bulletin on television because it is a good way for them to keep themselves informed while still being able to interact with other family members or simply to relax after a long working day. Also, it might well be the case that the more superficial news and information coverage on radio and television would provide some people with a general reference to events of the day, which will stimulate them to seek deeper analysis and more background information from the Internet or the next morning newspaper, or both. For those with strong need for and orientation to news and information, these differences in use contexts and information intensity across media are good reasons to seek all available sources at different times and places throughout the day.

On this basis, three hypotheses are proposed as three components to answer RQ5:

H7.1: Online news and information users use traditional sources more frequently than non-users of Internet news and information.

H7.2: Frequent users online news and information use traditional sources more frequently than non-frequent users of online news and information.

H7.3: Online news and information usage is more associated with news and information seeking from more information-intensive sources.

Methods

This chapter is based on a secondary data analysis of the 2003 Australian Survey of Social Attitudes (AUSSA), a national survey conducted from August to December 2003. This is the first of an ongoing series of national surveys of the social attitudes and behaviours of adult Australians. Data collection was conducted by an inter-university research team and directed out of the Australian National University from August to December, 2003, employing a stratified systematic random sample from the 2002 Australian Electoral Roll (Gibson et al, 2004). The dataset is publicly available on the Australian Social Science Archive's website at http://ssda.anu.edu.au/. Using a stratified, systematic, random sample from the 2002 Australian Electoral Roll, the survey achieved an overall response rate of 42%, with a final sample size of 4270.

The survey asked respondents numerous questions relating to beliefs about Australian society and national identity, and attitudes and behaviours with respect to major institutions, such as the family, the criminal justice system, the mass media, work, and education (see Wilson et al, 2005). Over twenty questions relating to Internet access, news and information uses and socio-demographic factors were employed for this book. The question related to news and information uses was worded as "How often do you use the following for news and information?", with seven media listed: "Commercial television", "ABC and SBS television", "Radio", "Newspapers", "Internet sites" "Talkback radio", and "News Magazines". The response categories included "never", "once a week or less", "several times a week" and "daily". These were numerically coded to indicate the number of times using a medium in an average week ("never" was treated as zero; "once a week or less" equalled one time a week; "several times a week" equalled three times/week; and "daily" equalled seven times/week).

There are several reasons why the 2004 survey dataset was not used in the current analysis. First, the 2003 AUSSA dataset is a very high-quality, nationally representative and large-sample dataset that is suitable to address the core research issue of the book. Second, this survey covered the uses of news and information, rather than news – and this is particularly relevant for studying the relationship between the Internet and traditional mass media, because the core business of a mass medium is not totally about news but is also about non-news information. In reality, with the vital emergence of new media, publishers and broadcasters around the world have been shifting their business mindset from a seeing themselves as news producers and disseminators to being "information companies" (Boczkowski, 2004). In other words, an examination of the relationship between traditional and online media in terms of both news and non-news information would produce more practical findings about the future survival of the old. In addition, the 2004 survey does not allow for a good analysis of the relationship between online and traditional news uses. Although the questionnaire asked all respondents about their uses of traditional news sources, the response categories of these questions were different between user groups: "very often", "often", "not very often" and "never" for online news users but "everyday", "several times a week", "several times a month" and "less often" for online news nonusers. This made comparing traditional news uses between users and nonusers of online news difficult, although there are statistical techniques that might help to address this problem.

In terms of data analysis methods, for the first two hypotheses, t-tests of mean weekly uses of traditional news and information were conducted for users versus non-users of online news and information; and for frequent users versus non-frequent users of online news and information. Frequent users were defined as those using the Internet for news and information several times a week or every day. It must be noted that non-frequent users of online news and information included both infrequent users and nonusers of it. For the third hypothesis, descriptive analysis of data from the first three tables was first carried out to explore the use of information-intensive sources across different levels of online news and information users. Then Pearson correlations between weekly use of online news and information with weekly use of each of the six traditional sources were explored – with attention to their statistical significance. A linear regression analysis of online news and information use as a function of all traditional news and information uses, sex, age, education, individual income and occupations was also undertaken to make sure that if the hypotheses were supported, the complementary relationship remained the same after controlling for major socio-economic factors.

After sample exclusions, the sample included 2804 Internet users (nearly 70% of the sample) used the Internet. About 59% of the sample had Internet access through home (and other places). About 37% had access through work (and other places). Three quarters of Internet users received online news and information. 25% of the whole sample were frequent Internet news and information users: its counterpart was 86% in the case of commercial television, 69% (public television), 85% (non-talkback radio), 25% (talkback radio), 66% (newspapers) and 12% (magazines).

Results

Before testing the three hypotheses, the relationship between Internet use and traditional news and information uses was explored. Table 7.1 shows the differences in mean weekly use of traditional online news and information between Internet users and non-users. No statistical difference was found between these two groups in their mean weekly use of news and information from radio and newspapers. Non-users, however, scored higher in their frequency of using commercial television (5.82 versus 5 times a week), public television (4.13 versus 3.81 times a week) and talkback radio (1.69 versus 1.37 times a week) for news and information. The only significant increase from Internet nonusers to users was found in the case of news magazines (0.77 to 0.91 times a week).

Table 7.2 splits the sample into adopters (or users) and non-adopters (non-users) of online news and information. Clearly, adopters tended to more frequently use most of the other sources for news and information (3.92 versus 3.66 times a week in the case of public television; 5.24 versus 4.88 for regular radio; 3.99 versus 3.47 for newspapers; and 1.04 versus 0.67 for news magazines). The only decrease from nonadopters to adopters was found for commercial television (5.36 versus 5.08 times a week) and no difference was detected in the case of talkback radio.

Table 7.1: Mean weekly use of traditional news and information among Internet users and non-users (times/week)

	Nonusers	Users	Net difference	p-value
Commercial television	5.82	5.01	0.81	<.001
Public television	4.13	3.81	0.32	=.001
Radio	5.11	5.14	0.03	>.05
Talkback radio	1.69	1.37	0.32	<.001
Newspapers	3.79	3.85	0.06	>.05
Magazines	0.77	0.91	0.14	<.01

Source: Australian Survey of Social Attitudes 2003

Table 7. 2: Mean weekly use of traditional news/information among online news and information users and nonusers (times/week)

	Nonusers	Users	Net difference	p-value
Commercial television	5.36	5.08	.28	<.001
Public television	3.66	3.92	.26	<.001
Radio	4.88	5.24	.36	<.001
Talkback radio	1.44	1.33	.11	>.05
Newspapers	3.47	3.99	.52	<.001
Magazines	.67	1.04	.37	<.001

Source: Australian Survey of Social Attitudes 2003

At a higher level of using online news and information (frequent usage), a similar picture emerges (Table 7.3) – the only major change was that frequent and non-frequent users of online news and information were no longer different in their use of news and information on public television. News and information from radio, newspapers and magazines remained more frequently used by those who frequently used the Internet for news and information: 5.32 versus 5.07, 4.19 versus 3.73 and 1.2 versus 0.79 respectively. All this suggests a clear complementary relationship: the more people use the Internet for news and information, the more they use traditional sources for this purpose.

Table 7.3: Mean weekly use of traditional news/information among frequent and non-frequent users of online news/information (times/week)

	Non-frequent Users	Frequent users	Net difference	p-value
Commercial television	5.32	5.15	0.17	>.05
Public television	3.89	4.02	0.13	>.05
Radio	5.07	5.32	0.25	<.001
Talkback radio	1.52	1.39	0.13	>.05
Newspapers	3.73	4.19	0.46	<.001
Magazines	0.79	1.20	0.41	<.001

Source: Australian Survey of Social Attitudes 2003

Furthermore, a preliminary look at the data in Tables 7.2 and 7.3 suggests that online news and information usage at both levels of adoption and frequent use are positively associated with more frequent use of more information-intensive traditional sources like radio, newspapers and news magazines. Moreover, reading across Tables 7.2 and 7.3 reveals that the frequency of using newspapers, the richest and most elaborate traditional news and information source, rose by 0.2 times a week from 3.99 at the adoption level of online news and information (shown in Table 7.2) to 4.19 at the frequent-usage level (shown in Table 7.3). In the case of the other print medium, the increase was 0.16 times a week (from 1.04 to 1.2). This also occurred to the information-poorer electronic sources but the change was smaller (0.1 times a week or less): from 5.08 to 5.15 for commercial television; 3.92 to 4.02 for public television; 5.24 to 5.32 for regular radio and 1.33 to 1.39 for talkback radio. Other supportive evidence includes the following facts:

o both adopters and frequent users of online news and information reported using the entertainment-oriented commercial television less often than their relevant opposite groups; and

o while the frequency of using public television for news and information was significantly less among adopters than non-adopters of online news and information, it became insignificant at the higher use level (frequent usage) of online news and information. This might be because public television is information-rich enough for the general online news and information population but not rich enough for the more information-oriented population of frequent online news usage.

For a systematic exploration of the issue, partial correlations between online news and information usage and the use of each traditional source were calculated. Table 7.4 shows that the only sources that were not significantly correlated with online news and information were commercial television and talkback radio. Commercial television was even negatively associated with the former although this is not statistically significant. All the other sources received positive correlation, with newspapers and magazines achieving the highest positive correlation coefficient (0.12 and 0.18), followed by radio (0.07) and public television (0.05). Although these correlation coefficients are not strong, they are all statistically significant.

Table 7.4: Correlations between mean weekly use of online news/information and mean weekly use of traditional sources

	Pearson's r	p-value
Commercial television	-0.015	>.05
Public television	0.050	=.001
Radio	0.070	<.001
Talkback radio	0.007	>.05
Newspapers	0.120	<.001
Magazines	0.180	<.001

Source: Australian Survey of Social Attitudes 2003

Together, the above findings suggest that the three hypotheses proposed for this chapter could be confirmed. At this stage, however, it is still unclear whether the data reflect a true channel relationship or a by-product of socio-structural factors such as sex, age and socio-economic status. The latter is quite likely because a detailed analysis of the dataset reveals that online news and information users were not only more likely to be young males living in urban areas and working in larger-size organizations but also enjoyed more socio-economic advantages: higher education; higher socio-economic status (including household income and how it is compared with the average rate, perceived social class, occupation and workplace positions); and higher perceived economic well-being (including current management of household income, the ease of finding a job similar to the current one, and the chance to improve living standards) (see Nguyen & Western, 2007 for more details).

In order to make sure of a true channel relationship, a linear regression model was derived for weekly online news and information usage on weekly uses of each of the six traditional sources, controlling for the five major socio-structural factors of sex, age, individual income, education and occupation. From the original nine major occupational groups classified by the Australian Bureau of Statistics (.1997.), three dummy variables were created, with each indicating whether respondents were professionals [managers/administrators, professionals and associate professionals] or skilled workers [tradespersons] or clerical practitioners). Unskilled/manual workers (labourers and intermediate workers) were used as the reference category. For education, four dummy variables were created (with one indicating the possession of a university degree, a certificate/diploma, a trade or apprenticeship qualification, a year-12 educational level), with less than year-12 education as the reference category. The sex variable was treated as a dummy, with one indicating a male and zero representing a female.

During the investigation, interactions between sex and all other independent variables were explored but only the sex-by-education interaction was statistically significant. These are retained in the final model (Table 7.5). The results of the final regression model show that, after controlling for the five important individual attributes, the relationship depicted in Table 7.4 remained the same: news and information reception from the most entertainment-oriented sources, talkback radio (beta = -0.014, p =0.36) and commercial television (beta =0.026, p = 0.07), did not have any significant relationship with the use of online news and information but all the others did and did in a positive direction. It is now safe to confirm the second, third and fourth hypotheses of the chapter.

Further analysis and discussion

This chapter aims to test the complimentary effect of the Internet on traditional media within the specific function of news and information utilities that is shared by all media. Contrary to persuasive evidence from previous user-centric studies (.Robinson et al 2000.; .Stempel et al 2000.), the findings from this survey do not support the more-more relationship between general Internet usage and traditional news and information usage. However, given that Internet users were not different from non-users in their use of more information-intensive sources like radio and newspapers and tended to use magazines more frequently, the findings do provide some evidence that the Internet population in general consists of information-oriented people, who are likely less frequently to use the entertainment-oriented (infotainment) sources of commercial television, public television and talkback radio.

Table 7.5: Linear regression model for weekly online news/information usage by weekly use of traditional source, controlling for sex, age, education, individual income and occupation (n = 3372)

	Coefficient	p-value
Commercial television	0.026	.07
Public television	0.059	< .001
Radio	0.028	<.05
Talkback radio	-0.014	.36
Newspapers	0.063	< .001
Magazines	0.240	< .001
Sex	0.032	.80
Age	-0.036	< .001
Individual income	-0.123	< .01
Professionals	0.551	< .001
Clerics	0.356	.001
Skilled workers	0.135	.35
Year 12	0.021	.95
Trade and apprenticeship	0.329	.49
Certificate/diploma	-0.249	.38
University degree (bachelor or higher)	-0.533	.30
Sex*Year 12	0.121	.60
Sex*Certificate/diploma	-0.224	.41
Sex*University degree	0.848	< .001
Intercept	2.030	< .001
Adjusted R^2	0.187	< .001

Source: Australian Survey of Social Attitudes 2003

In terms of the cross-media news and information usage, however, a clear more-more pattern was found: there is a significantly positive, although weak, association between traditional news and information and online news and information uses (at both levels of general adoption and frequent usage). It appears that online news and information usage reinforces the use of traditional sources, especially those information-intensive sources like newspapers and magazines. These findings are in line with a study by Althaus and Tewksbury (2000.), who surveyed 520 American undergraduate students to find that Web news usage was positively associated with newspaper reading but no significant correlation was found in the former's relationship with television watching. In a more recent work, Dutta-Bergman (2004.) incorporated audience involvement, selective exposure and the theory of the niche to find not only that online news adopters are avid information users who substantially seek news from available sources but also that there is strong congruence in the use of online and offline sources in seven news content domains (politics, sports, business, science and health, international affairs, government and entertainment) before and after controlling for demographic factors such as age, sex, education and income.

All this provides strong evidence against claims that the Internet as a "powerful" news and information medium would replace traditional sources in the long run. Rather, because of their strong news and information orientation or need and the many differences in use contexts and information quality between media, online news and information users would use all available sources. The more-more relationship could happen in two scenarios, explored below.

In the first scenario, people with a strong need for news and information adopt the Internet for this purpose at least without reducing their use of traditional sources. The chance for this scenario of increasing budget is quite high because media time spending is not necessarily constant. The time increase in total news and information usage might come from a number of sources such as time previously spent on entertainment on television or radio (Bromley & Bowles, 1995.), sleep hours and other personal-care activities (eating and grooming) as well as family-care (shopping, child care, house cleaning etc.) and even travel time (Robinson et al, 2000.). It could also come from curtailing non-media, free-time social activities, although the study by Robinson et al (2000.) did not support this (because active Internet users were also found to be more sociable).

To this, we need to add another possible source of time, which results from the nature of the Internet as an efficient time-saving multi-purpose medium. Instead of spending much time driving to a bank to make a transaction, for example, an Internet user can easily log on the Web and accomplish it in a matter of minutes. This means Internet usage reduces time spent on traditional, non-media, non-free-time activities and this, in turn, increases time for Internet usage. In other words, Internet adopters can divert more time resources from non-media activities to their online usage while still fulfilling their needs for these activities. The total time spent on media would increase as the result. That is to say, the all-or-nothing phenomenon has an even better chance to occur in the Internet age. As information-oriented junkies, online news and information users allocate this time increase for this purpose rather than entertainment.

However, as noted above, the more-more pattern found in this study does not definitely affirm that people would adopt and use online news and information without reducing their time for traditional news and information usage. The second scenario is that online news and information users might originally have a higher budget for news and information than non-users and thus a reduction in this budget does not lead to a change in their profile of information junkies in comparison to non-users. This is especially worth noticing in the context that this investigation is based on a secondary data analysis of a survey that was originally not intended to investigate media usage and thus used only crude measures of frequency. The point to reiterate here is that even if a displacement effect is under way; that is, even if they have to reduce time on traditional news and information usage to compensate for online news and information use, strongly information-oriented users would put a limit on this reduction of time spent.

What, then, will happen when the Internet becomes the primary news and information source? In order to explore this, the sample was split again for statistical tests between two groups: one that includes those who had reportedly relied the most on the Internet for news and information (104 respondents or 2.5% of the sample) and those who had not. Table 7.6 shows the distinction between the two groups in their patterns of traditional news and information usage, based on significance testing for differences in their mean weekly use of traditional sources. No significant difference was found in the case of magazine reading, but those who relied on the Internet the most for news and information reported significantly less frequent use of all the other sources. However, the levels of using traditional sources among these people are not at all insubstantial. The means of 3.85 times a week for commercial television, three times a week for public television and

Table 7.6: Mean weekly use of traditional news/information among those who do and do not rely the most on the Internet for news/information (times/week)

	Not relying on Internet the most for news/information	Relying on Internet the most for news/information	p-value
Commercial television	5.31	3.85	<.001
Public television	3.95	3.00	<.001
Radio	5.15	4.52	<.05
Talkback radio	1.50	0.78	<.01
Newspapers	3.88	2.69	<.001
Magazines	0.91	0.73	>.05

Source: Australian Survey of Social Attitudes 2003

4.52 times a week for radio among those who relied the most on online news and information are quite considerable in the context that a score of 3 was coded for "several times a week".

The only medium being used below this point is newspapers (2.69) but this is not too far below 3. In proportional terms, almost half (48%) of those relying on the Internet the most for news and information still use newspapers for the same purpose at least several times a week; the level classified as "frequent usage" in this study (data not shown). In other words, despite their ultimate reliance on the Internet for news and information, people still find other sources helpful and use them substantially to complement what they receive from the Internet. All traditional sources would experience some decline (that is, be partially displaced) but would have their own right to coexist.

Conclusion

All in all, this chapter suggests that a positive answer to the fifth research question of this book ("Is there a complementary relationship between online news and information and traditional sources?"). It shows that the historical coexistence of old and new media will continue in the Internet age. At least within the provision of news and information, instead of driving out old media, the Internet will complement them in serving the seemingly insatiable news and information needs among a substantial segment of society. Decline of traditional news and information usage might be under way, especially when the Internet becomes the most relied-on news and information source – but it is unlikely for any replacement (absolute displacement) to occur.

Chapter 8

The future of online news: social, economic and professional implications of this work

In the 1980s, amidst the uptake of electronic publishing alternatives, William Chilton, president and publisher of *The Charleston Gazette*, declared that technologies are so "unyielding" that they "(move) on with (their) own laws and momentum, which human beings adapt to whether we want or not" (quoted in Boczkowski, 2004). In the early 1990s, following the emergence of the web, the Internet went "from a technonovelty to a chic media cliché ... within barely 12 months" (quoted in Kyrish, 1996, p.17), stimulating a massive wave of online migration in the traditional news industry that makes online news appear like a sudden overnight emergence. All this was rooted in the same mindset as Chilton: the "power" of online news would effortlessly attract users and could drive the old news out of existence. This book, however, has highlighted the need to be cautious about this line of technologically determinist thinking. While the view of technologies as a driver of social changes should not be totally dismissed, it is essential to think of this relationship in terms of a reciprocal process: technological power potentially enhances human life but the extent to which this potential can materialise and create changes to human life depends largely on how human beings – particularly technology creators and technology users – assess, develop and adjust to fit it in their existing social world.

As this book has shown, the Internet as a news medium is not a revolution coming from nowhere. Despite its seeming sudden emergence in the 1990s, online news has a 160-year evolutionary history that developed from simple consumer telegraphic news services to telephone-based audio news services to the faxed newspaper to videotex to web news. Some of the pre-web online news forms enjoyed immediate successes, some were dead from their early days, some were off and on again, and some are still surviving in today's digital age. This is because technologies do not always translate into market demands but are subject to a range of social, economic, cultural and political conditions. As Silverstone (1995, p. 63) pointed out:

> Revolutions are evolutions in disguise. They are hard won. And needs have to be created. They do not simply merge fully formed from natural desires, innocent perceptions or even previous experiences.

Or as Raymond Williams argued, a technical invention only gains some social significance once it has been chosen for investment and production, "processes which are of a general social and economic kind, within existing social and economic relations, and in the specific social order" (quoted in Lister et al, 2003, p. 190). The problem is that despite the instruction of history, media practitioners and critics alike tend to place an undue emphasis on technological power and return to the same hopes and fears about what technologies can help and harm.

In investigating the dynamic of online news diffusion, this study has indirectly explored its potential development and impact, with many implications for the future of online news and journalism. This chapter summarises the study's major findings and uses them to analyse these implications. First, it summarises the current state of play and presents a forecasting model of online news consumption growth in the future, taking into account all the technical and socio-structural factors explored in this book (online news attributes, social locators, news orientation/behaviour, innovativeness, and Internet experience). Second, based on the data on the effect of online news attributes, I will make some projections and suggestions about good online news practices in its unfolding second development stage. Throughout this, some concerns will also be raised about the possible continuation of the adverse effect of the media's fear-driven innovation culture on the shape of online news in the near future. Third, I will present a detailed discussion of the implications of these developments of online news for the well-known digital divide. Fourth, the chapter discusses the normative implications of the recent rise of participatory publishing for the future of the public sphere and journalism. At the end, a range of other potential consequences and implications of online news diffusion that are not explored in this work – including the future of the digital divide, the possible transformation of old news forms, potential problems for journalism professionalism – will be briefly discussed as a way to call for future research.

Implication 1: the potential diffusion of online news among the public

This book, particularly Chapter 4, has shown that the Internet as a news medium has gained a mainstream status in most developed segments of the world since the early 2000s. In Australia, by September 2004, online news had reached about a third of the adult population and had made an important contribution to shaping the perception and understanding of public affairs among over one-fifth. Not less importantly, this penetration of online news has shown no sign of stopping, with the size and substance of the online news audience still growing around the globe. In order to predict this potential development in the future, there is a need to build a model that charge the factors influencing online news adoption/use.

Concerning this, I posited elsewhere a forecasting model for the potential development of online news, based on data from a global review of online news consumption in its first seven or eight years (Nguyen, 2003). This model (Figure 8.1) encompassed four groups of direct predictors of online news adoption/use: demographics, bandwidth, Internet experience and use locations. Accordingly, all these factors have a direct influence on online news use, indicated by the continuous arrows. Further, close relationships between some of these direct factors, indicated by the discrete arrows, make them more decisive as indirect influences on the potential adoption/use of online news in the future. In the light of this work's in-depth theoretical development and empirical findings, however, this model has turned out to be too simplistic. For example, the influence of online news

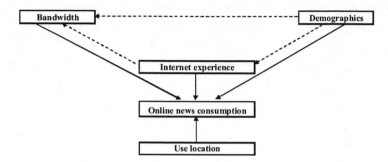

Figure 8.1: Nguyen's (2003) forecasting model of online news consumption

features or news needs and habits was not taken into account in the model. Therefore, a fuller, more exhaustive and more complex model on the dynamics of online news adoption/use has been developed and is depicted in Figure 8.2.

As can be seen, on the background of this model are the individual's social locators (age, sex, jobs, education, income, living area etc.) that determine four groups of factors with a direct influence on how and why he/she adopts and uses online news. These include (1) news orientation and its associated use patterns; (2) innovativeness (the degree to which one is receptive to new technologies); (3) experience with the Internet (the degree to which one can access, use, master, enjoy and depend on the Internet for daily activities); and (4) perceived online news attributes. Between these direct determinants are at least six relationships that make the dynamics of online news adoption/use complex. From the bottom up, the six elements of the model and their mutual relationships are recapitulated below:

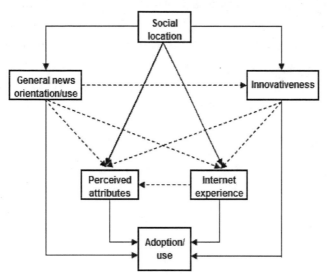

Figure 8.2: A forecasting model of online news adoption/use

Adoption/use: In this model, adoption/use refers to the way online news is integrated into daily life, which encompasses a range of behaviours and attitudes related to online news use, including the decision to adopt it, its use levels, and the extent to which one is affectively and cognitively attached to it. As shown throughout Chapters 5 and 6, the effect of each group of direct determinants varies from one aspect of adoption/use to another.

Perceived attributes of online news: Technical features are obviously a crucial factor in the adoption/use of online news and are the technological basis for much of hype surrounding it in the 1990s. However, the intrinsic technical advantage of online news can only materialise when it is *appreciated* to be advantageous by potential adopters.

Within this study, Chapters 4 and 5 found that despite the many opportunities for accidental exposure on the web, there is compelling evidence to make several important conclusions. First, most of the nine online news features being explored (no cost, more news choices, multitasking, immediacy, in-depth and background information, diversity of viewpoints, customisation, "have my say" ability and ability to exchange news and current affairs with peers) are being used because they are appreciated (i.e. are not used ritualistically). Second, they not only contribute to online news adoption decision but also play a primary role in shaping at least one aspect of the post-decision behaviours explored in this study (use frequency, time spending on online news in a typical session, perceived importance of online news, perception of the Internet as the best news source to serve one's news needs, and self-identification as online news fans). The particular effect of each attribute and its implications for online news practices will be discussed in details in the next section. It must be noted, however, that the effect of online news attributes on use frequency and time spending wears off when they are controlled for the attachment variables – i.e. online news attributes influence use levels via determining attachment levels, especially the cognitive dependence on online news.

While not explored in detail in this book, online news content should be considered part of perceived attributes. Indeed, content and technical features go together in formulating perceptions of and motivations for using online news. For example, an individual who likes sports will be more likely to use the Internet to check for sport score updates and other related information than one who does not. If this is not well supplied on the web, the sport fan might well turn to television for what he/she needs. In other words, technical features are an integral part of online news content. Future research should further explore this integration.

Internet experience: Although under the same label as in the 2003 model, Internet experience here is much more broadly understood as a catch-all term referring to different aspects of Internet access and use. In essence, "bandwidth", "use locations" and "Internet experience", depicted as direct drivers in Figure 8.1, are subsumed under "Internet experience" in the new model. It has a direct effect on online news adoption/use because it improves the chance for one to use and become gradually attached to it – via, for example, enhanced Internet skills, more accessibility to the Internet (e.g. both at work and at home), broadband connections, dependence on the Internet and so on. Part of this direct effect of Internet experience comes from its effect on how one perceives and appreciates online news advantages (represented by the discrete arrow between these two boxes). Within this study, Chapter 6 suggests the following major future trends in relation to this diverse group of determinants:

- o Online news is more likely to be adopted among Internet users who (1) have Internet access at more than one place; (2) have broadband connections and, among broadband users, have broadband connections at more than one place; (3) have used the Internet for a longer time; (4) are more dependent on the Internet in daily life; (5) use the Internet more frequently; (6) understand the Internet more; (7) use the Internet more frequently for all non-news purposes (entertainment and relaxation, e-commerce, personal contact, interaction with other online news users, searching non-news information for work, study and other purposes). In terms of unique contributions, perceived level of understanding the Internet and non-news Internet use frequency are significant positive predictors.

- o Among adopters, online news is likely to be used more frequently by those who (1) have broadband connections; (2) have used the Internet for a longer time; (3) use the Internet more frequently; (4) understand the Internet more; and (5) use the Internet more frequently to search non-news information for work, study and other purposes. As for unique effect, perceived level of understanding the Internet, general Internet use frequency and non-news Internet use frequency are primary contributors to online news use frequency.

- o Also among adopters, online news is more likely to be perceived as an important/essential part of daily Internet use by those who (1) have Internet access at more than one place; (2) have broadband connections at more than one place; (3) use the Internet more frequently; and (4) use the Internet more frequently for entertainment and relaxation and for searching non-news information for work, study and other purposes. In terms of unique contribution, non-news Internet use frequency is the only significant positive predictor.

News orientation and its associated behaviours: This group of factors has a strong direct influence on online news adoption/use because it encompasses an individual's needs for news, skills in using it as well as the extent to which news is integrated in his/her daily life. It has a widespread influence on all the other groups of direct determinants. General news use, for example, could have an important effect on innovativeness because an individual with more news/information consumption is more likely to be earlier in obtaining knowledge and understanding about innovations, including online news and its utilities. By the same token, it can have an impact on Internet experience because the more news and information one consumes, the more likely he/she is to be aware of technical innovations and to obtain how-to knowledge related to his/her Internet use. Also, because of this knowledge, he/she might have been earlier in adopting the Internet and thus is more likely to be an Internet veteran. Meanwhile, news orientation, including the subjective value given to news, could influence how one appreciates online news attributes – e.g. an individual with no general preference for immediacy might not much appreciate the capacity of updates on the web.

This study found the following major trends related to news orientation/behaviour:

o Online news is more likely to be adopted by Internet users who (1) have a stronger need for the two hard news categories of international affairs and national/state politics; (2) have less need for news about culture/the arts and about local community affairs; (3) are news junkies; (4) more enjoy keeping up with the news; (5) receive news more frequently (but not necessarily spend more time on news); (6) wish they had more time to follow the news; and (7) discuss news and current affairs with peers more frequently either in face-to-face or telephone talks. Of these, enjoying keeping up with the news and being news junkies are likely the primary factors that have a significant or almost significant positive unique contribution to online news adoption.

o Among adopters, online news is likely to be used more frequently by those who (1) have a stronger need for news about international affairs, national/state politics, economics (including business and finance); (2) have less need for news about social problems (crime/disasters/accidents) and culture/the arts; (3) more enjoy keeping up with the news; (4) receive news more frequently (but not necessarily spend more time on news); and (5) discuss news and current affairs more frequently when meeting peers. In terms of unique effect, enjoyment of keeping up with the news and exchanging news and current affairs are positive predictors of on online news frequency. However, those who use online news more frequently are also those who spend less time on news in general.

o Also among adopters, online news is likely to be perceived as an important or essential part of daily Internet use by those users who (1) have a stronger need for not only the four hard news categories of international affairs, national/state politics, economics and science, technology and health but also a stronger overall news need; (2) are news junkies; (4) receive news more frequently (but not necessarily spend more time on news); and (5) discuss news and current affairs with peers either in face-to-face or telephone talks. As for unique contribution, being a news junkie, general news use frequency and news exchange are significant predictors.

It is also in this news orientation/behaviour arena that the complementary, rather than replacement, effect of the Internet on traditional media can be argued for. Although this book explored this complementary relationship in the general domain of news and information, the user-centric theoretical perspective underlining this relationship (Chapter 7) can well be applied to the more specific news realm. Indeed, much of this user-centric perspective is an expansion of the theoretical discussion that bolstered the influence of general news orientation/behaviour on online news adoption/use in Chapter 6. Thus, we can project with confidence that because each news source offers a distinctive set of gratification opportunities, based on their content profile and use context, people with a strong news orientation and a heavy pattern of news uses will continue to use traditional sources – especially intensive sources like newspapers – substantially after adopting and integrating online news into their daily life. Certainly, as pointed out in Chapter 7, a displacement effect cannot be ruled out. The fact that both online news adopters and frequent users in the 2004 survey received news more frequently but were not different from their counterparts in the average daily amount of time spending on news (Chapter 6) suggests that there might have been some reallocation of time and probably attention. But the crucial point is that the Internet will not drive any established medium out of existence. All media will compete but, at some point in time, will compromise to coexist in human life.

Innovativeness: Although this factor was not empirically investigated with direct survey data in this book, the review of relevant literature in Chapter 3 provides a firm ground to include it in the model. There was also some evidence from the 2004 survey to indirectly support this. This was found when I explored how the adoption of a cluster of new media technologies/services (subscription to a pay TV service; subscription to a pay online service; having more than one computer at home; having a laptop; having a DVD player; having an MP3 player; having a digital camera; having a mobile phone with a built-in camera; and having a Personal Digital Assistant) was associated with online news adoption, use frequency and attachment level. The findings indicate that this new media cluster index (alpha = .63) was a significant predictor of online news adoption ($p < .001$) and its perceived importance ($p < .02$), although it only marginally predicted use frequency ($p = .09$) (data not shown).

Similar conclusions have been found among adopters of other new media technologies (see, for example, Atkin, 1993; Ettema, 1989; Jeffres & Atkin, 1996; Lin, 1998; Li & Yang, 2000; Lin, 2001; Li, 2003). Some researchers (Cameron, 2004; Rainie & Horrigan, 2003; Rhee & Kim, 2004; Australian National Office for the Information Economy, 2004; Zhou & He, 2002a) have attributed this cluster adoption phenomenon to the home effect (e.g. the presence and number of children with educational and informational needs, the status of new technologies as communal household assets). Others (e.g. Lin, 2001) argued that this is a matter of functional similarity: new media technologies tend to be adopted in clusters because they are functionally related, complementing or supplementing each other in serving similar media-related needs. Still some others (Atkin, 2002; Jeffres & Atkin, 1996, LaRose & Atkin, 1992; Neuendorf et al, 1998) have come up with the argument that the way people integrate technologies into their daily life is actually determined by the compatibility of these technologies with their existing behavioural patterns, regardless of their needs for, past experiences with and beliefs in them. Accordingly, the adoption of media clusters is a matter of "lifestyle".

In whatever explanation, however, new media cluster adoption "can be subsumed under the umbrella of habits ..., whether those are how one uses the media, the lifestyle one pursues, the communication needs one has, and so on" (Reagan, 2002, p. 81). It follows from this that the ownership of new media clusters can be seen as an indicator – or the manifest behaviour – of what I term a *modern media orientation*, understood here as the tendency that an individual is enthusiastic about and ready for new media technologies. As the term itself suggests, modern media orientation is a function of innovativeness (in the sense that it indicates the willingness to try and adopt new technologies – either because of needs or lifestyle or simply pro-technology attitudes). More specifically, modern media orientation and new media clusters tend to go together and can be seen as equivalent to what Migley and Dowling (1978) called "inherent innovativeness" (a novelty-seeking orientation) and "actualised innovativeness" (the willingness to take risks and adopt new technologies). The former is a precondition for the latter. From another perspective, the pro-technology orientation can reflect what is called open-processing innovativeness – a cognitive style that indicates an individual's openness to new experiences and places thanks to their intellectual, perceptual and attitudinal characteristics, as opposed to domain-specific innovativeness (the tendency to learn about and adopt innovations within a more specific domain of interest) (Citrin et al, 2000; Hui & Wan, 2004).

In short, the positive correlation between new media cluster and online news adoption/use found in the 2004 survey provides evidence for the strong influence of innovativeness on the latter and thus its presence in the suggested model of online news adoption/use dynamics is both theoretically and empirically justified. In a similar vein, it could be argued that people with a higher degree of innovativeness might be more enthusiastic about and/or capable of receiving messages about new media technologies and services, such as online news, and might form a favourable attitude to their attributes more quickly. Also because of this general pro-technology attitude, they are likely to have been among the first Internet adopters and thus to have more experience with the Internet.

Social locators: Although representing the same variables as demographic factors in Figure 8.1, social locators here are seen as indirect, rather than direct, determinants of online news adoption/use. As it has been clear by now, social locators generate different socio-economic and psychological situational factors (e.g. news needs and skills) that lead to different news orientation/use patterns, different levels of willingness to try new technologies, different experiences with the Internet, and different perceptions of what web news is good/bad at – all of which lead to different decisions regarding online news adoption/use. Although they conceptually have little direct influence on the adoption/use behaviours (i.e. there is no direct arrow from social locators to online news adoption/use), the strong influence of social locators on the four groups of direct influencers make them an important group of predictors of online news adoption/use. Within this study, the following major trends could be suggested:

o Online news is more likely to be adopted among Internet users who are males, are younger, live in metropolitan areas, work full-time, are active white-collar workers or higher professional occupations, and (quite possibly) have more education. In terms of unique contribution, online news adoption is likely to be determined by being a male, being younger and being a professional.

o Among adopters, sex is the only significant predictor of online news frequency, with males being likely to use it more frequency. Together, however, these demographic variables do not predict online news use frequency.

o Also among adopters, online news is likely to become an important/essential part of those who live in a metropolitan area. However, when the seven social locators are controlled together, it appears that users with more education but less income are more likely to use the Internet for news more frequently.

All in all, taking into account only the primary determinants (those with a significant unique contribution) within each group of socio-structural variables in the book, we could identify the following trends for the future:

o Online news is more likely to be adopted by Internet users who are males, are younger, live in metropolitan areas, are professionals, more enjoy keeping up with the news, have a higher level of understanding the Internet, and use the Internet for more non-news Internet purposes.

o Among adopters, online news is likely to be more frequently used by those who, regardless of their social locators, more enjoy keeping up with the news, more frequently discuss news and current affairs with peers, have more years of Internet experience, use the Internet more frequently, and use the Internet for more non-news purposes. These frequent users, however, tend to spend less time on news in general.

o Also among adopters, online news is more likely to be perceived as an important or essential part of Internet usage by those who are more educated, are news junkies, use news more frequently, exchange news and current affairs with peers more frequently, and use the Internet for more non-news purposes. These users, however, tend to have lower income than infrequent users.

In addition, the advantageous features of online news are more likely to be appreciated as reasons for using it by those who are younger, use news more frequently, exchange news and current affairs with peers more frequently and use the Internet, and use the Internet for more non-news purposes. However, quite strikingly, online news users living in metropolitan areas, having higher income and spending more time on news per day are likely to be less appreciative of the collective "power" of online news (Chapter 6).

Towards a further future, the model suggests that if a few decades ago, the nascent television medium immediately saw rosy years ahead as its early adopters were dominantly young media-savvy people, the same thing could be hoped for online news. As I argued elsewhere: "This young generation, growing up with more skills, enjoyment and dependence in relation to computers and the Internet, will more and more rely on the web as their source of news. The Internet is the news medium of the future in this sense" (Nguyen, 2003).

Implication 2: online news practices for the second stage and their potential economic impediments

The potential diffusion of online news depends not only on public responses to it but also on how media actors use and appropriate its potential. With the news public around the globe having shown a positive response to online news, Chapter 2 shows that traditional news organisations, now feeling even more threatened than the 1990s, have been actively catching the wave to make up their time lost in the online news world in its first decade. Since 2005, generous resources have been made available for their online businesses, signalling that online journalism is entering a more substantive development stage – one in which a strong commitment to capitalising on the diverse potential of online news is seen as the way for traditional news businesses to ensure a sustainable development.

What, then, should be focused on, further promoted and/or improved to foster a further diffusion of online news in this unfolding development stage? How can online news professionals harness its socio-technical potential to maximise their success in the years ahead? The original user data in this work suggest several practical ideas, briefly outlined below:

First, immediacy seems to be the defining attribute of online news and needs to be given a high priority. Within the 2004 survey, the ability to get updated news at any time is the most crucial contributing medium factor, scoring the highest mean as a reason for online news adoption and, after statistical control for other attributes, being the only variable that makes a significant contribution to every of the online news behaviours and attributes being explored (see the previous section). In addition, the timeliness and updatedness of online news was given the highest satisfaction score, above its presentation format, diversity of news content, depth of coverage and different viewpoints (Chapter 4). Also, the majority (70%) of online news users in the sample had visited news sites a few times a day to check up-to-the minute news and almost half (47%) would go to the Internet first had they heard something of great interest had just happened. All this is well in line with findings by previous studies (Abdulla et al, 2002; Conway, 2001; Nozato, 2002, Salwen et al, 2005, Schweiger, 2002; Washingtonpost.com, 2005; and the Pew Internet Project's recent surveys). Thus, to foster a wider adoption and more substantial use of online news, its practitioners might need to focus more on providing continual 24-hour news services.

Second, news speed needs to be provided at the same time as news substance. As seen in chapter 5, the appreciated immediacy and content richness of online news tend to co-vary, suggesting that people looking for updates will look for depth as well. As reasons for online news use, the availability of in-depth/background information and that of more news choices came third and fourth respectively in mean scores (Chapter 4). When statistically controlled for other attributes, they made a unique significant contribution to

242

the perceived importance of online news and the time budget for it (Chapter 5). Also, the vast majority (90%) of users had clicked on links for in-depth/background information and nearly three quarters had visited a number of sites for the same news item (Chapter 4). Thus, along with continuous updates to keep users coming back frequently, online news practitioners might be able to generate more substantial traffic and/or increase users' time on their sites by at least taking advantage of the Internet's hypertextual links and unlimited space to provide further details (including raw materials) and/or organise content into themes and/or special (temporary and permanent) sections. Taking advantage of social media technologies to elicit a diversity of news perspectives from the public should also be seen as a key content development strategy.

Third, the ease/convenience of online news use should be promoted. The specific features generating this characteristic such as its 24/7 availability, the ability to combine news use with other online purposes have been found to be among the most crucial assets of online news in research by Chan and Leung (2005), Conway (2001), Salwen et al (2005), the Nielsen//NetRatings study for Washingtonpost.com (2005) and the Pew Internet Project. Within this research, the ability to multitask was ranked second as a reason for online news use (chapter 4) and, after statistical control, was a unique contributor to its use frequency (chapter 5). Also, subscription to email alerts of general news was among one of the few behaviours that made a significant unique contribution to online news frequency (Chapter 5). While much of the use convenience of online news is inherent to the Internet itself (Chapter 3), these data suggest that the provision of services that further improve this – such as email news alerts, RSS feeds, opportunities for users to make a news service their home page, or news options on portal or social-network sites – will play an important role in attracting users and keeping them coming back to news sites. It might also be a good strategy to maintain and improve news recommendation options – such as Digg – so that users can pick and post stories of their interest to external websites. The combined dissemination of news via the web, podcasting, handheld technologies and others -- i.e. multiple-platform publishing – is another option.

Finally, although the data do not seem to suggest that participation opportunities – arguably the most unique attribute of online news (Chapter 3) – are compelling enough to drive online news use, their role should not be depreciated. In Chapters 4 and 5, we saw that the ability to talk back to the media and the ability to discuss news with other users were ranked at the bottom of medium-centric reasons for online news adoption, and, after being controlled for other appreciated attributes, made little significant contribution to its use and attachment levels. While this might appear disappointing for those enthusiastic about the democratic nature of online news, it does not necessarily mean that user-journalist and user-user interactions are not attractive. As pointed out in Chapter 4, the insignificant contribution of participation opportunities in this study might be due to the fact that by the time of the survey, public participation was still a small part on most news sites. Additionally, the fact that 71% of users in the sample had passed some first-hand accounts to peers suggests that users indeed are keen on harnessing the Internet to distribute their news and views and obtain social gratifications from it if they are given the chance. All this, coupled with the unprecedented rise of participatory publishing in the past ten years (Chapter 4), suggests that building and improving interactivity-based services that offer users opportunities to be part of the news flow via so-called Web 2.0 technologies is a wise business strategy for online news ventures in the coming years. At least, as noted above, encouraging public participation will improve the content richness of news sites. There are many other, and normative, reasons for journalism to be serious about public participation on the web, to be discussed in detail in the next section.

With all these user data and implications in mind, I was immediately attracted to a model for the 21st century newsroom that I came across when this book came to its close. Proposed by British academic Paul Bradshaw of Birmingham City University on his popular Online Journalism Blog, the model assumes that "the strengths of the online medium are essentially twofold, and contradictory: speed, and depth" (Bradshaw, 2007), an assumption strongly supported by the user data in this book. Thus, Bradshaw called for practitioners to "think mobile and email updates, think moblogs, (and) think Twitter" (for speed) at the same time at thinking about its hypertextual and pull properties (for depth and breadth). An ideal operation model for online newsrooms is depicted in Figure 8.3. Accordingly, the life cycle of a news event will spread along the following extensive seven-step process of content sharing, updating and adding via multiple platforms:

1. Alert: As soon as an event unfolds, an alert is sent out to instantly notify subscribers to SMS news services or email updates as well as users of Twitter or Facebook and the like. For Bradshaw, "this shows you 'own' the story ... and drives readers to your website, newspaper or broadcast".

2. Draft: Following the alert is a draft report, something that is "too rough for print or broadcast" but is "perfect for blogs". With updated basic details such as initial names, places and sources, this draft can keep the "Alert" readers on the site, bring more readers and improve search engine rankings via words spread in the blogosphere. It can also be used to receive feedbacks on details from those close to or affected by the event.

3. Article/Package: "At this stage, the draft turns into a package with higher production values, and which could be online, in print, broadcast, or all of those."

4. Context: In this stage, the unlimited space and the powerful hyperlinks of the web are utilised to provide users with instant and extensive contextual information that traditional media do not enjoy or can only do so on a limited basis. Here, traditional-medium reports should refer users to the online resource for more contextual details.

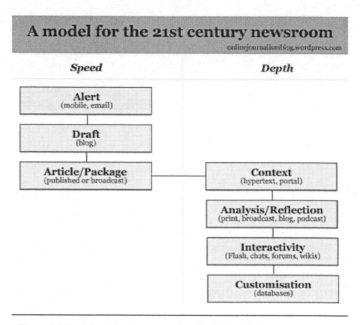

Figure 8.3: Paul Bradshaw's proposed model for the 21st century newsroom

5. Analysis/Reflection: The analysis comes after the report, drawing on the almost instant reaction of online participants on blogs and forums onsite or offsite, especially information from "the informed and the affected". Also in this process, the story's writer could reflect on the whole experience on his/her blog and/or might use podcasts to invite discussion and debate.

6. Interactivity: At this stage, the users should be provided with opportunities to be engaged and further informed through engagement, via facilities such as forums, wikis, live chats and flash combinations of hypertext, video, audio, animation and databases. Bradshaw maintains that while this is often laborious and expensive, it can generate a "long tail" resource that keeps users coming back to the site in the long run.

7. Customisation: Here, users' wishes to tailor the information to their own need are honoured via tools such as email/RSS updates of that particular story, social recommendation or searchable databases.

While the model might look idealistic to some critics, it provokes a great deal of thoughts on how news practitioners can harness the power of online news to provide users with a "total experience" (Chapter 3) and thereby to obtain their commercial and professional aims. It is not only well in line with the audience and market data in this book but also commensurate with the normative nature of journalism as a discipline of verification, whose ultimate job is to use objective methods to get the facts straight and then put them together in a meaningful way so that people can make sense of the world (Kovach & Rosenstiel, 2001). It will, in other words, assist online journalists to effectively and efficiently perform the two distinctive functions of journalism that Walter Lippmann (1922) envisioned nearly nine decades ago: providing the news ("to signalise an event") and telling the truth ("to bring to light the hidden facts, to set them into relation with each other, and make a picture of reality upon which man can act"). For these reasons, Bradshaw's model could serve as an ultimate aim for which online newsrooms should strive in the long term.

The question is whether online practitioners are willing to do this. With all the above in mind, we can see that most of the recently renewed online strategies of traditional news outlets – producing content for multiple platforms, adding original content such as multimedia and web-first breaking news, building interactive communities and so forth (Chapter 2) – are much on the right track. Online practitioners today are much more technically and professionally prepared than their 1990s counterpart, having learnt a great deal from a decade of failures and successes. This could and should prompt a strong hope for many more innovative online news services to arrive in the years ahead. That is, however, not to paint an all-too-optimistic picture. There is still a fundamental issue to be concerned about when thinking about the future of online news: the potential adverse effect of the still defensive innovation culture behind the new development stage of online news.

As detailed in Chapter 2 and summarised above, much of the recent active move by the traditional media stems less from an excitement about the socio-technical possibilities of online news than from a renewed and intensified fear of the Internet's potential ability to push them to the path of dinosaurs. Thus, if history is a prologue, we should not be too over-optimistic about online news development in the years ahead because, as seen in the videotex experience and the first decade of web news (Chapters 1 and 2), the feeling of being threatened by new technologies can lead traditional newspeople to focus most of their strategic thinking on defending their well-being rather on exploring the new in a creative and proactive manner. Thus, despite the recent signs of positive changes, the potential negative impact of this "being faithful by being faithless" innovation approach on the fate and shape of online news is still something that online journalism scholars and practitioners should continue to closely watch.

More specifically, what we will need to monitor is the likely continuation of the tension between the determination to build an innovative online news artefact and the reluctance resulting from the fear that this can "kill" the still profitable existing businesses. We have to be concerned about this because there is much evidence that the massive resources spent on online news since the mid-2000s are still part of defensive business strategies. For example, when he was still the CEO of Fairfax in Australia, Fred Hilmer (now Vice-Chancellor of the University of New South Wales) saw multiple-platform publishing as a crucial strategy more to preserve traditional markets via building good relationships with readers in an age of media segmentation than to build better online news services:

> (Readers) start to use other forms of media because the first law of media is that media segments (sic). You keep them in the *Herald* brand through convergence. We're seeing this particularly with the Internet. One of the interesting spin-offs is that the Internet has become quite a significant channel for driving print subscriptions because people like the brand (quoted in Quinn & Quinn-Allan, 2005, p. 10).

Hilmer's successor, Dr David Kirk, set three strategic priorities for the recently renamed Fairfax Media (Chapter 2), the first and most crucial of which is to "defend and grow our newspapers" (Kirk, 2006). And when the primary aim is to protect the old, anything new is likely to be done with the caution that it cannot become a direct competitor to the old (Chapter 2). Thus, would the recent impressive resources spent on online news continue in the coming years, given that fully-fledged online news services are likely to result in a direct threat to the still profitable traditional products? This point becomes more critical in the light that as users migrate on to the web, they seem to "normalise" their online news experience, being driven more by its capacity for traditional news qualities such as immediacy, news diversity and depth of coverage than by its unique features (Chapter 5). Meanwhile, as long-time online business consultant Vin Crosbie of Digital Deliverance estimated in 2006, "newspapers need between 20–100 readers online to make up for losing just one print reader" (quoted in Bleyen & Van Hove, 2007).

The further problem is that traditional news practitioners, although now technically and professionally prepared, are not yet commercially ready to build independent online news businesses. Despite being used in one way or another by the majority of news sites, paid content does not seem to work well (Bleyen & Van Hove, 2007; Herbert & Thurman, 2007) – even the *New York Times* had to remove its pay wall to make all its long-blocked content free from September 2007 and the *Wall Street Journal* under its new owner, Rupert Murdoch, decided to open its opinion and commentary pages for free use in January 2008. Meanwhile, advertising is tough in the online world, with a large proportion being now in the hand of search engines (Chapter 2), and is still something that traditional newspeople have not fully understood and/or mastered. In their in-depth interviews on multimedia and convergence with major British news editors in June-July 2007, for instance, Thurman and Lupton (2008) found that although these editors showed a willingness to invest" in online video news, "no clear picture emerged of what sort of video will be popular or profitable" and "it remain(ed) to be seen whether the advertising revenue they hope for (would) come to the national, generic content providers in a world of increasing consumer control, niche content, and fragmented attention". Other potential revenue sources – such as reader donations – might be good for small sites but would probably make little significant financial contribution to the big (and often greedy) news companies.

Thus, it might be over-optimistic to believe that traditional news organisations would be willing to devote all necessary resources to developing an excellent online news artefact that threatens their traditional "bread and butter" sources but makes insufficient returns. The fact remains that online news sites still depend very much on the economic health of their traditional siblings. Vin Crosbie's adept observation in 2004 – that "newspapers online and newsprint editions aren't Siamese twins: the newsprint editions can exist without the online editions -- but online editions can't exist without newsprint editions" – is still valid today. In short, until traditional newspeople find and establish distinctive revenue models for independent online news businesses, it will remain hard to predict how the social shape of online news will evolve in the market in the next decade or so. An important research direction in the coming years, therefore, might be to identify good-practice cases in which the old journalism and business routines and mindsets are overcome and/or well accommodated with the diverse potential of online news.

Implication 3: a widening digital divide

In exploring the past and present of online news to forecast its potential development via the above social and technical factors, this research has in effect shown the social impact of the new news form. The fact that online news has been quite deeply integrated into the daily life of a substantial part of the global public is in itself a demonstration of this impact. However, with this penetration of online news into daily life and its promising future has come the fact that it seems to be widening the so-called "digital divide" – the information gap between different socio-economic strata caused by advances in digital technologies within (and between) societies around the world. Like its development in other countries, online news has diffused within a more socio-economically advantaged circle of the Australian public, with the majority of its users being younger males, living in a metropolitan area, working full-time, belonging to white-collar or higher-prestige occupational groups, having more formal education, and having more household income (see above). Similar profiles of online news and information users have been found in elsewhere too (Compaine, 2001; Nguyen & Western, 2006; Norris, 2001). As D. Johnson put it, "the Internet can give power to the less powerful, and it can increase the power of the already powerful. It all depends on who uses the Internet and how" (quoted in Mason & Hacker, 2003, p. 44).

Since the Internet in general and online news in particular are still in their early diffusion stage, the question is whether the above gap will disappear when these innovations approaches their saturation point in the familiar S-shaped curve (Chapter 3) in the future. For many scholars, the answer to this question is yes and the so-called digital divide is nothing to worry about. A key figure in this debate is Benjamin Compaine, who collected and edited a thorough series of empirical and critical studies to dismiss the notion of the digital divide, which he claimed to be "not the issue to expend substantial amounts of funds nor political capital" (Compaine, 2001a, p. xvi). In this volume, *The Digital Divide: Facing a Crisis or Creating a Myth?*, Compaine published a piece he wrote in the early 1980s to question "whether these warnings (about information gaps) are sound, or are merely good copies for the mass media, or are the creation of some academics with little tie to the real world, or are serving to further the political and social agenda of a cadre with a particular ideology" (Compaine, 2001b, p. 105). One of his major arguments, drawn from media history, is that all information gaps will be eventually eliminated as access to information increases and the skills to use it becomes less demanding over time:

> In the mass media, history shows that the colonial press was structured for the educated elite. A series of cultural and technological developments which started to emerge in the 1830s created the conditions for the mass audience penny press. The spread of newspapers, like many cultural innovations, followed an S curve.
>
> In the earliest days of radio, a user had to have a modest technical bent to use the medium, tinkering with the crystal set. With improvements in the technology and the development of programming, the radio spread rapidly. Instalment plans allowed households of modest means to purchase a radio. Even during the Depression the number of radio sets grew.
>
> Television followed a similar pattern. As with other innovations, prices came down rapidly as production volume increased. In 1950, a small black and white television cost about $3000 in 1984 dollars. Today, a larger screen colour model can be had for $300 or even less" (Compaine, 2001b, pp. 112-113).

By the same token, Compaine (2001a) contended that as the Internet will play a crucial role in the future and thus will be used by people from all walks of life, those worrying about the digital divide might be creating a modern legend:

> Are there stakes for democracy? Yes and no. In the long term – perhaps over 25 years – new ways of communication will become mainstream and prevalent. What is today the Internet, that is, a packet-switched multi-node network utilising both wired and wireless components, will likely become *a* – if not *the* – primary carrier. So access to that network will be critical. On the other hand, what is the likelihood that this network will indeed become universal and central to communications if virtually everyone did not first have access to it?

> Will people need high-tech skills to participate in this democracy in the future? Probably not. In fact, probably less than is needed today .... And the skill level to use intelligent devices keeps getting lower. Even programming is easier today with higher level languages than the totally foreign machine languages that were needed in the earliest years of computing (Compaine, 2001a, p. xv-xvi).

Other scholars support this in the context of recent Internet development. They believe that SES variables will become less important in the take-up of information technologies, especially Internet technologies, as they accelerate their diffusion and become cheaper, more available and more familiar. Neuendorf et al. (1998) contended that "a convergence of users" should be expected to correspond to a world of no discontinuous innovations, where the "hardware" of an innovation is linked to established delivery systems. According to Powell (2001), a combination of "dirt-cheap" Internet access and the costs of computers "approaching the costs of television sets" (p. 309) have led to the end of the 1990s digital divide in the 21st century. In terms of the skills needed for Internet use, Lloyd Morrisett (2001, p. x) argued that the Internet is by its nature a remover of its technical barriers:

> No technology, in itself, will ever eliminate the differences that arise among people who effectively utilise a technology and those who do not. The Internet, however, is a technology that can give people the opportunity to learn the very skills that maximise the value of the technology. Internet content can be created that allows everyone the opportunity to learn to read, and as readers, take full advantage of the cornucopia of information resources that exist and are being created. The divide between those who can read well and those who cannot is a real divide. Rather than being a 'digital divide', the Internet can be a road to information freedom.

These arguments have received some empirical support from recent work, which has identified a less influential role of demographic factors such as income and education in the adoption of the Internet (Rhee & Kim, 2004), web-streaming (Kwak et al., 2004; Lin, 2004; Tanaka, 2000) as well as other types of online services (Lin, 2001). In short, the digital divide is more a "digital delay" and would disappear as Internet connectivity normalises (Xavier, 2001, p. 6).

This research, however, does not seem to support the disappearance of the existing information gap in the digital age. For one thing, the mindset underlining the hope for a gradual disappearance of the digital divide is, in essence, a technologically determinist one, which this book has consistently argued to be at least naïve. Certainly, these arguments make their own case and should not be totally discredited because as we have seen, technologies are the fundamental infrastructure on which social changes take place. The Internet is a powerful vehicle that has shown its values in the information society and it is not too over-optimistic to think of it as *a* primary communication medium of the future. But again, from a micro user-centric perspective, it could be argued that access to technologies is not and will never be enough. The fact that this study found an existing socio-economic gap between online news users and non-users *within the Internet population* is in itself supportive of this view.

This becomes clearer in the light of the theories underlining the model in Figure 8.2. It is essential to think of the digital divide not as a new problem peculiar to the online world, but, rather, as an old problem that might be worsened by the Internet. This is because the use of online news (and non-news information) is substantially determined by a labyrinth of beyond-access socio-psychological factors that form their news (and information) orientation – such as needs, reading skills and social networks. These factors are deep-seated in different patterns of social stratification and have long shown their impact in the offline world. Newspapers, for example, are accessible to everybody today; yet they tend to be used more by those with higher SES who usually have stronger needs for serious news and information and have enough cognitive resources to process this information. In contrast, the universally accessible television medium is more a domain of news and information for people with a more limited possession of education and other socio-economic resources (see Chapter 6). And as the Internet as an information-intensive medium penetrates daily life, it tends to have been adopted and used for news and information by those who substantially use and depend on other information-intensive sources.

The information gap, in short, will not fade away when the access and skill issues are solved in the digital age, because it is by nature a very human issue, not a technological one. As D. Johnson put it: "The Internet can give power to the less powerful, and it can increase the power of the already powerful. It all depends on who uses the Internet and how" (quoted in Mason & Hacker, 2003, p. 44). Indeed, "digital divide" seems to be a technologically obsessed term that conveys a wrong sense of a unique negative outcome of digital technologies. The term tends to orient us too much to the technology associated with it and too far away from the human nature of the issue. Thus, what is at stake and is more worthy of concerns is the extent to which and the way in which digital technologies, particularly the Internet, is facilitating the widening of this gap – and I think Pippa Norris is more than correct when putting forth the following argument:

> The interesting question is not whether there will be absolute social inequalities in Internet access; of course there will be, as in every other dimension of life. Alexander Graham Bell's commercial telephone service was launched in the United States in 1877, nevertheless today in America, more than a century later, there remain pockets of racial inequality in access to household telephones. Cable TV started to become available in the mid-1960s but today, due to choice or necessity, only two-thirds of American households are connected, along with about half of all households in industrialised nations. Given substantial inequalities in the old mass media, it would be foolishly naïve to expect that the Internet will magically transcend information poverty overnight. The more intriguing series of questions (…) concern whether there are special barriers to digital technologies, such as greater complexity or costs, and whether relative inequalities in Internet use will be similar to disparities in the penetration rates of older communication technologies (Norris, 2001; reprinted in Webster, 2004, p. 279).

And when touching these questions, we will see the information gap in the Internet era might become an increasingly serious social problem. Here, the concept of Internet experience in Figure 8.2 could be taken as a starting point. The model suggests that online news adoption/use changes over time, along with changes in Internet experience, which has both primary effect (on adoption/use) and secondary effect (on perceived attributes and news orientation). This suggests, for instance, that those who adopt the Internet earlier and/or use it more substantially will be more adept in using the medium for news purposes. Thus, those who are already online at the time a non-user "joins the crowd" are likely to have reached a more advanced level of using the medium when the novice becomes used to it. This gap will keep going unless (1) the technical skills needed to use the medium is almost the same over time (like turning on/off a television set and switching the channel with a remote controller); or (2) the novice speeds up his/her Internet use, spending more time and other resources to learn to use the medium and to keep up with veterans. Both of these scenarios seem to be unlikely even in mere technological terms. The Internet is very different from other media in that it follows what Lister et al. (2005, p. 180) called "the logic of upgrade culture":

> Differential (or non-universal) access is objectively a feature of the Internet. The Internet will never work like the pre-deregulated television where all shared more or less the same kind of technology, could access the same channels and all experience the same TV texts. Universal access in this case built out of the technology by the logic of upgrade culture – that is to say there will always be better software and faster computer architecture creating uneven access conditions.

More particularly, while advances in other media have more to do with improved quality (e.g. from black-and-white to colour television), advances in information technologies like the Internet are aimed at increasing their capacities for complex tasks (Mason & Hacker, 2003). Within the online news realm only, the four-year course of this book has seen the introduction or the takeoff of a range of new technologies – weblogs, podcasting, RSS feeds, and searchable news aggregators like Google News or Topix.com, just to name a few (Chapter 3). That has not included the increasing popularity of many infrastructure technologies (such as wireless Internet) and the famous Moore's law that suggests computer chips double their processing power every 18 to 24 months. And to keep up with these continuous advances based on the Internet infrastructure, users have not only to possess good resources but to accumulate a set of sophisticated digital skills.

Rogers foresaw this problem in the 1980s, when he argued that the increasingly rapid introduction sequence of new communication technologies in the market could only increase the overall degree of information equality because as one begins to reach widespread adoption, another may be creating a new set of widened gaps (Rogers, 1986). Thus, to continue the above example, at the time the novice user has enough resource to have access to ADSL broadband connection, for instance, many of the veterans might have long been enjoying the many benefits of wireless broadband. In other words, there is no single S-curve in the online world – the dynamic diversity of Internet technologies and services means that *successive S-curves* are always on the way and those with more access and skills related to the Internet would be more likely to be able to keep up with the changes. And to accumulate these increasingly complex skills, as Figure 8.2 shows, they need to have more socio-psychological resources to be able to take up the Internet and its related technologies right in the first place. Thus, later adopters of online technologies, who are generally less socio-economically and psychologically resourceful than earlier adopters (Chapter 5), will be left further and further behind.

This has not factored the fact that in the interactive online environment, earlier adopters seem to be crucial shapers of successive new technologies. As it has become clear, people use online news-related technologies in ways that reflect their news orientation – e.g. their needs, tastes and their cognitive skills. In the online world, they not only do it by themselves but also share them with other people with the same orientation. Over time, these exchanges between earlier adopters increase their skills and resources. A few decades ago, Pierre Bourdieu (1986) discussed this under the concept of "social capital" – "the aggregate of the actual or potential resources which are linked to possession of a durable network of more or less institutionalised relationships of mutual acquaintance and recognition". More importantly, via their interaction, earlier adopters gradually establish a distinct set of "supervening market demands" that would become the guideline for technology producers to create new products. Clearly, these market demands reflect the skills, resources and orientation of earlier adopters. Thus those who are missed out in the early chain of online communication will be left behind. As Mason and Hacker (2003, p. 48) contended, a process of power reproduction is taking place and "those already possessing sophisticated resources and skills continue to shape the technology".

From a producer-centric perspective, can competitive market forces serve as an antidote to the information gap of the digital age? As interests in the online world resurge, many would hope that online news/information providers will make their best attempt to appeal to the audience in order to exchange its attention for advertising dollars. Theoretically, this is correct. Practically, it is probably not. Certainly, as this study has consistently argued, media actors would follow what users need and integrate users' needs and tastes into online news services. The kind of users they tend to follow, however, is not the general public but those whom advertisers like. In Australia, for example, Channel 10 has been enjoying a huge success after its near-bankruptcy in the early 1990s by caring less about maximising the overall audience and more about the 16-39 age group (Flew & Gilmour, 2006; Turnbull, 2006). Also, as mentioned in Chapter 3, with news audience being fragmented in an increasingly diversified media landscape, media corporations have been adopting a "get more out of less" strategy – one focusing on small markets of highly educated and affluent audiences, rather than on the general public (Kovach & Rosenstiel, 2001). With the move to neo-liberal public policies and the loosening of cross-media ownership under the Howard Government, as well as the speeding investment in online news by major traditional players, the situation does not seem to allow for an easy sanguineness.

With the above having been said, however, I do not want to be a cyber-pessimist. While the information gap in the digital age will hardly level off over time and while it would be a little naive to expect corporate media to play a vital voluntary role to fix this social exclusion, the model in Figure 8.2 suggests that it can be narrowed down through the facilitation of public policies and regulations. First, some aspects of Internet experience can be addressed in policies relating to the digital divide. A universal and low-cost provision of broadband connections to regional and rural areas seems to be crucial here as it potentially enhances all other aspects of Internet experience – it could result in an increase in the enjoyment of Internet usage, in the chance or motivation to more substantially use online services, and consequently in more understanding of and dependence on the medium for daily purposes. Also, taking advantage of early adopters and other change agents to provide technical education and training in disadvantaged communities would help in many ways. Second, with the concept of perceived attributes and news orientation/behaviour in Figure 8.2 in mind, it would become obvious that providing good access to the technology and improving awareness and skills in using it would become meaningless if online news/information is perceived to be not useful enough.

Therefore content regulations and policies should encourage the production of such content that is geared to needs and tastes of low-SES people. For instance, the provision of local and community content and/or the enhancement of native-language programs might be helpful for rural areas and ethnic minorities. How this can be done is a matter of debate and choice but one major way is to maintain and enhance the online operation of public broadcasting services like the ABC and SBS in Australia or the BBC in the UK.

The argument that public broadcasters are becoming redundant in the age of digital market – one reason for governments to keep funding for these organisations either stable or increasingly reduced in a time they need more money to invest in new media ventures (Jacka, 2006) – is only a myth. The technology does facilitate the diversity of news content and perspectives and the catering of niche audiences, but commercial media, who are still the dominant online news sources, would not be so keen on those consumers who do not deliver some money value. As seen in Chapter 2, the news organisations which have been most active in employing and exploiting online news potential are public service broadcasters.

Implication 4: journalism in the wake of participatory publishing

This work has shown that in addition to the widespread rise of online news consumption, a combination of technological and social developments has resulted in a shift of news and information production from an institutionalised and industrial activity into a mode of popular expression. By tapping the power of the Internet and other new technologies to transform itself from mere news consumers into "prosumers", the public as the traditional underdog in the news and information flow has paved the way for a potentially better democracy. As signalled above, the normative importance of this development for the future of journalism and the public sphere is so immense that it would be a mistake to end this book without a detailed discussion of this importance.

The rise of the new decentralised information order on the Internet has led many people to question the fate of journalism. As the need for the media as the third party to mediate in the communication of public affairs is no longer inevitable, the power to govern the public sphere no longer belongs solely to the media, which generates many speculations about the demise of journalism. However, participatory publishing (PP), when closely examined, can intensify the crucial role of journalism – a more reactive and responsive journalism, to be exact – in the information age. This is because as much as online communities have proved to be potentially powerful in improving public debates, they are also potentially detrimental to the health of the fledgling online public sphere, making the need for professional mediators not at all diminishing but more essential.

One way to see this is to use the notion of an ideal public sphere envisioned by Jürgen Habermas (1996). Accordingly, an ideal public sphere is "a domain of our social life" to which everybody can access in principle and in which "such a thing as public opinion can be formed" through the governance of rational and critical discussions of matters of general interest by "(autonomous) private persons coming together to form a public" (Habermas, 1996, p. 398) – a dream shared by early netizens like William Quick, who coined the term "blogosphere" deliberately with the Latin root "logos" to imply "logic and reasoning" (Hiler, 2002). The reality of online participation, however, is that as netizens assemble and, in Habermas's words, "express and publicise their opinions freely", they do not always unite. To use the classic analytic triad of online communities (Lister et al, 2003, p. 174), people now have a shared space and probably some common relationship but there is nothing to guarantee shared values. Because of this, the ethics of participatory discourses – the acknowledgement and articulation of other feelings, races and values in seeking a universal agreement of moral standards (Wilson, 2004) – are not always met in the online public sphere.

Although the power of public participation online has materialised in many recent social and political events (Chapter 4), empirical research has shown that electronic discussions both before and after the introduction of the web do not always work toward consensus, can be short-lived with little impact and can easily turn into "dialogues of the deaf" that might lead nobody to anywhere (Arteton, 1987; Brants, Huizenga & van Meerten, 1996; see also works cited in Tsagarousianou, Tambini & Bryan, 1998). In many cases, the border between participation and ideological abuse and sensational responses is a hair-thin line. Australian blogger and author Sophie Masson noted that "some people seem to only respect 'free speech' if you agree with them", arguing:

> At its best, blogging, for the writer, can be a terrific experience, enabling you to have genuine discussions with readers, and engage in the kind of thoughtful and illuminating speculation that can often inspire new ideas and new trains of thought in you. However, that is the ideal situation, and it's rare, and precious. All too often, what the comments box turns into is a kind of dialogue of the deaf, with the original post hopelessly lost in a welter of tangents, parti pris positions, shouting matches, and a certain amount of intellectual bullying which I have found quite intimidating at times. It's not that I'm a stranger to unpleasant missives - if you write publicly anywhere, you've got to expect negative as well

as positive feedback - but I think *the medium itself has an atmosphere which makes people confrontational* (Masson, 2005; emphasis added).

This might become even more serious by the removal of the need to reveal identities in the lack of face-to-face interaction, which, while providing people with more freedom to express what they truly think and do, are potentially conductive to dangerous abuse at the same time.

The online public sphere, thus, is far from operating on the strength of autonomous and rational arguments which scientifically filter, in Habermas's language, "public opinions" (those based on scientific reasoning) from "mere opinions" (those based on established cultural norms or collective prejudices). In some cases, it could even result in what Senft (2000) called the "cult of public opinion" – not "the court of public opinion". This is worsened by the fact that, as discussed in Chapter 3, the easy publishing environment of the web – the launching pad of online participation – ironically provides a fertile land for many rumours, hoaxes and cheating games to freely circulate and for many individuals and organisations with vested interests (including, among others, politicians, celebrities and public relations corps) to sway public opinion. Rebecca Blood – a most authoritative voice in the world of weblogs – is radically correct in declaring: "The weblog's greatest strength – its uncensored, unmediated, uncontrolled voice – is also its greatest weakness" (quoted in Lane, 2002).

These characteristics of the online public sphere make responsible journalism – one that is both reactive and responsive to public concerns – all the more needed in an online environment. At a time when people have a potentially powerful means as much to reach "universal agreement" via critical discussions as to become irrational, the need for the professional moderation and facilitation of a responsible journalism to avoid further social and ideological fragmentation is still here to stay, if not intensified. When a former CBS gift shop clerk can quickly become an Internet personality and a millionaire just by continuously posting unchecked rumours surrounding politics, showbiz and the weather in the so-called Drudge Report, a responsible journalism would be more important to a public being swamped in an information overload. And when technologies allow ordinary people to even fool the whole global media system (such as Benjamin Vanderford's self-produced beheading video clip that purported to be Nick Berg execution in 2003), the gate-keeping function of the press is strengthened rather than becomes obsolete.

This, however, is not to encourage a "professional colonisation" of the online public sphere and to call for preserving a top-down model of communication between journalists and citizens. Rather, it is a call for a process in which journalists are no longer mere agenda-setters but also let the public set the agenda for themselves. That is, in addition to seeing their professional duty and obligation as informing and educating the public, journalists now would need to be directly informed and educated by the public in their daily operation. This represents a compromise in a two-step process: online participants initiate their dialogues; then journalism responds and works together with them so that these concerns can arrive in the broader democratic decision-making context. This asynchronous coordination between mainstream journalism and PP is well reflected in the biggest scoops of online participation so far. For example, OhmyNews initiated the attacks on American military presence in South Korea in the summer of 2002 and the mainstream media followed suit: the outcome of all this – the regime change and the national movement against the American presence (Chapter 4) – was the result of joint efforts between OhmyNews and mainstream media, which spread the former's messages far beyond its comparatively small, although huge-in-number, community to the general Korean population. A similar development was seen in the fall of Trent Lott (Chapter 4).

In order to achieve this mutual coordination, journalism has to abandon its long-held ignorance of public needs and concerns that has substantially contributed to its declining credibility (noted in Chapter 3). From bulletin boards, online forums to weblogs and collaborative websites, the long trend of declining media credibility has been declared to be a considerable motive and imperative for the public to join the recent rise of PP. Pew studies found that the unprecedented growth of the American blog audience in 2004 was attributable to two kinds of blogs – those on recent political affairs and those on media affairs such as the "Rathergate" and the Sinclair Broadcast Group's retreat from plans to broadcast a program critical of John Kerry to avoid an advertising boycott (Rainie, 2005; Cornfield et al, 2005). In understanding this, journalists might then appreciate that if public pressure has been the key weapon of journalism in dealing with other powers, then it is time for journalism as a power centre to feel its sharpness. And if public service is what journalists claim for their professional status and – in the last analysis – the economic pillar of the news business, they have to adapt to this new ecosystem and act responsibly.

It would be an imperative, therefore, to recognise a very simple fact: journalism is a paradoxical profession. Professionals must have some autonomy over their clients (Henningham, 1990) – but unlike doctors or lawyers, journalists serve a client base that would not easily accept the role of laymen waiting for specialist guidance. In the fledgling online public sphere, the public also wants it in the other way round – people want to use their freedom and creativity to inform and educate their traditional news feeders. Thus, the most assured way for journalists to enhance their place in the heart and mind of their clients in this interactive and decentralised environment is attention, attention and attention to public concerns. After all, journalists' professional power is more charismatic than formal – it is gained more through trust and respect than specialist expertise and is based on a reliance on clients' needs and demands as the supreme service orientation (Henningham, 1990). In the interactive online world, a journalism that is out of the public's touch will not be able to build up any influence, which has become more than essential for the economic and professional success of the news media. As Phillip Meyer (2005) argued, an influence-based business model – one that creates a sharp countermeasure to the increasingly blur line between journalism and pseudojournalism – is "the only way to save journalism" in a time when "the pure audience is drifting away as old readers die and are replaced by young people hooked on popular culture and amusement".

Embracing PP not only guarantees a sustainable development in the long run but also generates immediate benefits. As theorised by Kovach and Rosenstiel (2001), the public is an interlocking body – with three levels of engagement: being involved, being interested and being uninterested. Everybody belongs to all three groups, depending on the issue. A computer engineer might be uninterested in and even ignorant of latest medical developments but is certainly an expert in new software related to his/her work. That is to say, in any issue, certain members of the public know more than journalists do

– and the web is a wonderful tool for the latter to fill the gap in a cost-saving way. When CBS was investigating the "Rathergate" in a hope to defend itself, ironically, it had to look to bloggers to locate a 1970s typewriter expert (Eberthart, 2005).

In addition, online participants are closer to news events and can pick up many things that traditional journalists miss or cannot update due to their limited resources. There are bubbles but deep in the information fog are what early blogger ObviousGuy calls "jewels of information and true news". There first-hand sources can "unearth the strange, the quirky, the interesting nugget that would have remained hidden" (Lasica, 2002). The scenario envisioned by Dan Gillmor – fifty pictures of a news event might be posted before print or broadcast photographers arrive on the scene (cited in Runnett, 2003) – is nothing far from reality. The rich, vivid and revealing graphic information flowing from citizens and tourists to mainstream television bulletins, news sites and newspapers around the world during the Burmese monks' demonstration in 2007, the Chinese crackdown on Tibetan dissidents in early 2008 and the recent Sichuan earthquake provides just a few examples of how "crowd-sourcing" – resorting to online communities as a point of reference for raw information and materials – can become an integral and crucial part of the future journalist's toolkit.

What if journalists still do not care? At the very least, the emerging "fifth estate" will act as the "gatekeeper of gatekeepers", using their collective power to correct it. In disseminating and interpreting news, online participants often redistribute professional news through hypertextual links across interest-sharing and like-minded communities with free and fearless comments. All this would result in what Allan (2005) referred to as "tipping points" – where a critical mass is formed and generates changes (Chapter 3). As blogger Chris Mooney (2003) argued:

> Some of the web's best known political bloggers … have become veritable journalistic power brokers due to their large online followings. A link on one of these bloggers' sites can catapult a previously unknown web writer into fame, or notoriety or both.

Evidence of this is not difficult to find. When the Jayson Blair plagiarist scandal was on the way, the executive editor of the *New York Times*, Howell Raines, was reportedly forced to resign partly due to aggressive pressure from influential American bloggers and their followers (Regan, 2003). The Rathergate (Chapter 4) is another spectacular example.

If this collective pressure still did not work in the end, the worst scenario might come: journalists would have to witness in pain their role diminishing in this age of easy publishing. If their needs are not well served and their concerns not addressed in one way or another, news audiences might turn to their communities for news. This is a new fair game: you need to attend to me so that I attend to you. Already, since the early 2000s, members of the public in many places have donated large amounts of money so that their favourite bloggers and citizen reporters to operate and to go out to do their own reporting (Hourihan, 2002; McGrady, 2007). At OhmyNews, a Harvard-trained scholar received a tip of more than $30,000 from readers of an article questioning the logic and wisdom of moving the nation's capital outside Seoul (McGrady, 2007). All this, along with the large followings of many citizen-news sites and the fact that advertisers have begun to tap the power of PP platforms, sounds a warning for journalism to make necessary adjustments in the wake of the online public sphere. As Rupert Murdoch admitted in his 2005 speech to the American Society of Newspaper Editors:

> What is happening right before us, in short, is a revolution in the way young people are accessing news. They don't want to rely on the morning paper for their up-to-date information. They don't want to rely on a God-like figure from above to tell them what's important. And to carry the religion analogy a bit further, they certainly don't want news presented as gospel.
>
> Instead, they want their news on demand, when it works for them. They want control over their media, instead of being controlled by it. They want to question, to probe, to offer a different angle. (…) One commentator, Jeff Jarvis, puts it this way: give the people control of media, they will use it. Don't give people control of media, and you will lose (Murdoch, 2005).

In short, as Anderson, Dardenne and Killenberg (1994, p. 15) put it, "journalism actually must become a communication discipline – which, ironically, is what it had thought it was all along".

Other potential consequences of online news and their implications: a call for research

This book, I believe, is a timely contribution to the still limited international literature on the diffusion and socio-political impact of online news. In addition to presenting a new and radical perspective on the evolutionary history of online news, the study contributes substantially to the literature on the socio-technical kinesis of new media diffusion by proposing two distinctive models for exploring online news adoption/use among the public (Figure 5.3 and Figure 8.2). In fact, the 8.2 model could be elaborated and modified to explore the adoption/use of many non-news online services within the context of Internet use. Internet experience, innovativeness, social locators and their inter-relationships would probably remain as determinants in the take-up of other online services, although their influences might be lessened or strengthened from one service to another. News orientation/behaviour might be changed to, for example, consumption capacity/habits if one needs to explore the adoption/use of online commerce services. Of course, there are other social determinants in these cases, which are not the subject of this research. The book, however, has not investigated many other potential consequences of online news that have important implications for the future of news in particular and for society in general. In this final section, I would like to briefly touch on some of these unexplored issues as a way to call for future research.

From a user-centric perspective, there are three sets of issues. First, this research has not explored in any depth is the way online news users have been reallocating their resources, especially attention and time, to adapt to the online news environment. Following Becker and Schoenbach (1989), we might ask what happen to other news and non-news behaviours after such a resource allocation. With the ubiquity of the Internet, does online news adoption/use lead to a shift in the ritual of news consumption – e.g. do users move their news use from a primarily at-home activity to an at-work one and if yes, what does this do to society in general and to work productivity in particular? Also, does private online news use lead to a reduction in the time spending on common activities with family members or friends such as watching television or going our for a movie? If yes, what are the social impacts of these changes? Or, as a substantial number of news outlets have offered news services to mobile devices, how do they redirect people's attention and affect the way they make sense of the world? If these technologies enjoy another sweeping penetration in the future, are we going to be further segmented? Will some people rely on SMS-length stories as the primary mode of news consumption? Or will they be used primarily just as news alerts that will lead users to websites for more details, as Bradshaw suggested above? And what does all this mean to the future of the citizenry and of democracy?

Second, also in relation to the reallocation of resources, research might need to pay more attention to the potential impact of online news on the transformation of traditional news media. Although this work has shown that online news and information users do not seem to use the Internet to replace other sources, the possibility for a displacement effect still exists (Chapter 7). How does this displacement process, if any, take place – and what gratifications opportunities do traditional media have in order to keep this displacement effect from becoming a replacement? Not less importantly, as need complementarity governs the user's behaviour in relation to different media, is the physical display vehicle to play any role? For instance, do the recent initial experiments with flat rollable digital papers in the US and Europe (Chapter 3) signal the beginning of the metamorphosis from wood-made paper to a paper made entirely of bits? As people can enjoy all the portability, the familiar look and the content of the print newspaper on a screen, does it matter that the wood-made newspaper disappears? Or as the computer is increasingly serving the function of the television set, would the latter still be a common feature in the lounge room of the home or would it be replaced by the TiVo? In short, to use Fidler's (1997) term, is there a *mediamorphosis* process under way? Why or why not?

The third set of issues that might be of interest is the nature and impact of the changing notion of news brought by the Internet. This book adopts the concept of "informational news" (Chapter 4) but its social shape and consequences are still open to question. What is informational news and what does it mean to the social construction of reality? There are at least two sub-groups of related issues that need further exploration:

First, as news is no longer the exclusive preserve of professional news media, the news provision landscape is rapidly diversifying and I have theoretically projected that this can either pave the way for a more rational and scientifically critical public sphere or generate a chaotic and anarchic public space that results in a more sensationalised and even more desensitised citizenry. There is, however, still a lack of empirical and systematic evidence regarding these theoretical perspectives. Does the exposure to the new rich and diverse repository of news in this "publish, then filter" – rather than "filter, then publish" (Shirky, 2002) – world actually improve our news knowledge and attitudes? If yes, to what extent and in what way? If no, what are the reasons and can we overcome existing problems over time? How do people filter facts from fiction and the sound from the unsound so that the truth can emerge in the online public sphere? More radically, can the truth emerge in this increasingly fragmented and potentially divided audience world, or are we entering a postmodern world where different truths exist in different segments of the population? In answering these questions, future research will be able to identify effective mechanisms that help to boost the social benefits and minimise the social harms of the hard-to-control world of weblogs, wikis, forums, social networks and the like.

The second sub-group of issues related to the concept of informational news is associated with a transformation of the traditional audience from mere readers, viewers or listeners into researchers. As Burnett and Marshall (2003, p. 161) argued: "The web presents itself as a repository of information that can be retrieved. It is up to the user to find the information via the many search engines that are available. News and information thus blend somewhat for the user as his/her activities can be likened to the traditional role of the researcher". Several questions arise from this. How can users as researchers cope with the information overload that might be worsened as the sheer volume of Internet content becomes increasingly immense while time spending on news-related activities remain stable? To what extent does serendipity – or accidental exposure – via searching (and other web activities) enhance our understanding of world? Also, the temporal dimension of news might be changing. For example, when one searches, finds and reads a news story written one year earlier, is it still news? It might well be a genuine news item to this "late user" but not to the journalist who writes this story and to those users who consume it around the time of its delivery.

Finally, from a producer-centric perspective, a wide range of professional issues deserve close monitoring and/or further exploration. For one thing, with online paid content being still something of a distant future, the likely increasing power of advertisers in the production of online news ought to be placed under constant watch. In the online world, the traditional "Great Wall" between advertising and editorial functions can easily fall (Alterman, 2000; Bita, 2001; Raouf, 1998). Advertising links can be embedded in editorial matters and audience privacy is tracked and shared with advertisers. It is becoming increasingly hard for online editors now have make pure editorial decisions. Research and anecdotal evidence points us to the fact that many online news practitioners are heavily involved in marketing and circulation activities (Bita, 2001; Singer, Tharp & Haruta, 1999). This is likely to become a bigger issue in a near future, given the recent ruthlessly profit-driven development of the news media in the Western world and the fact that news sites are still struggling to attract online advertising. As advertisers are in the driver's seat now, can and how can news providers assure their audience of their journalistic integrity? If this cannot be guaranteed in a transparent way, it might result in more dissatisfaction and even disdain among a public that has already been very critical of the media.

Also posing challenges to journalism professionalism is the current shift to multiple-platform news publishing (Chapter 2). Does this mean that every future journalist has to become a "Mr Know Everything" – i.e. a multi-skilled reporter – and, if yes, what does this mean to the division of labour and control structure in the newsroom? These are worrying because media owners seem to like multi-skilling for both economic and political reasons. Sanders (2003, p. 135) noted a dangerous trend in which editors address the conflict between turning a profit and doing good journalism by finding ways to cut costs through "spurious multi-skilling". More aptly, Bob Franklin (2005) pointed out in his McJournalism theory that using technologies to multi-skill journalists not only creates economic efficiency but also places more control in the hand of owners because less teamwork and more individual operation will isolate journalists and remove them from a collective culture, reducing their bargaining power. Michael Bromley contended that multi-skilling "contains the potential for the final fragmentation of journalism, en-skilling some as 'entrepreneurial editors' but de-skilling others to the status of machine hands and extensions of the computer" (quoted in Sanders, 2003, p. 135). Meanwhile, the National Union of Journalists in the UK (2007) described the nature and development pace of multimedia working as "all at once exhilarating, terrifying, baffling, inspiring and damaging". These and other consequences of the multi-platform phenomenon must be a serious concern for scholars in journalism and mass communication, sociology and political sciences alike.

Other normative issues might emerge out of the way in which online journalists exploit the potential of the web in the years ahead. For instance, the user data in this research show that practitioners might need to focus on providing continual 24-hour news services to foster a wider adoption and more substantial use of online news. This, however, could generate serious problems as competition to be the first in the speedy online environment could mean less time to guarantee the substantive quality of news (Seib, 2001). If journalists are under constant pressures to compete for breaking news with a plethora of mainstream and non-mainstream players, there is a risk that their gate-keeping and verification will become less efficient or even weakened. Consider, for example, the way Matt Drudge outran *Newsweek* to break the Clinton-Lewinsky story, and forced the news magazine – which had been holding up the account to verify some facts – to post it online soon afterwards. The implication is huge. The good news in relation to that risk, as shown above, is that the online news public seems to expect news speed at the same time as news substance. An important mission for journalism research in the years ahead, then, is to identify efficient and effective editorial practices and strategies that online journalists employ to guarantee this often expensive combination.

Or, if journalism is to become an authentic communication discipline as discussed above, do journalists have to adopt new professional values to cope with the new nature of the news public? How can journalists as listeners, discussers, forum leaders and moderators build an intimate relationship with their audiences without losing their upheld values of objectivity, fairness and balance? In an increasingly polarising media atmosphere, how can journalists become competent in moderating and facilitating healthy public debates without losing compromise? Could blogging journalists both "think and write" at the same time? How could and should they be different from ordinary citizens who blog? What are the possible strategies for online journalists to use to guarantee that "the urge to comment" does not "replace the need to verify" (Kovach & Rosenstiel, 2001, p. 140)? How can this "personal journalism" with its informal writing style be added to the established body of journalism knowledge, especially its elaborate and well-crafted news writing skills? At the very least, these issues will invite some radical theoretical and practical changes to how journalism is taught and studied and will generate a great deal of tough challenges. But it is exactly this toughness that renders online journalism research and education more exciting, more rewarding, and more worthwhile.

References

Abdulla, R., Garrison, B., Salwen, M., Driscoll, P. & Casey, D. (2002). "The credibility of newspapers, television news and online news." Paper presented at the annual convention of the Association for Education in Journalism and Mass Communication. Miami Beach, August 9, 2002.

Abrahamson, D. (1998). "The visible hand: Money, markets and media evolution." *Journalism and Mass Communication Quarterly.* 75(1), pp. 14-18.

Abrahamson, E. & Rosenkopf, L. (1993). "Institutional and competitive bandwagons: Using modelling as a tool to explore innovation diffusion. *Academy of Management Review.* 18(4), pp. 487-517.

Ahlers, D. (2006). "News consumption and the new electronic media." *Press/Politics,* 11(1), pp. 29-52.

Ajzen, I. (1991). "The theory of planned behaviour." *Organisational Behaviour and Human Decision Processes.* No 50, pp. 179-211.

Aldisardottir, L. (2000). "Research note: Global medium – local tool? How readers and media companies use the web." *European Journal of Communication.* 15(2), pp. 241-251.

Allan, S. (2006). *Online News: Journalism and the Internet.* London: Open University Press.

Allen, K. (1999). *The Crystal Ball: A look at how the Internet will change journalism in the future.* Retrieved March 30, 2001 from http://www.carleton.ca/jmc/cujo/showcase/allnews/crystal.htm.

Alterman, E. (July 3, 2000). "Independence: An endangered species." *The Nation,* p.10.

Althaus, S. & Tewksbury, D. (2000). "Patterns of Internet and Traditional News Media Use in a Networked Community." *Political Communication.* 17(1), pp. 21-45.

American Press Institute (2006). "Newspaper Next: Blueprint for transformation." Retrieved April 15, 2007 from http://www.newspapernext.org.

Anderson, B. & Tracey, K. (2002). "Digital living. The impact (or otherwise) of the Internet on everyday British life". In B. Wellman & C. Haythorntwaite (eds.), *The Internet in Everyday Life*, pp. 139-163. Oxford: Blackwell.

Anderson, C. (July 1995). "The Internet." *The Economist*, p. 5.

Anderson, R., Dardenne, R. & Killenberg, G. (1994). *The Conversation of Journalism.* London: Praeger.

Appleyard, B. (1999). "Under the net." *New Statesman.* 128 (4457), p. 56.

Arbitron NewMedia (1999, October 6). "Web no threat to traditional media: Radio, television, Internet often used simultaneously." Press Release. Retrieved November 24, 2004 from http://internet.arbitron.com/mainfiles/web_no_threat.htm.

Aronson, S. H. (1977). "Bell's electrical toy: What's the use? The sociology of early telephone usage." In I. Pool (ed.), *The Social Impact of the Telephone.* Cambridge: The MIT Press.

Arteton, F.C. (1987). *Teledemocracy: Can Technology Protect Democracy?* London: Sage.

Atkin, D. & LaRose, R. (1994). "Profiling call-in users." *Journal of Broadcasting & Electronic Media.* 38(2), pp. 217-227.

Atkin, D. (1993). "Adoption of cable amidst a multimedia environment". *Telematics and Informatics.* 10(1), pp. 51-58.

Atkin, D. (1995). "Audio information services and the electronic media environment." *The Information Society.* 11, pp. 75-83.

Atkin, D., Jeffres, L. & Neuendorf, K. (1998). "Understanding Internet adoption as Telecommunications Behaviour." *Journal of Broadcasting & Electronic Media.* 42 (4), pp. 475-490.

Audit Bureau of Verification Services (2005, April 11). "Online advertising market grows 64% in 2004". Press Release.

Australian Broadcasting Authority (1996). *Investigation into the Content of Online Services.* Canberra: ABA. Retrieved March 14, 2001 from http://www.aba.gov.au/newspubs/documents/olsfinal.pdf.

Australian Broadcasting Authority (2001). "Internet@home - What do Australian users want?." Retrieved May 11, 2002 from http://www.aba.gov.au/internet/research/home/index.htm.

Australian Bureau of Statistics (1997). *Australian Standard Classifications of Occupations.* 2nd Edition. Canberra, Australia: Australian Bureau of Statistics..

Australian Bureau of Statistics (2004). "Innovation and Technology Update." *Bulletin No. 11.* Retrieved April 30, 2005 from http://www.abs.gov.au.

Australian Bureau of Statistics (2005b). "Household use of information technology." Retrieved May 11, 2006 from from http://www.abs.gov.au.

Australian Bureau of Statistics (2006). "Business use of information technology, 2004-2005". Retrieved 11 May, 2006 from from http://www.abs.gov.au.

Balnaves, M., Green, K., Shoesmith, B., Lim, B. & Hwee, B. (2003). "Push, pull, layering and blogs: User behaviour in the online medium." In M. Rao (ed.), *News Media and New Media*, pp. 124-145. Singapore: Eastern Universities Press.

Baptista, R. (1999). "The diffusion of process innovations: a selective review." *International Journal of the Economics of Business*. 6(1), pp. 107-129.

Bardoel, J. (1996). "Beyond Journalism: A Profession between Information Society and Civil Society." *European Journal of Communication*, 11(3), pp. 283-302.

Barnhurst, K. (2002). "News geography and monopoly: The form of reports on US newspaper Internet sites." *Journalism Studies*. 3(4), pp. 477-489.

Barr, T. (1985). *The Electronic Estate: New Communications Media and Australia.* Victoria: Penguin Books.

Becker, L. & Schoenbach, K. (1989). "When media content diversifies: anticipating audience behaviours." In L. Becker and K. Schoenbach (eds). *Audience Response to Media Diversification: Coping with Plenty*, pp. 1-27. London: Lawrence Erlbaum.

Becker, L., Dunwoody, S. & Rafaeli, S. (1983). "Cable's impact on the uses of other media." *Journal of Broadcasting*. 27(1), pp. 127-140.

Beville, H. (1948). "The challenge of new media: television, FM and facsimile." *Journalism Quarterly*, 25(1), pp. 3-11.

Bita, N. (2001). "Is cyberspace bad news?" *The Australian*. March 22. *Media* section, pp. 6-7.

Bleyen, V. & Van Hove, L. (2007). "Western European newspapers and their online revenue models: an overview." *First Monday*, 12(12). Retrieved January 10, 2008 from http://www.uic.edu/htbin/cgiwrap/bin/ojs/index.php/fm/article/viewArticle/2014/1899.

Black, C. (2000). "Don't write off newspapers yet." Retrieved April 21, 2001, from http://www.wan-press.org/guest.column/black.html.

Blondheim, M. (1994). *News over the Wire: The Telegraph and the Flow of Public Information in America, 1844-1897.* Cambridge: Harvard University Press.

Blood, R. (2000). "Weblogs: a history and perspectives." Retrieved July 18, 2002 from http://www.rebeccablood.net/essays/weblog_history.html.

Blumler, J. & Katz, E. (eds.) (1974). *The Uses of Mass Communications: Current Perspectives on Gratifications Research.* Beverly Hills: Sage.

Blumler, J. (1978). "The role of theory in uses and gratifications studies." *Communication Research*. 6(1), pp. 9-36.

Boczkowski, P. (2004). *Digitising the News: Innovation in Online Newspapers.* Cambridge, Massachusetts: The MIT Press.

Bogart, L. (1964). "The mass media and the blue-collar worker." In A. Shostak and W. Gomberg (eds). *Blue Collar World: Studies of the American Worker*, pp. 416-428. Englewood Cliffs: Prentice Hall.

Bogart, L. (1989). *Press and Public: Who Read What, When, Where, and Why in American Newspaper.* 2nd Ed. Hillsdale: Lawrence Erlbaum Associates.

Bogle, D. (September 26, 2001). "Information overload." *The Australian.* Media section, p.12.

Bolter, J. D. & Grusin, R. (2000). *Remediation: Understanding New Media,* The MIT

Bourdieu, P. (1986). "The forms of capital." In J. Richardson, *Handbook for Theory and Research for the Sociology of Education*, pp. 241-258. London: Greenwood Press.

Bowman, S. & Willis, C. (2003). *We Media: How Audiences Are Shaping the Future of News & Information.* Retrieved September 19, 2003 from http://www.ndn.org/webdata/we_media/we_media.htm.

Bradshaw, P. (2007, January 27). "Trinity Mirror head speaks of 'garlic bread moment'." Retrieved January 31, 2007 from http://ojournalism.blogspot.com/2007/01/trinity-mirror-head-speaks-of-garlic.html.

Bradshaw, P. (2007, September 17). "A model for the 21st century newsroom: pt1 – the news diamond". Retrieved January 29, 2008 from http://onlinejournalismblog.wordpress.com/2007/09/17/a-model-for-the-21st-century-newsroom-pt1-the-news-diamond/.

Brand, J. & Pearson, M. (2001). "The newsroom versus the lounge room: Journalists' and audiences' views on news." *Australian Journalism Review.* 23(2), pp. 63-89.

Brand, J., Archbold, D. & Rane, H. (2002). "Sources of news and current affairs." Retrieved March 23, 2003 from http://www.aba.gov.au/tv/research/projects/sources/stage2/pdf/aud_stage2.pdf.

Brants, K., Huizenga, M. & van Meerten, R. (1996). "The new canals of Amsterdam: an exercise in local electronic democracy." *Media, Culture and Society.* 18(2), pp. 233-247.

Briggs, A. (1977). "The pleasure telephone: A chapter in the prehistory of the media". In I. Pool (ed.), *The Social Impact of the Telephone.* Cambridge: The MIT Press.

Bromley, R. & Bowles, D. (1995). "Impact of Internet on use of traditional news media." *Newspaper Research Journal.* 16(2), pp. 14-27.

Brown, C. (June 1999). "The state of the American Newspaper: Fear.com." *American Journalism Review*. Retrieved June 3, 2001 from http://www.ajr.org/Article.asp?id=3230.

Bruns, A. (April 11, 2005). "Online produsers dish up the news." *Online Opinion*. Retrieved June 12, 2005 from http://www.onlineopinion.com.au/view.asp?article=3333.

Brusselle, R., Reagan, J., Pinkleton, B. & Jackson, K. (1999). "Factors affecting Internet use in a saturated-access population." *Telematics & Informatics*. 16, pp. 45-58.

Bucy, E. & Gregson, K. (2001). "Media participation: A legitimising mechanism of mass democracy." *New Media & Society*, 3(3), pp. 357-380.

Burnett, R. and Marshall, P. (2003). *Web Theory: An Introduction*. NY: Routledge

Butler, K. and Kent, K. (1983). "Potential impact of videotext on newspapers." *Newspaper Research Journal*. 5(1), pp. 3-11.

Cameron, A. (2004). "Factors affecting broadband adoption and demand: a comparative study between metropolitan and regional Australia". *Telecommunications Journal of Australia*. 54(2), pp. 53-60.

Cameron, G., Curtin, P., Hollander, B., Nowak, G. & Shamp, S. (1995). "Electronic newspapers: towards a research agenda." Retrieved April 15, 2004 from http://www.empiricom.org/glensite/PDF_articles/EPAPER.COX.doc.

Carey, J. (1982). "Videotex: The past as prologue." *Journal of Communication*. Spring, pp. 12-17.

Case, D. (2002). *Looking for Information. A Survey of Research on Information Seeking, Needs and Behaviour*. San Diego: Academic Press.

Caselli, F. & Coleman, W. (2001). "Cross-country technology diffusion: the case of computers." *American Economic Review*. 91(2), pp. 328-335.

Chan, J. & Leung, L. (2005). "Lifestyles, reliance on traditional news media and online news adoption." *New Media & Society*, 7(3), pp. 357-382.

Chan-Olmsted, S. & Park, J. (2000). "From on-air to online world: examining the content and structures of broadcast TV stations' websites." *Journalism and Mass Communication Quarterly*. 77(2), pp. 323-339.

Chen, W., Boase, J. & Wellman, B. (2002). "The global villagers: comparing Internet users and uses around the world." In Barry Wellman & Carolyne Haythorntwaite (eds.), *The Internet in Everyday Life*, pp. 74-113. Oxford: Blackwell.

Cheong, W. (2002). "Internet adoption in Macao." *Journal of Computer-Mediated Communication*. 7(2). Retrieved August 11, 2002 from http://www.ascusc.org/jcmc/vol7/issue2/macau.html.

Chyi, H., I. & Larosa, D. (1999). "Access, use and preferences for online newspapers." *Newspaper Research Journal.* 20(4), pp. 2-13.

Citrin, A., Spritt, D., Silverman, S. & Stern, D. (2000). "Adoption of Internet shopping: the role of consumer innovativeness." *Industrial Management and Data Systems.* 100(7), pp. 294-300.

Coats, R. (2002). 'Power users: A profile of online newspaper consumers." Retrieved September 10, 2002 from http://www.digitaledge.org/specialreports.html.
Cohen, N. (February 28, 2008). "A web-only news operation gets its due." *International Herald Tribune.* Retrieved March 10, 2008 from http://www.iht.com/articles/2008/02/24/business/blogger.php.

Colton, A. (1912). "The telephone newspaper – new experiment in America." *Telephony*, March 30, pp. 391-392. Retrieved June 15, 2005 from http://earlyradiohistory.us/telenew3.htm.

Compaine, B. (2001). "Information gap: Myth or reality?" In B. Compaine (ed.), *The Digital Divide: Facing a Crisis or Creating a Myth?*, pp. 105-118. Cambridge, MA: The MIT Press.

Conway, M. (2001). "Cybernewsers, deserters and includers: an analysis of Internet news users and the effect on traditional news media use." *Proceedings of the Annual Meeting of the Association for Education in Journalism and Mass Communication (84th, Washington, DC, August 5-8, 2001)* – Communication Technology and Policy Division. Retrieved March 30, 2005 from http://eric.ed.gov/ERICDocs/data/ericdocs2/content_storage_01/0000000b/80/0d/9d/ec.pdf.

Cook, T. (April 4, 2005). "State of play: blogging and podcasting in Australia today." *Online Opinion.* Retrieved June 12, 2005 from http://www.onlineopinion.com.au/view.asp?article=3307.

Cornfield, M., Carson, J., Kalis, A. & Simon, A. (2005). "Buzz, blogs, and beyond: The Internet and the national discourse in the Fall of 2004." Retrieved September 12, 2005 from http://www.pewinternet.org/ppt/BUZZ_BLOGS_BEYOND_Final05-16-05.pdf.

Covvey, H. & McAllister, N. (1982). *Computer Choices.* MA: Addison-Wesley.

Crosbie, V. (2004). "What newspapers and their websites must do to survive." *Online Journalism Review*, March 4. Retrieved April 7, 2004 from http://www.ojr.org/ojr/business/1078349998.php.

D'Haenens, L., Jankowski, N. & Heuvelman, A. (2004). "News in online and print newspapers: differences in reader consumption and recall." *New Media & Society.* 6(3), pp. 363-382.

Davis, F. (1989). "Perceived usefulness, perceived ease of use, and user acceptance of information technology." *MIS Quarterly.* 13(3), pp 319-340.

Davis, W. (2005, May 4). "Forrester: Online ad spend to reach $14.7 billion in 2005." Retrieved May 5, 2005 from http://publications.mediapost.com/index.cfm?fuseaction=Articles.san&s=29840&Nid=13 277&p=294184..

Davison, E., & Cotten, S. (2003). "Connection discrepancies: Unmasking further layers of the digital divide." *First Monday.* 8(3). Retrieved March 23, 2005 from http://www.firstmonday.org/issues/issue8_3/davison/..

Day, M. (March 2, 2006). "Internet profits the next logical step for papers." *The Australian*, p. 14.

Defleur, M. & Ball-Rokeach, S. (1989). *Theories of Mass Communication.* Fifth edition. New York: Longman.

Denison, T. (April 1901). "The telephone newspaper." *World's Work,* pp. 640-643. Retrieved June 15, 2004 from http://earlyradiohistory.us/telenew1.htm..

Deuze, M. (2001). "Online journalism: Modelling the first generation of news media on the web." *First Monday*, 6(10). Retrieved September 24, 2004 from http://www.firstmonday.org/issues/issue6_10/deuze/..

Dueze, M. & Dimoudi, C. (2002). "Online journalists in the Netherlands: towards a profile of a new profession." *Journalism*, 3(1), pp. 85-100.

Dibean, W. Garrison, B. (2005). "Online newspaper market size and the use of world wide web technologies." In M. Salwen, B. Garrison & P. Driscoll (eds.), *Online News and the Public*, pp. 257-276. Mahwah: Lawrence Erlbaum.

Dimmick, J. & Rothenbuhler, E. (1984). "The theory of niche: Quantifying competition among media industries." *Journal of Communication.* Winter, pp. 103-119.

Dimmick, J. (2003). *Media Competition and Coexistence: The Theory of the Niche.* Mahwah: Lawrence Erlbaum Associates.

Dimmick, J., Chen, Y. & Li, Z. (2004). "Competition between the Internet and traditional news media: the gratification-opportunities niche dimension." *Journal of Media Economics.* 17(1), pp. 19-34.

Dizard, W. (2000). *Old Media, New Media: Mass Communications in the Information Age.* New York: Longman.

Donohue, G., Tichenor, P., & Olien, C. (1979). "Mass media and the Knowledge Gap: A hypothesis reconsidered." *The Public Opinion Quarterly.* 34(1), pp. 3-23.

Dotinga, R. (April 25, 2005). "Newspapers struggle to avoid their own obit." *The Christian Science Monitor,* Retrieved 23 September, 2005 from http://www.csmonitor.com/2005/0425/p02s01-usgn.html..

Dozier, D. & Rice, R. (1984). "Rival theories of electronic newsreading." In Ronald Rice (ed.), *Communication, Research, and Technology*. London: Sage Publications.

Dryburgh, H. (2001). "Changing our ways: why and how Canadians use the Internet." Retrieved September 21, 2002 from http://www.statcan.ca/english/research/56F0006XIE/56F0006XIE.pdf.

Dube, J. (February 15, 2005). "RSS for journalists." Retrieved March 23, 2005 from Poynter News Service at http://www.poynter.org/column.asp?id=32&aid=78383.

Dupagne, M. & Green, R. (1996). "Revisiting the Principle of Relative Constancy: Consumer Mass Media Expenditures in Belgium." *Communication Research*. 23(5), pp. 612-635.

Dupagne, M. (1994). "Testing the relative constancy of mass media expenditures in the United Kingdom." *The Journal of Media Economics*. 7(3), pp. 1-14.

Dupagne, M. (1997). "Beyond the Principle of Relative Constancy: Determinants of consumer mass media expenditures in Belgium." *The Journal of Media Economics*. 10(2), pp. 3-19.

Dutta-Bergman, M. (2004). "Complementarity in consumption of news types across traditional and new media." *Journal of Broadcasting & Electronic Media*, 48(1), pp. 41-61.

Dutton, Bill & Helsper, Ellen (2007). "The Internet in Britain 2007." Retrieved January 4, 2008 from http://www.oii.ox.ac.uk/research/oxis/OxIS2007_Report.pdf.

Dutton, W., Gennaro, D. & Hargrave, A. (2005). "The Internet in Britain." Retrieved August 31, 2005 from http://www.oii.ox.ac.uk/research/.

Eastin, M. & LaRose, R. (2000). Internet self-efficacy and the psychology of the digital divide. *Journal of Computer-Mediated Communication*, 6(1). Retrieved January 24, 2006 from http://jcmc.indiana.edu/vol6/issue1/eastin.html.

Eberthart, D. (January 31, 2005). "How blogs torpedoed Dan Rather." *NewsMax*. Retrieved September 11 2005 from http://www.newsmax.com/archives/articles/2005/1/28/172943.shtml.

Eid, M. & Buchanan, C. (2005). "North America: Multiplying media in a dynamic landscape." *First Monday*, 10(11). Retrieved 15 April, 2006 from http://www.firstmonday.org/issues/issue10_11/eid/.

Eijck, K. & Rees, K. (2000). "Media orientation and media use: Television viewing behaviour of specific reader types from 1975 to 1995." *Communication Research*. 27(5), pp. 574-616.

Este, J. & Sainsbury, M. (June 15, 2006). "Web before print for Guardian." *The Australian*, p. 16.

Ettema, J. & Kline, F. (1997). "Deficits, differences, and ceilings: contingent conditions for understanding the knowledge gap." *Communication Research*, 4(2), pp. 179-202.

Ettema, J. (1989). "Interactive electronic text in the United States: Can videotext ever go home again?" In J. Salvaggio & J. Bryant (eds.), *Media Use in the Information Age: Emerging Patterns of Adoption and Consumer Use,* pp. 105-124. London: Lawrence Erlbaum.

European Commission (2000). "Europeans' participation in cultural activities." Retrieved March 15, 2003 from http://europa.eu.int/comm/public_opinion/archives/eb/ebs_158_en.pdf.

European Commission (2002). "Eurobarometer 57." Retrieved March 15, 2003 from http://europa.eu.int/comm/public_opinion/archives/eb/eb57/eb57_en.htm.

European Commission (2003). "Eurobarometer 58." Retrieved April 24, 2003 from http://europa.eu.int/comm/public_opinion/archives/eb/eb57/eb57_en.htm.

Ewart, J. & Gregor, S. (2001). "Online journalists need more than the ABC's of journalism: the skills and attributes for online news." *Australian Journalism Review,* 23(1), pp. 43-56.

Ewart, J. (2003). "News connections: Regional newspapers and the web." Transformations. 7 (September). Retrieved June 21, 2004 from http://transformations.cqu.edu.au/journal/issue_07/article_01.shtml.

Fairfax (2005). Fairfax Annual Report 2005. Retrieved June 21, 2006 from http://www.fxj.com.au/announcements/sep05/Fairfax%20AR%20web.pdf.

Fardi, P. (March 2000). "The dotcom braindrain." *American Journalism Review.* Retrieved on June 7, 2001 from http://ajr.org/Article.asp?id=313.

Farhi, P. (May 17, 1992). "The networks stage a comeback." *Washington Post,* p. H-1.

Federal Communications Commission. (2000). *FCC Issues Report on the Availability of High-Speed and Advanced Telecommunications Services.* Retrieved April 30, 2002 from http://www.fcc.gov/Bureaus/Common_Carrier/News_Releases/2000/nrcc0040.html.

Ferguson, D. & Perse, E. (2000). "The world wide web as a functional alternative to television." *Journal of Broadcasting & Electronic Media.* 44(2), pp. 155-173.

Fidler, R. (1997). *Mediamorphosis: Understanding New Media.* London: Pine Forge.

Fidler, R. (1998). "Life after 2001: Redefining print media in the cyberspace." Retrieved March 27, 2001 from http://www.futureprint.kent.edu/articles/fidler01.htm

Fidler, R. (1999). "Newspapers in 2020: Paper vs. digital delivery and display media." Retrieved on March 27, 2001 from http://www.futureprint.kent.edu/articles/fidler04.htm.

Finberg, H. (2006). "Broadband power drives news use." Retrieved January 6, 2007 from http://www.poynter.org/content/content_view.asp?id=98747.

Findahl, O. 2001. "Swedes and the Internet Year 2000." Retrieved July 12 2002 from http://www.worldinternetinstitute.com/filer/swedes_and_the_internet_2000.pdf.

Fishbein, M. & Ajzen, I. (1972). *Beliefs, Attitudes, Intentions and Behaviour: an Introduction to Theory and Research.* Massachusetts: Addison-Wesley.

Fishbein, M. (1967). "Attitude and the prediction of behaviour." In M. Fishbein (ed.), *Readings in Attitude Theory and Measurement.* New York: Wiley.

Fishbein, M. (1968). "An investigation of relationships between beliefs about an object and the attitude towards that object." *Human Relationships.* No 16, pp 233-240.

Fitzgerald, T. (October 15, 2002). "Web the place for office folks." Retrieved on October 17, 2002 from http://209.61.190.23/news2002/oct02/oct15/2_tues/news4tuesday.html.

Fitzgerald, W. G. (June 22, 1907). "A telephone newspaper." *Scientific American*, p. 507. Retrieved June 15, 2005 from http://earlyradiohistory.us/telenew5.htm.

Flew, T. & Gilmour, C. (2006). "Television and pay TV." In S. Cunningham & G. Turner (eds.), *The Media and Communications in Australia*, pp. 175-192. Sydney: Allen & Unwin.

Frank, R. (November 2000). "Future unclear." *The New Leader*, p.52.

Franklin, B. (2006). "'McJournalism': The McDonaldization Thesis and Junk Journalism." Retrieved 15 January, 2008 from http://www.unet.univie.ac.at/~a9807630/STEP6SS2006/Franklin.pdf.

Galloway, J. & Meek, F. (1981). "Audience uses and gratifications: An expectancy model." *Communication Research.* 8(4), pp. 435-449.

Garneau, G. (1996). "The web: next step in interactive agenda." *Editor & Publisher*, February 17. Retrieved November 6, 2001 from InfoTrac database.

Garneau, G. (June 6, 1992). "Pittsburgh strike in its third week: papers moving to alternate means of distribution." *Editor & Publisher*. Retrieved on November 6, 2001 from InfoTrac database.

Genova, B. & Greenberg, B. (1979). "Interests in news and the Knowledge Gap." *The Public Opinion Quarterly.* 43, pp. 79-91.

Gibson, R., Wilson, S., Denemark, D., Meagher, G. & Western, M. (2004). *The Australian Survey of Social Attitudes, 2003.* Canberra: Australian Social Science Data Archive, The Australian National University.

Gilder, G. (1994). *Life after Television.* New York: W. W. Norton & Company.

Giles, D. (2003). *Media Psychology*. London: Lawrence Erlbaum.

Gillin, B. (2003). "A blog goes silent, and the world holds its breath." Retrieved June 6, 2003 from http://www.siliconvalley.com/ (no longer available online).

Gillmor, D. (2003). "Here comes We Media". *Columbia Journalism Review*. May/June. Retrieved March 20 from http://www.cjr.org/archives.asp?url=/03/1/gillmor.asp..

Graber, D. (1989). *Mass Media and American Politics*. 3rd. ed. Washington, DC: CQ Press.

Green, L. (2002). *Communication, Technology and Society*. London: Sage.

Greenan, N. & Guellect, D. (1998). "Firm organisation, technology, and performance: An empirical study." *Economics of Innovation and New Technology*. 6(3), pp. 313-347.

Greenspan, R. (2002). "American surfers keep it simple." Retrieved October 20, 2002 from http://cyberatlas.internet.com/big_picture/geographics/article/0,,5911_1466661,00.html.

Grossberg, L., Wartella, E. & Whitney, D. (1998). *MediaMaking: Mass Media in a Popular Culture*. New York: Sage Publications.

Guardian Unlimited (July 15, 2003). "Operation weblog." Retrieved July 18, 2003 from http://politics.guardian.co.uk/egovernment/comment/0,12767,998683,00.html.

Gunter, B. (2003). *News and the Net*. Mahwah, NJ: Lawrence Erlbaum

Guo, Z. (2000). "Media use habits, audience expectations and media effects in Hong Kong's first legislative council election." *Gazette*. 62(2), pp. 133-151.

Habermas, J. (1996). The transformation of the public sphere's political function." In W. Outhwaite (ed.), *The Habermas Reader*. Cambridge: Polity Press.

Hagen, I. (1994). "Expectations and consumption patterns in TV news viewing." *Media, Culture & Society*. 16(4), pp. 415-428.

Hall, B. (2003). "Innovation and diffusion." Retrieved March 30, 2004 from http://elsa.berkeley.edu/~bhhall/papers/Diffusion_Ch18_BHHfinal.pdf.

Hall, J. (2001). *Online Journalism: A Critical Primer*. London: Pluto Press.

Hallin, D. (1986). "We keep America on top of the world." In T. Gitlin (ed.), *Watching Television*, pp 9-41. New York: Pantheon.

Harris Interactive (2001). "Internet grows as primary source of news and information in weeks following September 11 attacks.." Retrieved June 10, 2002 from http://www.online-publishers.org/opa_harris_crisis.pdf.

Hellwig, O., & Lloyd, R. (2000). *Sociodemographic Barriers to Utilisation and Participation in Telecommunications Services and their Regional Distribution: a Quantitative Analysis*. Canberra: National Centre for Social and Economic Modelling.

Henningham, J. (1992). "Journalism's threat to freedom of the press." University of Queensland Inaugural Lecture, St Lucia: University of Queensland Press.

Henningham, J. (1998). "Ideological differences between Australian journalists and their public." *Press/Politics*. 3(1), pp. 92-101.

Herbert, J. & Thurman, N. (2008). "Paid content strategies for news websites: An empirical study of British newspapers' online business models." *Journalism Practice*, 1(2), 208-226.

Hiler, J. (2002). "Blogosphere: the emerging media ecosystem." Retrieved June 10, 2003 from http://www.microcontentnews.com/articles/blogosphere.htm.

Hirschman, E. (1986). "Humanistic inquiry in marketing research: Philosophy, method and criteria." *Journal of Marketing Research*. 23(2), pp. 237-249.

Hoag, L. (1998). "Growing U.S. audience reads news on net." *Editor & Publisher*, 131, p. 8. Retrieved April 24, 2001 from InfoTrac.

Horrigan, J. & Rainie, L. (2002). "The broadband difference" Retrieved August 12, 2002 from http://www.edisonresearch.com/I9_FinalPresentation_1%20per%20page.pdf.

Horrigan, J. (2006). "Online news." Research report with the Pew Internet & American Life Project. Retrieved June 30, 2006 from http://www.pewinternet.org/PPF/r/178/report_display.asp.

Horrigan, J. (2007). "Broadband: What's All the Fuss About?" Retrieved January 4, 2008 from http://www.pewinternet.org/PPF/r/224/report_display.asp.

Hourihan, M. (August 18, 2002). "Blogging for dollars: giving rise to the professional blogger." Retrieved June 18 2003 from http://www.oreillynet.com/pub/a/javascript/2002/08/12/megnut.html.

Howard, P., Rainie, L. & Jones, S. (2001). "Days and nights on the Internet." *American Behavioural Scientist*. 45, pp. 383-404.

Hsia, H. (1989). "Introduction." In J. Salvaggio & J. Bryant (eds.), *Media Use in the Information Age: Emerging Patterns of Adoption and Consumer Use,* pp. xv-xxviii. London: Lawrence Erlbaum.

Australian Bureau of Statistics (2005a). "Internet Activity, Australia, March 2005." Retrieved 11 May, 2006 from from http://www.abs.gov.au.

Hui, T. & Wan, D. (2004). "The role of consumer innovativeness in the adoption of Internet shopping in Singapore." *The Internet Business Review.* Retrieved on August 14, 2005 from http://www.csu.edu.au/faculty/commerce/jib/issues/issue01/iss01_wan.pdf.

Interactive Advertising Bureau (2007, May 25). "Search accounts for 40% of US online ad revenues." Press Release. Retrieved April 15, 2008 from http://www.browsermedia.co.uk/2007/05/25/search-accounts-for-40-of-us-online-ad-revenue/.

Ives, N. (April 26, 2005). "Newspapers find national ads a tough sell." *The New York Times.* Retrieved April 27, 2005 from http://www.nytimes.com/2005/04/26/business/media/26adco.html?ex=1272168000&en=00e7f095d47303fd&ei=5090&partner=rssuserland&emc=rss..

Jacka, E. (2006). "The future of public broadcasting." In S. Cunningham & G. Turner (eds.), *The Media and Communications in Australia*, pp. 344-356. Sydney: Allen & Unwin.

Jackson, S. (June 2, 2005). "Verdict a boost for TV and websites." *The Australian*, p. 16.

James, M., Wotring, C. & Forrest, E. (1995). "An exploratory study of the perceived benefits of electronic bulletin board use and their impact on other communication activities". *Journal of Broadcasting & Electronic Media.* 39(1), pp. 30-50.

Jeffres, L. & Atkin, D. (1996). "Predicting use of technologies for communication and consumer needs." *Journal of Broadcasting & Electronic Media*, 40, pp. 318-330.

Johnson, T & Kaye, B. (1998). "Cruising is believing? Comparing Internet and traditional sources on media credibility." *Journalism & Mass Communication Quarterly.* 75(2), pp. 325-340.

Johnson, T. & Kaye, B. (2002). "Webelievability: a path model examining how convenience and reliance predict online credibility." *Journalism and Mass Communication Quarterly*, 79(3), pp. 619-642.

Katz, E., Blumler, J. & Gurevitch, M. (1974). "Uses and gratifications research." *The Public Opinion Quarterly*, 37(4), pp. 509-523.

Katz, E., Gurevitch, M. & Haas, H. (1973). "On the use of the mass media for important things." *American Sociological Review.* 38 (April), pp. 161-181.

Katz, J. & Rice, D. (2002). *Social Consequences of Internet Use: Access, Involvement and Interaction.* Massachusetts: Massachusetts Institute of Technology.

Kauffman, M. (August 1, 1994). "Just the fax, please." *Management*, p.37.

Kayany, J. & Yelsma, P. (2000). "Displacement effects of online media in the socio-technical contexts of households." *Journal of Broadcasting & Electronic Media.* Spring, pp. 215-229.

Kaye, B. & Johnson, T. (2002). "Online and in the know: uses and gratifications of the web for political communication." *Journal of Broadcasting & Electronic Media.* 46(1), pp. 54-72.

Kidman, A. (2002). "War of the websites." Retrieved July 25, 2002 from http://news.com.au/common/story_page/0,4057,4770112%5E421,00.html.

Kieve, J. (1973). *The Electric Telegraph: A Social and Economic History.* Newton: David & Charles.

Kirk, D. (2006). "How Fairfax is repositioning itself in the new media landscape." Retrieved November 5, 2006 from http://www.fxj.com.au/announcements/oct06/NatlPressClubSpeech.pdf.

Kiss, J. (January 11, 2005). "CBS sacks four after blogs trigger Rathergate." Retrieved September 11, 2005 from http://www.journalism.co.uk/news/story1195.shtml.

Klopfenstein, B. (1989). "Problems and potential of forecasting the adoption of new media." In J. Salvaggio & J. Bryant (eds.), *Media Use in the Information Age: Emerging Patterns of Adoption and Consumer Use,* pp. 21-41. London: Lawrence Erlbaum.

Kovach, B. & Rosenstiel, T. (2001). *The Elements of Journalism.* New York: Three Rivers Press.

Kovaric, W. *Web Design for the Mass Media.* Retrieved June 12, 2005 from http://www.radford.edu/~wkovarik/design/ch1.html.

Kwak, N., Skoric, M. M., Williams, A. E., & Poor, N. D. (2004). "To broadband or not to broadband: the relationship between high-speed Internet and knowledge and participation." *Journal of Broadcasting & Electronic Media.* 48(3), pp. 421-445.

Kyrish, S. (1994). "Here comes the revolution – Again evaluating predictions for the information superhighway." *Media International Australia.* No 74, pp. 5-13.

Kyrish, S. (1996). "From videotex to the Internet: lessons from online services 1981-1996." Retrieved September 9, 2001 from http://www.latrobe.edu.au/teloz/reports/kyrish.pdf.

Lacy, S. & Noh, G. (1997). "Theory, economics, measurement, and the Principle of Relative Constancy." *The Journal of Media Economics.* 10(3), pp. 3-16.

Lane, B. (February 2, 2003). "Welcome to bloggers' world." *The Weekend Australian.*

LaRose, R., & Eastin, M. (2004). "A social cognitive theory of Internet uses and gratifications: toward a new model of media attendance." *Journal of Broadcasting & Electronic Media,* 48(3), pp. 358-377.

Lasica, J. D. (2002a). "Blogging as a form of journalism." *Online Journalism Review.* Retrieved March 12, 2003 from http://www.ojr.org/ojr/workplace/1017958873.php.

Lasica, J. D. (2002b). "Weblogs: a new source of news." *Online Journalism Review.* Retrieved March 12, 2003 from http://www.ojr.org/ojr/lasica/1019165278.php.

Lasica, J. D. (2002c). "When bloggers commit journalism." *Online Journalism Review.* Retrieved March 12, 2003 from http://www.ojr.org/ojr/lasica/1032910520.php.

Lasica, J. D. (May 1997). "When push comes to news." *American Journalism Review.* Retrieved on March 30, 2001 from http://www.ajr.org/Article.asp?id=701.

Lasica, J. D. (November 1996). "Net gain." *American Journalism Review.* Retrieved August 24, 2001 from http://ajr.org/Article.asp?id=2217.

Lasswell, H. (1948). "The structure of and function of communications in society." In L. Bryson (ed.), *The Communication of Ideas.* New York: Harper & Row.

Lee, P. & Leung, L. (2004). *Assessing the displacement effects of the Internet.* Paper presented at the International Conference on Internet Communication in Intelligent Societies. School of Journalism & Communication, Chinese University of Hong Kong, July 8-10.

Lefcowitz, E. (2001). "Retrofuture: The information highway to nowhere." Retrieved September 21, 2001 from http://www.retrofuture.com/videotex.html.

Lent, A. (2000). "Livin' la Vida Internet: Sure, you've got information close at hand, but what (does) it do for your quality of life?" *PC World.* January 11. Retrieved November 24, 2004 from http://www.pcworld.com/news/article/0,aid,14746,00.asp.

Leung, L. & Wei, R. (1998). "Factors influencing the adoption of interactive TV in Hong Kong: Implications for advertising." *Asian Journal of Communication.* 8(2), pp. 124-147.

Levinson, P. (2003). *Realspace: the Fate of Physical Presence in the Digital Age, On and Off Planet.* London: Routledge.

Levy, M. & Windahl, S. (1985). "The concept of audience activity." In K. Rosengren, L. Wenner & P. Palmgreen (eds). *Media Gratifications Research: Current Perspectives*, pp. 109-122. Beverly Hills: Sage Publications.

Levy, M. & Windal, S. (1984). "Audience activity and gratifications: A conceptual Clarification and exploration." *Communication Research.* 11(1), pp. 51-78.

Levy, S. (August 26, 2002). "Living in the Blog-osphere." *Newsweek.* Retrieved October 10, 2002 from Expanded Academic ASAP.

Li, S. & Yang, S. (2000). "Internet shopping and its adopters: Examining the factors affecting the adoption of Internet shopping." Paper presented at the 35th Annual Conference by the School of Journalism and Communication at the Chinese University of Hong Kong. Hong Kong, July.

Li, S. (2003). "Electronic newspaper and its adopters: examining the factors influencing the adoption of electronic newspaper in Taiwan." *Telematics and Informatics.* 20, pp. 35-49.

Li, S. (2004). "Internet shopping and its adopters: Factors in the adoption of Internet shopping." In P. Lee, L. Leung & C. So (eds.), *Impact and Issues in New Media: Towards Intelligent Societies.* Cresskill: Hampton Press.

Li, X. (2006a) (ed). *Internet Newspapers: the Making of a Mainstream Medium.* London: LEA Publishers.

Li, X. (2006b). "News priority issues in print versus Internet newspapers." In Li (2006a), pp. 261-282.

Lin, C. & Salwen, M. (2006). "Utilities of online and offline news use." In Li (2006a), pp. 209-225.

Lin, C. & Jeffres, L. (1998). "Factors influencing the adoption of multimedia cable technology." *Journalism and Mass Communication Quarterly*, 75(2), pp. 341-352.

Lin, C. & Jeffres, L. (2000). "Comparing distinctions and similarities across websites of newspapers, radio stations and television stations." *Journalism & Mass Communication Quarterly.* 77(4), pp. 555-573.

Lin, C. (1994). "Exploring factors for home videotext adoption." In J. Hanson (ed.) *Advances in Telematics*, vol 2, pp. 111-121. New York: Ablex.

Lin, C. (1998). "Exploring personal computer adoption dynamics." *Journal of Broadcasting & Electronic Media*, 42(1), pp. 95-112.

Lin, C. (2001). "Audience attributes, media supplementation, and likely online service adoption." *Mass Communication & Society.* 4(1), pp. 19-38.

Lippmann, W. (1922/1997). *Public Opinion.* New York: Free Press.

Lister, M., Dovey, J., Giddings, S., Grant, I. & Kelly, K. (2003). *New Media: A Critical Introduction.* London: Routledge.

Liu, C., Day, W., Sun, S. & Wang, G. (2002). "User behaviour and the 'globalness' of the Internet: from a Taiwan users' perspective." *Journal of Computer-Mediated Communication.* 7(2). Retrieved August 11, 2002 from .http://www.ascusc.org/jcmc/vol7/issue2/taiwan.html..

Logue, T. (1979). "Teletext: Towards an information utility?" *Journal of Communication.* Autumn, pp. 19-33.

Loweweinstein, A. (April 11, 2005). "Alternative media is the only way forward." Retrieved June 12, 2005 from .http://www.onlineopinion.com.au/view.asp?article=3327..

Lowry, W. & Choi, J. (2006). "The web news story and cognitive flexibility." In Li (2006a), pp. 99-120.

Luft, O. (2008, February 29). "Birmingham Post goes 'web-first' with site relaunch." Retrieved March 1, 2008 from http://www.journalism.co.uk/2/articles/531115.php.

Lule, J. (1998). "The power and pitfalls of journalism in the hypertext era." *The Chronicle of Higher Education,* 44(48), pp. B7-B8.

MacLean, S. (April 28, 2005). "Print learns to love the web." *The Australian*, pp. 15& 20.

Maholtra, Y. & Galletta, D. (1999). "Extending he technology acceptance model to account for social influence: theoretical bases and empirical validation." *Proceedings of the 32nd Hawaii International Conference on System Sciences.* Retrieved March 20, 2005 from http://www.brint.org/technologyacceptance.pdf.

Manning, P. (2007, January 24). "Fairfax boss was troubled by left-leaning editorial culture." *The Australian.* Retrieved January 30, 2007 from http://theaustralian.news.com.au/story/0,20867,21108534-7582,00.html?from=public_rss.

Marcus, J. (October 2000). "When to make the link?" *American Journalism Review.* Retrieved on May 7, 2001 from http://www.ajr.org/Article.asp?id=442.

Martin, N. (September 1995). "Fax publishing: fast facts." *Communication World.* Retrieved November 6, 2001 from InfoTrac database.

Marvin, C. (1988). *When Old Technologies Were New.* New York: Oxford University Press.

Mason, S. & Hacker, K. (2003). "Applying communication theory to digital divide research." *IT & Society,* 5(1), pp. 40-55.

Massey, B. & Levy, M. (1999). "Interactivity, online journalism and English-language web newspapers in Asia." *Gazette*, 61(6), pp. 523-538.

Masson, S. (April 4, 2005). "Wikis, blogs, moblogs, and more." *Online Opinion.* Retrieved June 12, 2005 from http://www.onlineopinion.com.au/view.asp?article=3303.

Mayne, A. (1982). *The Videotex Revolution.* Hampshire: The October Press.

McAdams, M. (1995). "The sad story of videotex." Retrieved November 5, 2001 from http://www.well.com/user/mcadams/videotex.html.

McCombs, M. & Eyal, C. (1980). "Spending on mass media." *Journal of Communication.* 30(1), pp. 153-158.

McCombs, M. (1972). "Mass media in the marketplace." *Journalism Monograph.* 24

McGrady, R. (2007, November 22). "Citizen media business issues." Retrieved January 31, 2008 from http://citmedia.org/blog/2007/11/22/citizen-media-business-issues-donations/.

McGuire, T. (2005). "Apocalypse Now! Reinventing the newspapers in the public interest." Speech at Washington and Loo University, May 3. Retrieved 15 April, 2006 from http://journalism.wlu.edu/Reynolds/mcguire.html.

McIlwaine, S. & Nguyen, A. (2005). "Science, democracy, journalism, technology." Proceedings of *Journalism and the Public* – Journalism Education Association's 2005 Conference, Gold Coast, November 29-December 3. Retrieved March 4, 2006 from http://live-wirez.gu.edu.au/jea.

McLeod, J., Bybee, C. & Durall, J. (1982). "Evaluating media performance by gratifications sought and received." *Journalism Quarterly.* 59(1), pp. 3-12.

McLeod, J., Scheufele, D. & Moy, P. (1999). "Community, communication and participation: the role of mass media and interpersonal discussion in local political participation." *Political Communication.* 16(3), pp. 315-336.

McQuail, D. (1997). *Audience Analysis.* Sydney: Sage Publications.

McQuail, D. (2000). *McQuail's Mass Communication Theory.* Sydney: Sage Publications.

McQuail, D., Blumler, J. & Brown, J. (1972). "The television audience: a revised perspective." In D. McQuail (ed.). *Sociology of Mass Communications: Selected Readings,* pp. 135-165. Harmondsworth: Penguin

Mensing. D. & Greer, J. (2006). "Above the fold: a comparison of the lead stories in print and online newspapers." In Li (2006a), pp. 283-302.

Meyer, E. (2000). "Net-working: Demand for online journalists is on the rise" Retrieved April 30, 2001 from http://ajr.newslink.org/emcol14.html.

Meyer, P. (2004). *The Vanishing Newspaper: Saving Journalism in the Information Age.* Columbia, MO: University of Missouri Press.

Migley, D. & Dowling, G. (1978). "Innovativeness: The concept and its measurement." *Journal of Consumer Research.* 4(2), pp. 229-242.

Mikaki, S., Kubota, F., Hashimoto, Y., Yoshii, H., Endo, K. & Ishii, K.. 2002. "Internet usage trend in Japan." Retrieved August 12, 2002 from http://media.asaka.toyo.ac.jp/wip/survey2001e/report2001e.pdf.

Money, S. (1979). *Teletext and Viewdata.* Britain: Newness Technical Books.

Montague, P. (1981). "The electronic newspaper." In Rex Winsbury (ed.), *Viewdata in action.* London: McGraw-Hill.

Mooney, C. (February 2, 2003). "How blogging changed journalism – almost." Retrieved May 7, 2003 from http://www.post-gazette.com/forum/comm/20030202edmoon02p1.asp.

Morris, M. & Ogan, C. (1996). "The Internet as mass medium." *Journal of Computer-Mediated Communication*, 1(4). Retrieved May 24, 2001 from http://jcmc.indiana.edu/vol1/issue4/morris.html.

Morrisett, L. (2001). "Foreword." In B. Compaine (ed.), *The Digital Divide: Facing a Crisis or Creating a Myth?*, pp. ix-x. Cambridge, MA: The MIT Press.

MSNBC (2001, January 7). "Internet growing as news medium, at times exceeding traditional media. Retrieved May 26, 2002 from http://www.msnbc.com/m/info/press/02/0107.asp.

Mueller, J. & Kamerer, D. (1995). "Reader preference for electronic newspapers." *Newspaper Research Journal*. 16(3), pp. 2-13.

Murdoch, R. (April 13, 2005). "The challenges of the online world." Speech to the American Society of Newspaper Editors. Washington DC. Retrieved 29 March, 2006 from http://www.thehoot.org/story.asp?storyid=Web202159222200Hoot110548%20AM1591&pn=1.

National Office of the Information Economy (2003). *Current State of Play, Australia's Scorecard*. Retrieved April 30, 2003 from http://www.noie.gov.au

National Union of Journalists (2007). "Shaping the future: Commission on multi-media working 2007." Retrieved January 12, 2008 from http://www.nuj.org.uk/innerPagenuj.html?docid=605.

Neal, C., Quester, P. & Hawkins, D. (1998). *Consumer Behaviour: Implications for Marketing Research*. Sydney: McGraw-Hill.

Negroponte, N. (1995). *Being Digital*. New York: Alfred K. Knopf.

Nelson, R., Peterhansl, A. & Sampat, B. (2002). *Why and How Innovations Get Adopted: A Tale of Four Models*. New York: Columbia University.

Neuendorf, K., Atkin, D. & Jeffres, L. (1998). "Understanding adopters of audio information innovations." *Journal of Broadcasting & Electronic Media*. 42(1), pp. 80-94.

Neuendorf, K., Atkin, D. & Jeffres, L. (2002). "Adoption of audio information services in the United States: a bridge innovation." In C. Lin & D. Atkin (eds), *Communication Technology and Society: Audience Adoption and Uses*, pp. 92-125. Cresskill, NJ: Hampton Press.

Newsam, S. (2007, March 1). "Will newspapers be the vinyl records of the media?" *Western Mail*, p. 30.

Newspaper Advertising Bureau of Australia (2000). "NABA facts 2000." Retrieved October 12, 2001 from http://newspaperbureau.com.au (no longer available online).

Newspaper Association of America (2001). "Leveraging newspaper assets: A study of changing American media usage habits – 2000 research report." Retrieved on March 30, 2001 from http://www.naa.org/marketscope..

Newspaper Association of America (2008). "Advertising expenditures." Retrieved April 1, 2008 from http://www.naa.org/TrendsandNumbers/Advertising-Expenditures.aspx.
Nguyen, A. (2008a). "Facing the 'fabulous monster': the traditional media's fear-driven innovation culture in the development of online news". *Journalism Studies*, 9(1), pp. 91-104. Retrieved February 27, 2008 from http://www.informaworld.com.

Nguyen, A. (2008b). "The contribution of online news attributes to its diffusion: An empirical exploration based on a proposed theoretical model for the micro process of online news adoption/use." *First Monday.* 13(4). Retrieved April 7, 2008 from http://www.uic.edu/htbin/cgiwrap/bin/ojs/index.php/fm/article/view/2127/1952.

Nguyen, A. (2007). "The interaction between technology and society: lessons learnt from 160 evolutionary years of online news." *First Monday*, 12(3). Retrieved March 20, 2007 from http://www.firstmonday.org/issues/issue12_3/nguyen/index.html.

Nguyen, A. & Western, M. (2006). "The complementary relationship between the Internet and traditional mass media: the case of online news and information." *Information Research.* 11(3), paper 259. Retrieved April 20, 2006 from http://informationr.net/ir/11-3/paper259.html..

Nguyen, A. & Western, M. (2007). "Socio-structural correlates of online news/information adoption and use." *Journal of Sociology,* 43(2), pp. 167-185.

Nguyen, A. (2003). "The current status and potential development of online news consumption: a structural approach." *First Monday.* 8(9). Retrieved September 4, 2003 from http://www.firstmonday.dk/issues/issue8_9/nguyen/..

Nguyen, A. (2006). "Journalism in the wake of participatory publishing." *Australian Journalism Review.* 28(1), pp. 143-156.

Nguyen, A., Ferrier, L., Western, M. & McKay, S. (2005). "Online news in Australia: patterns of use and gratification." *Australian Studies in Journalism.* 15, pp. 5-34.

Nie, N., Hillygus, D. & Erbring, L. (2002). "Internet use, interpersonal realtions and sociability: a time diary study." In Barry Wellman & Carolyne Haythorntwaite (eds), *The Internet in Everyday Life*, pp. 215-243. Oxford: Blackwell.

Niedźwiedzka, B. (2003). ".A proposed model of information behaviour.." *Information Research*, 9(1), paper 164. Retrieved 10 March 2006 from http://informationr.net/ir/9-1/paper164.html.

Nielsen, J. (1997). "How people read on the web." Retrieved June 30, 2005 from http://www.useit.com/alertbox/9710a.html.

Noh, G. & Grant, A. (1997). "Media functionality and the Principle of Relative Constancy: An explanation of the VCR aberration." *The Journal of Media Economics.* 10(3), pp. 17-31.

Norris, P. (2001). *Digital Divide: Civic Engagement, Information Poverty, and the Internet Worldwide.* Cambridge: Cambridge University Press.

Nozato, Y. (2002). "Credibility of online newspapers." Paper presented at the annual convention of the Association for Education in Journalism and Mass Communication. Miami Beach, August 9, 2002. Retrieved March 23, 2004 from http://www.inma.org/subscribers/papers/2002-nozato.pdf.

Nua.com News (2002). "French employees go online at work." Retrieved from http://www.nua.ie/surveys/index.cgi?f=FS&cat_id=6. on 11/10/2002.

O'Regan, T. (1993). *Australian Television Culture.* Sydney: Allen & Unwin.

Online Publishing News (2001). "News continues to be a highly valued commodity for Internet users." Retrieved July 12, 2002 from http://www.onlinepublishingnews.com/htm/n20011126.059586.htm.

Oostendorp, H. & Nimwegen, C. (1998). "Locating information in an online newspaper." *Journal of Computer-mediated Communication.* 4(1). Retrieved on August 30, 2002 from http://jcmc.indiana.edu/vol4/issue1/oostendorp.html.

O'Toole, K. (2000). "Study offers early look at how Internet is changing daily life." Retrieved March 29, 2006 from http://www.stanford.edu/dept/news/pr/00/000216internet.html.

Outing, S. (1999). "Why online journalism is a great career choice." *Editor & Publisher.* May 1, p.49.

Outing, S. (2001). "Attack's lessons for news web sites." Retrieved October 10, 2001, from http://www.editorandpublisher..com. *Stop the Presses* column.

Palmgreen, P. & Rayburn, J. (1985). "An expectancy-value approach to media gratifications." In K. Rosengren, L. Wenner & P. Palmgreen (eds). *Media Gratifications Research: Current Perspectives.* Beverly Hills: Sage Publications.

Palmgreen, P. (1983). "The uses and gratifications approach: A theoretical perspective." *Media Panel Report.* No 30, November. Lunds Universitet & Högskolan I Vxäjö.

Palmgreen, P., Wenner, L. & Rayburn, J. (1980). "Relations between gratifications sought and obtained: a study of television news." *Communication Research.* 7(2), pp. 161-192.

Palser, B. (May, 2001). "Virtual wite-out ." *American Journalism Review*. Retrieved June 16, 2001 from http://www.ajr.org/article.asp?id=187.

Papacharissi, Z. & Rubin, A. (2000). "Predictors of Internet use." *Journal of Broadcasting & Electronic Media*. 44(2), pp. 175-196.

Patten, D. (1986). *Newspapers and New Media*. New York, NY: Knowledge Industry Publications.

Pavlik, J. (1998a). *New Media Technology: Cultural and Commercial Perspectives*. Sydney: Allyn and Bacon.

Pavlik, J. 2000. "The impact of technology on journalism." *Journalism Studies*. 1(2), pp. 229-237.

Peng, F., Tham, N. & Xiaoming, H. (1999). "Trends in online newspapers: a look at the US web." *Newspaper Research Journal*. 20(2), pp. 52-63.

Pew Research Centre for the People and the Press (2002a). "Public's news habits little changed by September 11." Retrieved September 30, 2002 from http://people-press.org/reports/display.php3?ReportID=156%2520..

Pew Research Centre for the People and the Press (2002b). "One year later: September 11 and the Internet." Retrieved from October 9, 2002 from http://people-press.org/reports/display.php3?ReportID=156%2520..

Pew Research Centre for the People and the Press (2005). "Public more critical of the press but goodwill persists." Retrieved July 23, 2006 from http://people-press.org/reports/display.php3?ReportID=248..

Pew Research Centre for the People and the Press (2006). "Online papers modestly boost newspaper readership." Retrieved July 23, 2007 from http://people-press.org/reports/display.php3?ReportID=282.

Picard, R. (1998). "The economics of the daily newspaper industry." In A. Alexander, J. Owers and R. Carveth (eds), *Media Economics: Theory and Practice*. 2nd edition. London: Lawrence Erlbaum Associates.

Piirto, R. (1993). "Electronic news." *American Demographics,* January. Retrieved November 6, 2001 from InfoTrac database.

Piirto, R. (1994). "Just the fax, ma'am." *American Demographics*. 16(11), p.6.

Piller, C. (March 31, 2003). "Who is blogger Salam Pax and is he alive?" *Chicago Tribune*. Retrieved March 31, 2002 from http://chicagotribune.com/technology/local/profiles/chi-030604blogger,0,4231426.story..

Pool, I. (1983). *Technologies of Freedom*. Cambridge, MA: Harvard University Press.

Pool, I. (ed.) (1977). *The Social Impact of the Telephone*. Cambridge: The MIT Press.

Powell, A. (2001). "Falling for the gap: Whatever happened to the digital divide?" In B. Compaine (ed.), *The Digital Divide: Facing a Crisis or Creating a Myth?*, pp. 309-314. Cambridge, MA: The MIT Press.

Price, V. & Cappella, J. (2002). "Online deliberation and its influence: the electronic dialogue project in Campaign 2000." *IT & Society*, 1(1), pp. 303-329.

Project for Excellence in Journalism. "The State of the News Media – 2008." Retrieved March 20, 2008 from http://stateofthenewsmedia.org/2008/about_the_study.php.

Prosser, J. (July, 1998). "The rise of online classifieds." *Online Journalism Review*. Retrieved June 7, 2001 from http://www.ojr.org/ojr/business/1017967473.php.

Quinn, S. & Quinn-Allan, T. (2005). "The worldwide spread of media convergence." Paper presented at the Journalism Education Association's 2005 Conference, Gold Coast, November 30-December 2.

Quinn, S. (2000). "The battle for Australia's eyeballs: An overview." *Online Journalism Review*. July. Retrieved on June 7, 2001 from http://ojr.usc.edu. *Feature* archive.

Quinn, S. (2005). "Making headlines." *The Sydney Morning Herald Online*. November 15. Retrieved November 16, 2005 from http://www.smh.com.au/news/livewire/making-headlines/2005/11/15/1132016799557.html.

Quittner, J. (1995). "The birth of way new journalism." Retrieved November 30, 2002 from http://hotwired.lycos.com/i-agent/ 95/29/ index4a.html (no longer available online).

Rainie, L. (2005). "Data demo: The state of blogging." Retrieved September 12 from http://www.pewinternet.org/PPF/r/144/report_display.asp.

Rainie, L. Fox, S. & Fallows, D. (2003). "The Internet and the Iraq War." Retrieved June 15, 2003 from http://www.pewinternet.org/reports/toc.asp?Report=87.

Raouf, N. (May 1998). "Editorial or advertorial: What's the difference?" *Online Journalism Review*. Retrieved May 17, 2001 from http://ojr.org/ojr/ethics/1017967444.php.

Rayburn, J. & Palmgreen, P. (1984). "Merging uses and gratifications and expectancy-value theory." *Communication Research*. 11(4), pp. 537-562.

Rayburn, J., Palmgreen, P. & Acker, T. (1984). "Media gratifications and choosing a morning news program." *Journalism Quarterly*. 61, pp. 149-156.

Readership Institute (2001). "The power to grow readership." Retrieved May 20, 2001 from http://www.naa.org/marketscope.

Reagan, J. (2002). "The difficult world of predicting telecommunication innovations: factors affecting adoption." In C. Lin & D. Atkin (eds), *Communication Technology and Society: Audience Adoption and Uses*, pp. 44-65. Cresskill, NJ: Hampton Press.

Reagan, J., Pinkleton, B., Chen, C. & Aaronson, D. (1995). "How do technologies relate to the repertoire of information sources?" *Telematics and Informatics*. 10, pp. 51-58.

Redden, G., Caldwell, N. & Nguyen, A. (2003). "Warblogging as critical social practice." *Southern Review*. 36(3), pp. 68-79.

Regan, T (2003). "Weblogs threaten and inform traditional journalism." *Nieman Reports*, 57(3): 68-70.

Rhee, K. & Kim, W. (2004). "The adoption and use of the Internet in South Korea." *Journal of Computer-mediated Communication*. 9(4). Retrieved August 30, 2004 from http://www.ascusc.org/jcmc/..

Rice, R., & Katz, J. E. (2003). "Comparing internet and mobile phone usage: digital divides of usage, adoption, and dropouts." *Telecommunications Policy*. 27, pp. 597-623.

Richards, B. (2007, November 30). "How an electronic newspaper becomes profitable." Retrieved March 8, 2008 from http://www.crosscut.com/media/9536/.

Robinson, J., Kestnbaum, M., Neustadtl, A. & Alvarez, A. (2000). "Mass media use and social life among Internet users." *Social Science Computer Review*. 18(4), pp. 490-501.

Rogers, E. & Scott, K. (1997). "The diffusion of innovations model and outreach from the National Network of Libraries of Medicine to Native American Community." Draft paper prepared for the National Network of Libraries of Medicine, Pacific Northwest Region, Seattle. December 10.

Rogers, E. (1986). *Communication Technology: The New Media in Society*. London: The Free Press.

Rogers, E. (2003). *Diffusion of Innovations*. Fifth edition. New York: The Free Press.

Rogers, E. (2004). "Diffusion of the Internet." In P. Lee, L. Leung & C. So (eds.), *Impact and Issues in New Media: Towards Intelligent Societies*. Cresskill: Hampton Press.

Roizen, J. (1980). "The technology of teletext and viewdata." In Efrem Sigel (ed.), *Videotext: The Coming Revolution in Home/Office Information Retrieval*. New York: Knowledge Industry Publications.

Rosalink, R. & Melinda, G. (1998). "Classifieds in crisis." Retrieved March 27, 2001 from http://ajr.newslink.org/rrcol.html.

Rosenberg, N. (1972). "Factors affecting the diffusion of technology." *Explorations in Economic History*. 10(1), pp 3-33.

Rothe, J., Harvey, M. & Michael, G. (1983). "The impact of cable television on subscriber and nonsubscriber behaviour." *Journal of Advertising Research*. 23, pp. 15-22.

Roy Morgan (2006a, May 25). "Online news continues to grow – Ninemsn number one for second year running." Press Release. Retrieved May 27, 2006 from http://www.roymorgan.com/news/press-releases/2006/498/.

Roy Morgan (2006b, December 16). "Australian media viewed with scepticism – TV remains first stop when chasing the news." Press release. Retrieved January 21, 2007 from **http://www.roymorgan.com/news/polls/2006/4117/index.cfm?printversion=yes**.

Roy Morgan (December 4, 2005). "Australians sceptical of the media." Retrieved December 16, 2005 from http://www.roymorgan.com/news/polls/2005/3952/.

Ruggiero, T. (2000). "Uses and gratifications theory in the 21st century." *Mass Communication and Society*. 3(1), pp. 3-37.

Runnett, R. (2003). "Blogging builds on connection between journalism, technology." Retrieved July 7, 2003 from http://www.journalism.co.uk/features/story604.html.

Salwen, M. (2005). "Online news trends." In M. Salwen, B. Garrison & P. Driscoll (eds.), *Online News and the Public*, pp. 47-79. Mahwah: Lawrence Erlbaum.

Salwen, M., Garrison, B. & Driscoll, P. (2005). *Online News and the Public*. Mahwah: Lawrence Erlbaum.

Samuel, G. (2005). *Media convergence and the changing face of media regulation*. Henry Meyer Public Lecture at the University of Queensland, May 19.

Sanders, K. (2003). *Ethics & Journalism*. London: Sage.

Saunders, C. (2002, October 10). "Study: Net hurts offline communications, media use." Retrieved April 24, 2005 from http://www.clickz.com/news/article.php/1480301.

Scheufele, D. & Nisbet, M. (2002). "Being a citizen online: new opportunities and dead ends." *Press/Politics*. 7(3), pp. 55-75.

Schierhorn, C., Wearden, S., Schierhorn, A., Endres, F., Tabar, P. & Andrews, S. (1999). "What digital formats do consumers prefer?" *Newspaper Research Journal*. 20(3), pp. 2-19.

Schiffman, L., Bednall, D., Cowley, E., O'Cass, A., Watson, J. & Kanuk, L. (2001). *Consumer Behaviour*: 2nd Ed. Sydney: Prentice Hall.

Schramm, W. (1949). "The nature of news." *Journalism Quarterly*. 26(3), pp. 259-269.

Schultz, T. & Voakes, P. (1999). "Prophets of gloom: Why do newspaper journalists have so little faith in the future of newspapers." *Newspaper Research Journal*. 20(2). Retrieved March 20, 2004 from http://www.findarticles.com/p/articles/mi_qa3677/is_199904/ai_n8848471.

Schulze, J. (2005a). "Online expansion now top priority." *The Australian*. August 12, p. 15.

Schulze, J. (2005b). "News ups online activity." *The Australian*. August 25, p. 17.

Schweiger, W. (2000). "Media credibility – Experience or image? A survey on the credibility of the world wide web in Germany in comparison to other media." *European Journal of Communication*. 15(1), pp. 37-59.

Seib, P. (2001). *Going Live: Getting the News Right in a Real-time Online World*. Lanham: Rowman & Littlefield.

Senft, T. (2000). "Baud girls and cargo cults." In A. Herman & T. Swiss (eds.), *The World Wide Web and Contemporary Culture*. London: Routledge.

Servon, L. (2002). *Bridging the Digital Divide: Technology, Community, and Public Policy*. Oxford: Blackwell Publishers.

Severin, W. & Tankard, J. (2001). *Communication Theories: Origins, Methods and Uses in the Mass Media*. Fifth edition. New York: Longman.

Shedden, D. (1998). "New media timeline." Retrieved August 31, 2001 from .http://www.poynter.org/research/nm/timeline..

Shirky, C (2002). "Broadcast institutions, community values." Retrieved March 15, 2004 from .http://www.shirky.com/writings/broadcast_and_community.html.

Shultz, T. (2000). "Mass media and the concept of interactivity." *Media, Culture and Society*. 22(2), pp. 205-221.

Siebert, F. (1956). "The libertarian theory of the press". In F. Siebert, T. Peterson & W. Schramm (eds), *Four Theories of the Press*, pp. 39-72. Urbana: University of Illinois Press.

Sifry, D. (April 2007). "State of the live web." Retrieved August 30, 2007 from . http://technorati.com/weblog/2007/04/328.html.

Silverstone, R. (1995). "Media, communication, information and the 'revolution' of everyday life." In Stephen Emmott (ed.*), Information Superhighway: Multimedia Users and Futures*, pp. 61-76. London: Academic Press.

Sinclair, L. (2004). "Web as commercial vehicle." *The Australian*, 2 December.

Singer, J. B. (2003). "Campaign contributions: online newspaper coverage of Election 2000." *Journalism and Mass Communication Quarterly*. 80(1), pp 39-56.

Singer, J. B., Tharp, M. & Haruta, A. (1999). "Online staffers: superstars or second-class citizens." *Newspaper Research Journal*, 20(3), pp. 29-47.

Smith, A. (1980). *Goodbye, Gutenberg: The Newspaper Revolution of the 1980s*. Oxford: Oxford University Press.

Smolkin, R. (2006). "Adapt or Die?" *American Journalism Review*, June/July. Retrieved January 6, 2007 from http://www.ajr.org/Article.asp?id=4111.

Snowden, C. (2003). "What's happening? Mobile communication technology and the surveillance function of news." *Transformations*. 7. Retrieved June 3, 2004 from http://transformations.cqu.edu.au/journal/issue_07/article_03.shtml.

Son, J. & McCombs (1993). "A look at the constancy principle under changing market conditions." *The Journal of Media Economics*. 6(2), pp. 24-36.

Sparks, C. (1999). "Newspapers, the Internet and the public sphere." *Review of Media, Information and Society*. April, pp. 51-67.

Specker, N. (1999). "Executive summary." 6th Interactive Publishing Europe Conference. November 17-19, Zurich/Switzerland. Retrieved May 8, 2001 from http://www.interactivepublishing.ch/99.sum_1.php.

Standage, T. (1998). *The Victorian Internet: The Remarkable Story of the Telegraph and Nineteenth Century's Online Pioneers*. New York: Berkley.

Stanford, S. (1983). "Comment on Palmgreen and Rayburn, 'gratifications sought and media exposure'". *Communication Research*. 10(2), pp. 247-251.

Stannard, B. (November 14, 1989). "Why Australia's media are on the nose." *The Bulletin*, p.8.

Star, S. & Bowker, G. (2002). "How to infrastructure". In L. Lievrouw & S. Livingstone (eds), *Handbook of New Media*, pp. 151-162. London: Sage.
Statistics Canada (2006). "Canadian Internet use survey." Retrieved January 9, 2007 from ***http://www.statcan.ca/Daily/English/060815/d060815b.htm***.

Statistics Norway (2005). "More Internet users, fewer newspaper readers." Press Release, April 25. Retrieved June 25, 2005 from http://www.ssb.no/english/subjects/07/02/30/medie_en/main.html.

Steinberger, P. (1984). "Urban politics and communality." *Urban Affairs Quarterly*. 20(1), pp 4-21.

Steinfield, C., Dutton, W. & Kovaric, P. (1989). "A framework and agenda for research on computing in the home." In J. Salvaggio & J. Bryant (eds.), *Media Use in the Information Age: Emerging Patterns of Adoption and Consumer Use*, pp. 61-86. London: Lawrence Erlbaum.

Stempel, G., Hargrove, T. & Bernt, J. (2000). "Relation of growth of use of the Internet to changes in media use from 1995 to 1999." *Journalism & Mass Communication Quarterly*. 77(1), pp. 71-79.

Stephenson, W. (1967). *The Play Theory of Mass Communication*. Chicago: University of Chicago Press.

Stokes, B. (1992). "Faxing a daily fix on Japanese news." *National Journal*, October 24. Retrieved on November 6, 2001 from InfoTrac database.

Stovall, J. (2004). *Web Journalism: Practice and Promise of a New Medium*. Boston: Pearson.

Sundar, S. (1998). "Effect of source attribution on perception of online news stories." *Journalism and Mass Communication Quarterly*. 75(1), pp. 55-68.

Sundar, S. (2000). "Multimedia effects on Processing and perceptions of online news: a study of picture, audio and video download." *Journalism and Mass Communication Quarterly*. 77(3), pp. 480-499.

Tanaka, K. (2000). "Motion pictures on the net: Streaming media industry, technology, and early adopters." Retrieved March 14, 2005 from http://www.isoc.org/inet2000/cdproceedings/4c/4c_2.htm.

Tapsall, S. (2001). "The media is the message." In S. Tapsall & C. Varley (eds.), *Journalism: Theory and Practice*. South Melbourne: Oxford University Press.

Teinowitz, I. (April 26, 1993). "Just the fax, ma 'am,' latest newspaper refrain." *Advertising Age*. Retrieved November 6, 2001 from InfoTrac database.

Tenopir, C. & Barry, J. (2000). "Are online companies dinosaurs?" *Library Journal*, 15 May, p. 44.

Tewksbury, D. & Althaus, S. (2002). "Differences in knowledge acquisition among readers of the paper and online versions of a national newspaper." *Journalism and Mass Communication Quarterly*. 77(3), pp. 457-479.

Tewksbury, D., Weaver, A. & Maddex, B. (2001). "Accidentally informed: Incidental news exposure on the World Wide Web." *Journalism and Mass Communication Quarterly*. 78(3), pp. 533-554.

The Age Online (2003, March 20). "Broadband use increasing but rate of take-up slowing." Retrieved March 24, 2003 from http://www.theage.com.au/articles/2003/03/20/1047749863541.html.

The Age Online (2005, November 10). "Online warning for papers." Retrieved November 12, 2002 from http://www.theage.com.au (no longer available online).

The Age Online (November 19, 2002). "Internet users to reach 655 million by year-end." Retrieved November 20, 2002 from http://www.theage.com.au/articles/2002/11/19/1037599406943.html.

The Australian (2005, November 17). "Stephen Ellis: net nerves hit newspaper sale," p. 12.

The Economist (US) (1999, July 17). "Caught in the web – Internet may mean the end of newspaper industry." Retrieved March 24, 2001 from InfoTrac database.

The Register (2004, May 27). "Broadband killed the TV star." Retrieved on March 24, 2005 from http://www.theregister.co.uk/2004/05/27/broadband_threatens_tv/.

The Times of India (2002, October 11). "Net third most popular source of information: study." Retrieved 12 October, 2002 from http://timesofindia.indiatimes.com/articleshow.asp?artid=17243868.

Thompson, G. (2003). "Weblogs, warblogs, the public sphere and bubbles." *Transformations*. 7. Retrieved October 20, 2003 from http://www.ahs.cqu.edu.au/transformations/journal/pdf/no7/thompson.pdf.

Thornburg, D. & Boccardi, L. (2005). *Report of the Independent Panel Review*. Retrieved February 11, 2005 http://www.rathergate.com/CBS_report.pdf.

Thurman, N. (2008). "Forums for citizen journalists? Adoption of user generated content initiatives by online news media." *New Media & Society*, 10(1), pp. 139-157.

Thurman, N. & Lupton, B. (2008). "Convergence calls: Multimedia news story-telling at British news websites". Paper presented to the 9th International Symposium on Online Journalism, University of Texas, Austin, USA, April 5. Retrieved April 30, 2008 from http://www.city.ac.uk/journalism/download_files/thurman_lupton_final.pdf.

Tichenor, P., Donohue, G., & Olien, C. (1970). "Mass media and differential growth in knowledge." *The Public Opinion Quarterly*. 34(1), pp. 158-170.

Tobler, H. (2002). "Study outlines computer use hazards." Retrieved November 1, 2002 from http://www.news.com.au/common/printpage/0,6093,5455128,00.html.

Tremayne, M. (2004). "The web of context: applying network theory to the use of hyperlinks in journalism on the web." *Journalism and Mass Communication Quarterly*. 81(2), pp. 237-253.

Tsagarousianou, R., Tambini, D. & Bryan, C. (1998). *Cyberdemocracy: Technologies, Cities and Civic Networks*. London: Routledge.

Tydeman, J., Lipinski, H., Adler, R., Nyhan, M. and Zwimerpfer, L. (1982). *Teletext and Videotex in the United States*. New York: McGraw-Hill.

U.S. Census Bureau (2002). "A nation online: how Americans are expanding their use of the Internet." Retrieved March 20, 2003 from http://www.ntia.doc.gov/ntiahome/dn/.

University of Southern California Centre for Digital Future (2008). "Annual Internet survey by the Center for the Digital Future finds shifting trends among adults about the benefits and consequences of children going online." Retrieved February 18, 2008 from http://www.digitalcenter.org/pdf/2008-Digital-Future-Report-Final-Release.pdf.

Utalkmarketing (2008). "Online is the future for newspaper ad models." Retrieved April 15, 2008 from http://www.utalkmarketing.com/pages/Article.aspx?ArticleID=4776&Title=Online%20is%20the%20future%20for%20newspaper%20ad%20models.

van Dusseldorp, M. (1998). "The Internet Age: Threat or opportunity for European printed press." Retrieved March 27, 2001 from http://www.futureprint.kent.edu/vandusseldorp01.htm.

Vargo, K., Schierhorn, C., Wearden, S., Schierhorn, A., Endres, F. & Tabar, P. (2000). "How readers respond to digital news stories in layers and links." *Newspaper Research Journal*. 21(2), pp. 40-54.

Walker, L. (2005). "It's a web buying spree for big media." *Washington Post*. September 8, p. D5.

Ward, I. & Cahill, J. (2007). "Old and New Media: Blogs in the third age of political communication." Paper presented at the Australasian Political Studies Association (APSA) Annual Conference 24th-26th September, Monash University.

Ward, M. (2002). *Journalism Online.* Oxford, Boston: Focal Press.

Wareham, J., Levy, A., & Shi, W. (2004). "Wireless diffusion and mobile computing: implications for the digital divide." *Telecommunications Policy*. 28, pp. 439-457.

Washingtonpost.com (2005). "The online news and information user: understanding media choices." Retrieved July 23, 2005 from http://www.washingtonpost.com/wp-srv/marketing/presentation/nielsen/content/frame.htm.

Wearden, S. & Fidler, R. (2001). "Crain's Cleveland business: evaluating an e-newspaper concept for tablet PCs." Retrieved September 24, 2003 from http://www.futureprint.kent.edu/articles/wearden03.htm.

Wearden, S. (1998). "Landscape vs. portrait formats: assessing consumer preferences." Retrieved March 23, 2002 from http://www.futureprint.kent.edu/articles/wearden01.htm.

Wearden, S., Fidler, R., Schierhorn, A. & Schierhorn, C. (1999). "Portrait versus landscape: Potential users' preferences for screen orientation." *Newspaper Research Journal*. 20(4), pp. 20-61.

Weibull, L. (1985). "Structural factors in gratifications research." In K. Rosengren, L. Wenner & P. Palmgreen (eds.). *Media Gratifications Research: Current Perspectives*. Beverly Hills: Sage Publications.

Weir, T. (1999). "Innovators or news hounds: A study of early adopters of the electronic newspaper." *Newspaper Research Journal*. 20(4), pp. 62-81.

Weiss, A., Meraz, S., Figur, N. & Poindexter, P. (2003). "Experience and Internet news: the real reason for the online news reading gender gap." Paper presented at the Association for Education in Journalism and Mass Communication's Annual Convention.

Kansas. Retrieved March 20, 2005 from .http://www.inma.org/subscribers/papers/2003-Weiss.doc..

Wenner, K. (2001, March). "Downsized dotcoms." *American Journalism Review.* Retrieved March 14, 2007 from http://www.ajr.org/article_printable.asp?id=455.

Wenner, L. (1985). "The nature of news gratifications." In K. Rosengren, L. Wenner & P. Palmgreen (eds). *Media Gratifications Research: Current Perspectives.* Beverly Hills: Sage Publications.

Williams, F., Strover, S. & Grant, A. (1994). "Social aspects of new media technologies." In J. Bryant & D. Zillman (eds). *Media Effects: Advances in Theory and Research,* pp. 463-482. London: Lawrence Erlbaum.

Wilson, S., Gibson, R., Denemark, D., Meagher, G. and Western, M. (2005). Forthcoming. *Australian Survey of Social Attitudes the First Report.* Sydney. University of New South Wales Press.

Wilson, T. & Walsh, C. (1996). *Information Behaviour: an Interdisciplinary Perspective.* Sheffield: University of Sheffield Department of Information Studies. Retrieved 29 March, 2006 from .http://informationr.net/tdw/publ/infbehav/index.html.

Wilson, Tom (1997). "Electronic publishing and the future of the book." *Information Research*, 3(2), paper 39. Retrieved 10 March 2006 from .http://informationr.net/ir/3-2/paper39.html.

Wilson, Tom (1999). "Models in information behaviour research." *Journal of Documentation.* 55(3), pp. 249-270. Retrieved 29 March, 2006 from .http://informationr.net/tdw/publ/papers/1999JDoc.html.

Wilson, Tony (2004). *The Playful Audience: From Talk Show Viewers to Internet Users.* Cresskill: Hampton Press.

Winseck, D. (1999). "Back to the future: Telecommunications, online information services and convergence from 1840 to 1910." *Media History.* 5(2), pp. 137-157.

Winston, B. (1998). *Media Technology and Society – A History from the Telegraph to the Internet.* London: Routledge.

Wollen, C. (2002). "A few thoughts about watching TV." ITC Future Reflections Workshop. Retrieved April 30, 2004 from .http://www.media.bournemouth.ac.uk/documents/henley.pdf.

Wood, W. & O'Hare, S. (1991). "Paying for the video revolution: Consumer spending on the mass media." *Journal of Communication.* Winter, pp. 24-30.

Wood, W. (1986). "Consumer spending on the mass media: The Principle of Relative Constancy reconsidered." *Journal of Communication.* Spring, pp. 39-51.

World Association of Newspapers (2006, June 5). "World press trends: newspaper circulation, advertising increases." Press Release. Retrieved June 6, 2006 from http://www.wan-press.org/article11185.html.

World Association of Newspapers (2007a). "World digital media trend: executive summary" Retrieved March 6, 2008 from http://www.wan-press.org/article14149.html.

World Association of Newspapers (2007b, May 8). "World press trends: newspaper circulation rises world-wide; number of new titles grows significantly." Press Release.

World Association of Newspapers (2008). "Investing in newspapers: executive summary." Retrieved March 6, 2008 from http://www.wan-press.org/article16373.html.

World Association of Newspapers. (2001). "The 2001 world press trends." Retrieved on April 21, 2001, from http://www.wan-press.org (no longer available online).

Wright, C. (1960). "Functional analysis and mass communication." *The Public Opinion Quarterly*. 24(4), pp. 605-620.

Wright, C. (1986). *Mass Communication: A Sociological Perspective.* Third edition. New York: McGraw-Hill, Inc.

Wu, H. & Bechtel, A. (2002). "Website use and news topic and type." *Journalism and Mass Communication Quarterly*, 79(1), pp. 73-86.

Xavier, D. P. (2001). *Bridging the Digital Divide: Refocusing on a Market-Based Approach – an APEC perspective.* Melbourne: APEC Study Centre

Yang, H. & Oliver, M. (2004). "Exploring the effect of online advertising on readers' perception of online news." *Journalism and Mass Communication Quarterly*. 81(4), pp. 733-749.

Zhou, J. & He, Z. (2002a). "Diffusion, use and impact of the Internet in Hong Kong: A chain process model." *Journal of Computer-mediated Communication.* 7(2). Retrieved August 11, 2003 from http://www.ascusc.org/jcmc/vol7/issue2/hongkong.html.

Zhou, J. & He, Z. (2002b). "Information accessibility, user sophistication, and source credibility: The impact of the Internet on value orientations in mainland China." *Journal of Computer-mediated Communication.* 7(2). Retrieved August 11, 2003 from http://www.ascusc.org/jcmc/vol7/issue2/china.html.

Zhou, J. & He, Z. (2002c). "Perceived characteristics, perceived needs and perceived popularity: Adoption and use of the Internet in China." *Communication Research.* 29(4), pp. 466-495.

Appendix: The 2004 news use questionnaire

Section A: General news usage (all users)

A1) How often do you get news from the media (i.e. read/watch/listen to news from newspapers, magazines, television, radio and the internet)?

☐ Everyday   ☐ Several times a week   ☐ Several times a month ☐ Less often

A2) On average, about how much time do you spend getting news a day?

☐ 15 minutes or less   ☐ 16-30 minutes   ☐ 31-60 minutes   ☐ Over 60 minutes

A3) In general, how much do you enjoy keeping up with the news?

☐ A good deal   ☐ Some   ☐ Not much   ☐ Not at all

A4) In general, would you describe yourself as a "news junkie" – someone who would miss the news very much if he/she couldn't get it for a substantial time?

    ☐ Yes   ☐ No

A5) Do you subscribe to the following?

• A daily newspaper	☐ Yes	☐ No
• A weekly news magazine (e.g. The Bulletin, Time)	☐ Yes	☐ No
• A special-interest magazine (e.g. People)	☐ Yes	☐ No
• A pay television service (e.g. Foxtel, Optus TV)	☐ Yes	☐ No
• A pay online service (e.g. America Online)	☐ Yes	☐ No

A6) Please respond to the following statements.

	Strongly agree	Agree	Neutral	Disagree	Strongly disagree
• *News is not as important today as it once was.*	5	4	3	2	1
• *I wish I had more time to follow the news.*	5	4	3	2	1
• *The Australian media help me a lot to follow the news.*	5	4	3	2	1
• *The Australian news media are fair.*	5	4	3	2	1
• *The Australian news media are biased.*	5	4	3	2	1
• *The Australian media cover news accurately.*	5	4	3	2	1

- *The Australian news media are dishonest.*   5   4   3   2   1
- *The Australian news media are trustworthy.*   5   4   3   2   1

A7) How strong do you find your need to follow the news types listed below?

	Very strong	Strong	Not very strong	Not at all strong
National/state politics	3	2	1	0
International affairs	3	2	1	0
Economics (including business/finance)	3	2	1	0
Sports and entertainment	3	2	1	0
Science/technology and health	3	2	1	0
Social problems (crime/disasters/accidents)	3	2	1	0
Culture and the arts	3	2	1	0
Local community affairs	3	2	1	0

A8) How often do you do the following?

	Very often	Often	Not very often	Never
Discuss news and current affairs with your peers (e.g. friends, colleagues, relatives etc.) when talking on the phone	3	2	1	0
Discuss news and current affairs with your peers when meeting them	3	2	1	0
Read editorial pages on newspapers	3	2	1	0
Read readers' opinion pages on newspapers	3	2	1	0
Watch participatory television shows (shows that invite viewers to call in to have their say)	3	2	1	0
Listen to talkback radio programs	3	2	1	0
Write letters to the editor	3	2	1	0
Call in talkback radio programs	3	2	1	0
Call in participatory TV shows	3	2	1	0

A9) Listed below are five attributes that people might look for when deciding which news source to choose. Please rank each of them in terms of their importance to you. Place 1 in the box next to the <u>most important</u> attribute and 2 in the second most important, and so on. If a listed item is <u>not</u> at all what you look for, place 0 in the corresponding box.

☐ Diverse range of news content (i.e. covering many topics)

☐ Timely and updated coverage

☐ In-depth coverage, including background information

☐ Different viewpoints in both news stories and opinion pieces

☐ Enjoyable presentation of news

A10) To what extent are you satisfied with the <u>diversity of news content</u> provided by the following media? Do not rate a medium if you never get news from it.

	Very satisfied	Satisfied	Neutral	Unsatisfied	Very unsatisfied
• Newspapers	5	4	3	2	1
• Magazines	5	4	3	2	1
• Radio	5	4	3	2	1
• Television	5	4	3	2	1

A11) Similarly, to what extent are you satisfied with the <u>depth of coverage</u> provided by the following media?

	Very satisfied	Satisfied	Neutral	Unsatisfied	Very unsatisfied
• Newspapers	5	4	3	2	1
• Magazines	5	4	3	2	1
• Radio	5	4	3	2	1
• Television	5	4	3	2	1

A12) Similarly, to what extent are you satisfied with <u>the way news is presented</u> in the following media?

	Very satisfied	Satisfied	Neutral	Unsatisfied	Very unsatisfied
• Newspapers	5	4	3	2	1
• Magazines	5	4	3	2	1
• Radio	5	4	3	2	1
• Television	5	4	3	2	1

A13) Similarly, to what extent are you satisfied with the <u>timeliness and updatedness</u> of news coverage in the following media?

	Very satisfied	Satisfied	Neutral	Unsatisfied	Very unsatisfied
• Newspapers	5	4	3	2	1
• Magazines	5	4	3	2	1
• Radio	5	4	3	2	1
• Television	5	4	3	2	1

A14) Similarly, to what extent are you satisfied with <u>the different viewpoints</u> represented in the following media?

	Very satisfied	Satisfied	Neutral	Unsatisfied	Very unsatisfied
• Newspapers	5	4	3	2	1
• Magazines	5	4	3	2	1
• Radio	5	4	3	2	1
• Television	5	4	3	2	1

A15) Some people say they feel overloaded with information these days, considering all the TV news shows, magazines, newspapers, and computer information services. Others say they like having so much information to choose from. How about you?

    ☐ I feel overloaded   ☐ I like having so much information   ☐ I can't say

A16) Do you own the following?

• More than one desktop computer	☐ Yes	☐ No
• A laptop computer	☐ Yes	☐ No
• A DVD player	☐ Yes	☐ No
• An MP3 player	☐ Yes	☐ No
• A mobile phone with a built-in camera	☐ Yes	☐ No
• A mobile phone only	☐ Yes	☐ No
• A digital camera only	☐ Yes	☐ No
• A Personal Digital Assistant (PDA)	☐ Yes	☐ No

A17) Do you use a VCR (video cassette recorder) at all?

    ☐ Yes, often   ☐ Yes, sometimes   ☐ No, never

A18) Do you use the Internet for any purposes at all?

    ☐ Yes → **Go to question A19.**

    ☐ No

---

a) Do you use computers for any purpose?   ☐ Yes   ☐ No

b) On a daily basis, do you have a chance to access the Internet at all?

    ☐ Yes, at work (office/school/university)

    ☐ Yes, at home

    ☐ Yes, at some other places (friends/relatives' houses, public library etc.)

    ☐ No

c) Why do you think you don't use the Internet? Please tick <u>all</u> that apply.

    ☐ I don't know what it is

    ☐ It looks too complicated

    ☐ I feel no need for it

    ☐ I cannot afford it

    ☐ Other (Please describe --

--)

> **d) Have you heard someone talking about the advantages and disadvantages of the Internet?**
>
> ☐ Yes, often   ☐ Yes, sometimes   ☐ No, never
>
> **e) Have you thought about connecting to the Internet in the future?**
>
> ☐ Yes   ☐ No
>
> └──────────→ In a near future?   ☐ Yes   ☐ No
>
> **Now go to section C on page 13.**

A19) How long have you been using the Internet?

☐ 1 year or less   ☐ Over 1-2 years   ☐ Over 2-3 years   ☐ Over 3-5 years   ☐ Over 5 years

A20) Where do you access the Internet?

☐ At work only   ☐ At home only   ☐ Both at work   ☐ Other places
(office/school/university)   and at home

A21) "Broadband" refers to different types of high-speed and 24-hour available Internet connection (those not through a dial-up telephone line). Where do you have, if any, Internet broadband connection?

☐ At work only   ☐ At home only   ☐ Both at work and home

☐ Other places   ☐ None   ☐ Not sure

A22) How often do you go <u>online</u> (i.e. log on to the Internet)?

☐ Everyday   ☐ Several times a week   ☐ Several times a month   ☐ Less often

A23) Which of the following statements applies to you <u>the most</u>?

☐ The Internet is an essential part of my life.

☐ The Internet will become an essential part of my life in a near future.

☐ The Internet might become an essential part of my life in a distant future

☐ The Internet would be unlikely to become an essential part of my life.

A24) To what extent do you believe you understand the Internet?

☐ A good deal   ☐ Some   ☐ Not very much

A25) How often do you use the Internet for the following purposes?

	Very often	Often	Not very often	Never
• Entertainment and relaxation (e.g. playing games)	3	2	1	0
• E-commerce (purchasing goods and using services such as finance and banking)	3	2	1	0
• Personal contact (e.g. emailing/messaging)	3	2	1	0
• Interaction with other online users (e.g.	3	2	1	0

attending forums, chat rooms)

• Getting news	3	2	1	0
• Searching non-news information for work/study	3	2	1	0
• Searching non-news information for other purposes	3	2	1	0

A26) What major purposes of your Internet usage are not mentioned above?

A27) Do you get news on the Internet at all?

    ☐ Yes → **Go to section B on the page 7.**

    ☐ No

> **Why do you think you use the Internet without getting online news? Please tick all that apply.**
>
>   ☐ Because online news is not convenient for me to use
>
>   ☐ Because the news I get from other sources is already enough.
>
>   ☐ Because I don't have enough time for news when going online
>
>   ☐ Because I don't trust information on the web
>
>   ☐ Because I find it tiresome reading on the computer screen.
>
>   ☐ Others (Please specify --
>
> ---
>
> ---
>
> --)
>
> **Now go to section C on page 13.**

Section B: Online news usage

B1) How long have you been getting news from the Internet?

☐ 1 year or less   ☐ Over 1-2 years   ☐ Over 2-3 years   ☐ Over 3-5 years   ☐ Over 5 years

B2) How often do you get news on the Internet?

   ☐ Everyday   ☐ Several times a week   ☐ Several times a month   ☐ Less often

B3) Please respond to the statement starting with *I get news online...*

	Strongly Agree	Agree	Neutral	Disagree	Strongly Disagree
... because I don't pay for it	5	4	3	2	1
... because I have more news choices on the Internet	5	4	3	2	1
... because I can combine getting news with other purposes online	5	4	3	2	1
... because I can look for in-depth and background information whenever I want	5	4	3	2	1
... because I can check for updated news whenever I want	5	4	3	2	1
... because I can get news tailored to my interest only	5	4	3	2	1
... because I can have my say to the news media	5	4	3	2	1
... because I can discuss news and current affairs with my peers	5	4	3	2	1
... because I can find different viewpoints on the Internet.	5	4	3	2	1

B4) Which type(s) of news sites do you visit? Please tick all that apply.

☐ Newspapers' sites (e.g. theage.com.au; theaustralian.news.com.au; nytimes.com etc.)

☐ Magazines' sites (e.g. bulletin.ninemsn.com.au etc.)

☐ Broadcasters' sites (e.g. abc.net.au, sbs.com.au, bbc.co.uk, cnn.com etc.)

☐ News agencies' sites (aap.com.au, reuters.com, afp.com etc.)

☐ Websites that accumulate news from a range of publications (e.g. news.com.au; f2.com.au; news.google.com; news.yahoo.com etc.)

☐ News sites offered by individuals/groups/organizations outside the mainstream media

☐ News/information exchange websites (e.g. online forums, chat rooms, newsgroups etc.)

☐ Others (Please specify ---

--)

B5) Please name your most favoured news website either by its name or its web address. ---

B6) As the result of events such as the 11/9 attacks, the Bali bombings, the war in Iraq, and terrorist threats, have you spent more, less or just about the same amount of time getting news on the web?

    ☐ More   ☐ Less   ☐ About the same   ☐ Not sure

→ **Was the first news story you got online <u>about</u> an event of this sort?**
       ☐ Yes   ☐ No   ☐ I can't remember

B7) Please choose the statement <u>most suited</u> to you from the following.
    ☐ News is an essential part of my Internet usage.
    ☐ News is an important part of my Internet usage.
    ☐ News is not an important part of my Internet usage.

B8) What time of the day do you typically go online for news?
  ☐ Before 9am   ☐ 9am-5pm   ☐ After 5pm to 12am   ☐ Whenever convenient

B9) Do you do the following?

• Subscribe to free email alerts of general news	☐ Yes	☐ No
• Subscribe to free email news alerts tailored to your own interests only	☐ Yes	☐ No
• Subscribe to a pay online <u>news</u> service	☐ Yes	☐ No
• Set up a personalized page offered by Internet services and online news providers (My Yahoo!, My MSN, My CNN etc.)	☐ Yes	☐ No
• Set your favourite news home page as the default front page of your web browser	☐ Yes	☐ No
• Receive news on a mobile device (e.g. cell phones etc.)	☐ Yes	☐ No

B10) Now please think about the last time you got news from the Internet…

    (a) When was it?
        ☐ Just today   ☐ Within the past few days   ☐ Within the past few weeks
        ☐ More than a month ago   ☐ I can't remember

    (b) Where was it?
        ☐ At work   ☐ At home   ☐ Other places   ☐ I can't remember

    (c) How did you start?
        ☐ I went deliberately to a news site to check the news of the day
        ☐ I heard something happened and visited a news site to check it.
        ☐ I got some news from other sources and went online for more details
        ☐ I got an interesting news item from a news email alert
        ☐ I got an interesting news item from a friend via an email message
        ☐ I happened to go across a news item while doing something else online
        ☐ I was linked to an interesting news item from a news/information trade network

☐ Other (Please specify---

--)

☐ I can't remember

(d) About how many minutes did you spend on news? -----------------------------------

(e) About how many minutes did you spend in that whole online session, including news usage? ---

(f) About how many news sites did you visit? ---

(g) How many of them are from <u>outside</u> Australia? --------------------------------

(h) Were you doing something else at the time (e.g. eating, chatting etc.)?
    ☐ Yes → **What was you doing?** ---
    ☐ No
    ☐ I can't remember

B11) Back to your normal usage… How often do you do the following when getting news online?

	Very often	Often	Not very often	Never
Use search tools to find news of your interest	3	2	1	0
Get up-to-the-minute news several times a day	3	2	1	0
Visit a number of sites for the same news item	3	2	1	0
Get audio news in addition to reading	3	2	1	0
Get video news in addition to reading	3	2	1	0
Scan/skim through news stories rather than read word by word	3	2	1	0
Print out some news items for later usage	3	2	1	0
Click on links to related stories for in-depth coverage (including background information)	3	2	1	0
Participate in online news polls	3	2	1	0
Find other perspectives from sources outside the news mainstream media	3	2	1	0
Go to an information exchange site to express your opinions	3	2	1	0
Send links to news stories to your peers	3	2	1	0
Receive links to news stories from your peers	3	2	1	0
Pass some news/information you have just witnessed/heard to others	3	2	1	0

B12) To what extent do you think online news has contributed to shaping the way you understand and think about public affairs?

☐ A good deal   ☐ Some   ☐ Not very much   ☐ No at all

B13) Have you heard of terms like weblogs or blogs?

☐ No

☐ Yes ⟶

    a) How often do you get news from weblogs?

    ☐ Very often   ☐ Often   ☐ Not very often   ☐ Never

    b) How often do you post comments on weblogs?

    ☐ Very often   ☐ Often   ☐ Not very often   ☐ Never

B14) To what extent are you satisfied with the Internet in terms of the following?

	Very satisfied	Satisfied	Neutral	Unsatisfied	Very unsatisfied
• The way news is presented	5	4	3	2	1
• Diversity of news content	5	4	3	2	1
• Different viewpoints	5	4	3	2	1
• Timeliness and updates	5	4	3	2	1
• Depth of coverage	5	4	3	2	1

B15) To what extent do you find the Internet helpful to follow the news types listed below?

	Very helpful	Helpful	Not very helpful	Not at all helpful
• National/state politics	4	3	2	1
• International affairs	4	3	2	1
• Economics (including business/finance)	4	3	2	1
• Entertainment/sport	4	3	2	1
• Science/technology and health	4	3	2	1
• Social problems (crime/disasters/accidents)	4	3	2	1
• Culture and the arts	4	3	2	1
• Local community affairs	4	3	2	1

B16) Apart from the Internet, how often do you receive news from the following?

	Very often	Often	Not very often	Never
• Newspapers	3	2	1	0
• Magazines	3	2	1	0
• Radio	3	2	1	0
• Television	3	2	1	0

B17) Since you adopted online news, has there been any shift in the <u>primary</u> time and location of your general news usage? Choose both "Yes" options if relevant.

☐ No, not at all.

☐ Yes, some time change (from ------------------------------ to ------------------------------)

☐ Yes some location change (from ---------------------------- to ------------------------------)

B18) Compared to when you didn't use online news, do you think the total amount of time you are spending on other news sources now is less, more or about the same?

☐ More ☐ Less ☐ About the same ☐ Not sure

B19) More specifically, please indicate which source is being spent less, more or about the same amount of time.

	More	Less	About the same	Not sure
• Newspapers	☐	☐	☐	☐
• Magazines	☐	☐	☐	☐
• Radio	☐	☐	☐	☐
• Television	☐	☐	☐	☐

B20) If right now, you heard something of great interest to you has just happened, which medium would you use <u>first</u> to get news about it?

B21) How often do you find yourself...

	Very often	Often	Not very often	Never
... being lost among too much information on the Internet?	3	2	1	0
... missing some important news that you should know after an online news session?	3	2	1	0
... being tired when getting news on the computer screen?	3	2	1	0
... encountering false news online?	3	2	1	0
... being irritated or insulted in an online news/information exchange network?	3	2	1	0
... being frustrated with advertising inserted in the body of online news stories?	3	2	1	0

B22) Which of the following labels would you consider yourself to be. Please tick <u>all</u> that apply.

☐ Newspaper fan ☐ Magazine news fan

☐ Radio news fan ☐ Television news fan

☐ Online news fan ☐ None

B23) Overall, which of the following media is <u>the best</u> to serve your news needs?

☐ Newspapers ☐ Magazines ☐ Television ☐ Radio ☐ Internet

B24) To what extent do you believe the Internet will become the <u>most important</u> news source in the future?

☐ A good deal ☐ Some ☐ Not very much ☐ Not at all

B25) Have you ever shared your experience of using online news to other people who do not use it?

    □ Yes, often   □ Yes, sometimes   □ No, never

B26) Now just a few questions about yourself before we finish. What's your sex?

    □ Male   □ Female

B27) What is your year of birth?   --

B28) What is your country of birth? --

B29) Which of the following best describe the area you now live in?

    □ A rural area/village   □ A small town   □ A large town

    □ A metropolitan area (including suburbs surrounding major cities)

B30) What is your current employment status?

    □ Full-time   □ Part-time   □ Not employed   □ Retired

B31) What type of job do you do?

    □ Professional   □ Administrator/Manager

    □ Agriculture worker (Farmer/Fisher/Miner)   □ Clerical/Sales

    □ Services   □ Trade person/Skilled worker

    □ Labourer   □ Student

    □ Home duties

B32) What's the highest level of education you have achieved so far?

□ Not complete secondary school   □ Completed secondary school

□ TAFE/Trade certificate □ University/CAE degree   □ Postgraduate

B33) And finally, we understand questions about incomes are personal and sensitive but it is very important for our analyses. Please indicate which of the following categories best describes your annual household income before tax.

□ Less than $20,000   □ $20,000 to less than $40,000

□ $40,000 to less than $50,000   □ $50,000 to less than $75,000

□ $75,000 to less than $100,000   □ $100,000 or more

Section C: News usage among non-users of online news

C1) How often do you get news from newspapers?

□ Everyday   □ Several times a week   □ Several times a month   □ Less often

C2) To what extent do you find newspapers helpful to follow the news types listed below?

	Very helpful	Helpful	Not very helpful	Not at all helpful
• National/state politics	4	3	2	1
• International affairs	4	3	2	1
• Economics (including business/finance)	4	3	2	1
• Entertainment/sport	4	3	2	1
• Science/technology and health	4	3	2	1
• Social problems (crime/disasters/accidents)	4	3	2	1
• Culture and the arts	4	3	2	1
• Local community affairs	4	3	2	1

C3) How much would you miss newspapers if they were no longer available?
□ A good deal □ Some □ Not very much □ Not at all

C4) How often do you listen to radio news?
□ Everyday □ Several times a week □ Several times a month □ Less often

C5) How often do you do something else (eating, drinking, driving, cooking, chatting etc.) when listening to radio news?
□ Very often □ Often □ Not very often □ Never

C6) To what extent do you find radio helpful to follow the news types listed below?

	Very helpful	Helpful	Not very helpful	Not at all helpful
• National/state politics	4	3	2	1
• International affairs	4	3	2	1
• Economics (including business/finance)	4	3	2	1
• Entertainment/sport	4	3	2	1
• Science/technology and health	4	3	2	1
• Social problems (crime/disasters/accidents)	4	3	2	1
• Culture and the arts	4	3	2	1
• Local community affairs	4	3	2	1

C7) How much would you miss radio if it were no longer available?
□ A good deal □ Some □ Not very much □ Not at all

→ How much would you miss radio news if radio networks no longer delivered it?
□ A good deal □ Some □ Not very much □ Not at all

C8) How often do you get news from magazines?
□ Every week □ Every month □ Every few months □ Less often

C9) To what extent do you find magazines helpful to follow the news types listed below?

	Very helpful	Helpful	Not very helpful	Not at all helpful
• National/state politics	4	3	2	1
• International affairs	4	3	2	1
• Economics (including business/finance)	4	3	2	1
• Entertainment/sport	4	3	2	1
• Science/technology and health	4	3	2	1
• Social problems (crime/disasters/accidents)	4	3	2	1
• Culture and the arts	4	3	2	1
• Local community affairs	4	3	2	1

C10) How much would you miss magazines if they were no longer available?

☐ A good deal   ☐ Some   ☐ Not very much   ☐ Not at all

C11) How often do you watch news on television?

☐ Everyday   ☐ Several times a week   ☐ Several times a month   ☐ Less often

C12) How often do you watch TV news with a remote controller at hand?

☐ Very often   ☐ Often   ☐ Not very often   ☐ Never

C13) How often do you do something else (eating, drinking, cooking, reading, chatting etc.) when watching TV news?

☐ Very often   ☐ Often   ☐ Not very often   ☐ Never

C14) To what extent do you find TV helpful to follow the news types listed below?

	Very helpful	Helpful	Not very helpful	Not at all helpful
• National/state politics	4	3	2	1
• International affairs	4	3	2	1
• Economics (including business/finance)	4	3	2	1
• Entertainment/sport	4	3	2	1
• Science/technology and health	4	3	2	1
• Social problems (crime/disasters/accidents)	4	3	2	1
• Culture and the arts	4	3	2	1
• Local community affairs	4	3	2	1

C15) How much would you miss TV if it were no longer available?

☐ A good deal   ☐ Some   ☐ Not very much   ☐ Not at all

→ How much would you miss TV news if TV networks no longer delivered it?

☐ A good deal   ☐ Some   ☐ Not very much   ☐ Not at all

C16) Which of the following labels would you consider yourself to be. Please tick <u>all</u> that apply.

☐ Newspaper fan   ☐ News magazine fan

☐ Radio news fan   ☐ Television news fan

☐ None

C17) Overall, which of the following media do you currently rely on <u>the most</u> for news and information about current affairs?

☐ Newspapers   ☐ Magazines   ☐ Television   ☐ Radio

→ Do you consider it <u>the best</u> medium to serve your news needs?

☐ Yes   ☐ No

C18) Have you heard someone talking about the advantages and disadvantages of <u>news on the Internet</u>?

☐ Yes, often   ☐ Yes, sometimes   ☐ No, never → **Go to question C20.**

C19) From what you have heard, how much do you believe the Internet will become an important news source in the future?

☐ A good deal   ☐ Some   ☐ Not very much   ☐ Not at all

C20) When getting news from newspapers/magazines/radio/television, how often do you find yourself in the following situations?

	Very often	Often	Not very often	Never
• Being frustrated for having to follow too many news items not of your interest	4	3	2	1
• Lacking in-depth, including background, information to follow some news stories	4	3	2	1
• Being annoyed by commercials inserted in the middle of TV/radio news bulletins	4	3	2	1
• Being unsatisfied for not getting enough updated news	4	3	2	1
• Being unsatisfied for not getting enough news of your interest	4	3	2	1
• Finding it difficult to arrange a time schedule suiting the timing of TV/radio news programs	4	3	2	1

C21) The Internet gives users an absolute control to minimise all the mentioned problems and offers some other much needed advantages. Would you consider doing something to explore this if you knew that?

☐ Yes   ☐ No   ☐ Not sure

C22) Now just a few questions about yourself before we finish. First, what's your sex?

☐ Male ☐ Female

C23) What is your year of birth? --

C24) What is your country of birth? --

C25) Which of the following best describes the area you now live in?

☐ A rural area/village ☐ A small town ☐ A large town

☐ A metropolitan area (including suburbs surrounding major cities)

C26) What is your current employment status?

☐ Full-time ☐ Part-time ☐ Not employed ☐ Retired

C27) What type of job do you do?

☐ Professional ☐ Administrator/Manager

☐ Agriculture worker (Farmer/Fisher/Miner) ☐ Clerical/Sales

☐ Services ☐ Trade person/Skilled worker

☐ Labourer ☐ Student

☐ Home duties

C28) What's the highest level of education you have achieved so far?

☐ Did not complete secondary school ☐ Completed secondary school

☐ TAFE/Trade certificate ☐ University/CAE degree ☐ Postgraduate

C29) And finally, we understand questions about incomes are personal and sensitive but it is very important for our analyses. Please indicate which of the following categories best describes your annual household income before tax.

☐ Less than $20,000 ☐ $20,000 to less than $40,000

☐ $40,000 to less than $50,000 ☐ $50,000 to less than $75,000

☐ $75,000 to less than $100,000 ☐ $100,000 or more

Wissenschaftlicher Buchverlag bietet

kostenfreie

Publikation

von

wissenschaftlichen Arbeiten

Diplomarbeiten, Magisterarbeiten, Master und Bachelor Theses
sowie Dissertationen, Habilitationen und wissenschaftliche Monographien

Sie verfügen über eine wissenschaftliche Abschlußarbeit zu aktuellen oder zeitlosen
Fragestellungen, die hohen inhaltlichen und formalen Ansprüchen genügt,
und haben **Interesse an einer honorarvergüteten Publikation**?

Dann senden Sie bitte erste Informationen über Ihre Arbeit per Email
an info@vdm-verlag.de. Unser Außenlektorat meldet sich umgehend bei Ihnen.

VDM Verlag Dr. Müller Aktiengesellschaft & Co. KG
Dudweiler Landstraße 125a
D - 66123 Saarbrücken

www.vdm-verlag.de